Administrative Structure and Policy in India

ADMINISTRATIVE STRUCTURE AND POLICY IN INDIA

Edited by

Gautam Vir

OMEGA PUBLICATIONS

NEW DELHI-110 002 (INDIA)

OMEGA PUBLICATIONS
4378/4B, G-4 JMD House
Murari Lal Street, Ansari Road
Daryaganj, New Delhi - 110 002
Phone : 65901906 (Off.)
e-mail : omega_publications@yahoo.com

Head Office :
78/3, Laxmi Garden
Near Satya Jyoti School,
Gurgaon (Haryana)
Mob : 9811787417

Administrative Structure and Policy in India

First Published : 2009

ISBN : 978–81–8455–160–0

PRINTED IN INDIA

Published by Mahendra Garg for Omega Publications, New Delhi-110 002 and Printed at Tarun Offset Press, Delhi-110053

Preface

The study of public administration as an independent discipline began only recently. As an activity public administration is as old as man himself. In the earliest stages of society we find the rudiments of administrative activity but no attention was paid for a long time to develop an independent science of public administration. In fact, even the term public administration did not exist earlier than the end of eighteenth century. Although we may find traces of administrative thought in the Arthasastra of Kautilya and the Prince of Machiavelli, yet these were just 'tips' to the ruler for maintaining his supremacy and security.

In a democracy, the importance of public administration is all the more great. The ideals of democracy—progress, prosperity and protection of the common man—can be obtained only through impartial, honest and efficient administration. The administrator is the essential servant of the new age which is becoming so complex that neither the bluster of the power politician nor the abundant goodwill of the multitude will avoid breakdown, if despite the adoption of right policies, wrong administrative steps are taken. An administrator should be capable and serve the masses with devotion and dedication. He should have "an agreeable personality, possess the ability to get along with the people, have character and integrity, have qualities of leadership and be able to make a high percentage of correct decisions without undue procrastination."

From what has been said above it is clear that public administration is a great social force in the life of a nation. The powerful and vital role played by it in the life of a nation led Ramsay Muir to remark that in England the minister is a tool in the hands of the permanent executive. While governments may come and go, ministries may rise and fall, the administration of a country goes on for ever. No revolution can change it and no upheaval can uproot it.

The major topics dealt in this book are : *Administration and Government Machinery; Performance of Public Enterprises; Development Administration; Public Service Ethics; District Administration; Structure of Personnel Administration; Ecology of Public Enterprises; Evolution of Civic Engagement; Administrative Relations; Planning for Administration; Policy of Legislative Control; Civil Service;* etc.

No doubt, these will serve the purpose of trainees and trainers, professionals and policy planners in the field. Since the sources of information are all secondary, we express our gratitude to the scholars whose works are cited or substantially made use of. We are thankful to all those who rendered ready help and cooperation while working on this project.

We express our gratitude to various scholars, teachers and friends for their assistance and guidance. Finally, we thank our publishers for bringing out this book in very limited time.

—Editor

Contents

1

Administration and Government Machinery

In India each state government has a Secretariat of its own, which is nerve centre of state Administration. The state Secretariat is headed by a Chief Secretary. In the Secretariat there are many departments and each one has a Secretary as its Head. He is assisted by many generalists at the state level and specialists in the field establishments. Then there are other officers who assist to Secretary in the discharge of his duties.

Organisation of Departments. There are no scientific means and methods for the organisation of department in the states. The departments are created and disbanded not on very sound and scientific basis. Usually however, a secretariat in a state has department of :

(a) General Administration.

(b) Home.

(c) Planning.

(d) Education.

(e) Revenue.

(f) Food and Agriculture.

(g) Animal Husbandry.

(h) Co-operation.

(i) Forests.

(j) Panchayat Raj.

(k) Finance.

(l) Health.

(m) Industries.

(n) Law.

(o) Transport.

(p) Irrigation and Power.

(q) Local Self-Government.

(r) Police, and

(s) Jails.

(t) Labour and Employment.

(u) Excise and Taxation etc

The States having scheduled castes and scheduled tribes population have department which deal with the problems connected with their welfare. Similarly states with sea shores have deparments of fisheries and so on. The creation of a new department is within the competence of state government and as such it is difficult to enumerate the departments which a state government can scientifically have or should have.

Organisation of State Secretariat. The state secretariat has people belonging different categories. These include—

(a) Chief Secretary.

(b) Sepcial Secretary.

(c) Secretary.

(d) Joint Secretary.

(e) Assistant Secretary.

(f) Officers on Special Duty.

(g) Deputy Secretary.

(h) Under Secretary.

(i) Superintendent.

(j) Assistant Superintendent.

(k) Lower Division Assistants.

(l) Upper Division Assistants.

(m) Typists, and

(n) Class IV employees.

But before we discuss their functions, it must be clearly understood that this organisation of state secretariat is not applicable to all the states. Since it is a common pattern, therefore, it is desirable to discuss it.

Chief Secretary. He is the head of secretariat set-up and responsible for the running of state administration. He controls the whole adminstration as well as the administrators. He enjoys a special status and position in the state. It has been discussed in detail in the next question.

Secretary. He is head of a department and usually belongs to IAS cadre. He is also adviser to his minister and works under the over all charge of Chief Secretary from whom he also receives instructions and guidance. He frames policies and programmes of his departments and acts as a link between the minister and his staff. He controls officers and staff working under him and ensures that the work in his department runs smoothly and efficiently. For all delays and other truoubles he is held responsible both by the Chief Secretary as well as the minister.

Special Secretary. Next to Secretary comes Special Secretary/Additional Secretary. The incumbent of this post is also a very senior officer. He holds charge of some items of work which he deals independently. He also deals with the minister direct and disposes of many cases at his own level. He howerver, works under the overall guidance and supervision of the Secretary, who can instruct him for doing a thing in a particular manner.

Joint Secretary. Next to Special/Additional Secretary comes Joint Secretary. In a department there can be one or two Joint Secretaries. A Jount Secretary is very senior civil servant. He also holds charge of items of work which he independently deals. He also receives his instructions from the Secretary of his department. He is under the administrative control of his Secretary.

Deputy Secretary. In the hierarchy then comes Deputy Secretary. He is also usually a person belonging to services. In a department there can be few Deputy Secretaries. Their number depends upon the nature of work in a department. Deputy Secretary disposes of several cases at his level and usually does not deal with the minister direct. All his files in the department to the minister are routed either through his Joint Secretary or Special/Additional Secretary or the Secretary.

Under Secretary. After Deputy Secretary, then comes Under Secretary, who supervises the work of two to three Sections. This post is filled up either by civil service people or by departmental promotion. He usually disposes of all routine matters at his level. He processes all the cases which are sent to his Deputy Secretary. He has not very many administrative powers. He seeks guidance from his superior officers on all matters of policy.

Assistant Secretary. An Assistant Secretary is the state secretariat does not enjoy any executive or administrative powers. He holds a gazetted rank. He deals with routine or establishment matters. His main function is to process cases beore these are sent to the higher officers.

Officer on Special Duty. An officer on special duty can be of any status. He is appointed for a particular work and as soon as his work is over, his post is abolished. This post is discretionary one.

Superintendent. As in the central secretariat we have Section Officers, so in the state secretariat are Superintendents. A Super-intendent is incharge of a section which in some cases is also called department. He maintains discipline in the section. He ensures that the files, where necessary have been opened and that all the papers have been processed.

Assistant Superintendent. Below the Superintedent comes Assistant Superintendent. He has both original as well as supervisory functions. Some of the papers received in the section are dealt with by him directly while in other cases papers are received by him from the assistants and he disposes them of.

Upper Division Assistants. Upper Discussion Assistants are very important persons in the Section/Department. They are recruited on the recommendations of Service Commission. They are supposed to maintain all fiels properly. In addition to this, they are also supposed to do all original work and do noting and drafting on the papers received in the section.

Lower Division Assistants. They assist the upper division assistants and maintain a record of the papers received in the section. They are also recruited through Public Service Commission. They keep the movement of the papers and files sent out of the section. They hold the fiels till there are needed by some superior official. One of their major responsibilities is to prepare statements and returns which are to go out of the section.

Other Staff. Then in the secretariat there are recorders who keep record of the papers and other documents. The typists who type papers and stenographers of different grades who help the officers in the discharge of their responsibilities.

An Assessment. In this way whole secretariat set-up is very elaborate. The organisation of course has its own problems. It is said that the progress of work is slow and the decision making process is not quick. On the other hand, the secretariat officers feel that they are over worked. The work which they are supposed to handle is beyond normal human capacity. They are left with no time to have any creative thinking. They also feel that the people, many a time, expect the secretariat to do a work which they are not supposed to do and which is the responsibility of the field establishments. There is also a complaint in the secretariat that officers are not allowed to decide cases on merits due to political interventions and considerations.

Whatsoever, the difficulties might be, in actual practice the citizen is not satisfied with the working of he state secretariat to the extent to which he should be. But the things have considerably improved and let us hope that these will improve further.

MINISTRIES AND DEPARTMENTS IN CENTRAL GOVERNMENT

As on 29th May, 1995, the Government consisted of the following ministries/departments under the Government of India (Allocation of Business) Rules, 1961—

1-3 Ministry of Agriculture :

(i) Department of Agriculture and Cooperation.

(ii) Department of Agriculture Research and Education.

(iii) Department of Animal Husbandry and Dairying.

4-5 Ministry of Chemicals and Fertilizers :

(i) Department of Chemicals and Petro-Chemicals.

(ii) Department of Fertilizers.

6-7 Ministry of Civil Aviation and Tourism :

(i) Department of Civil Aviation.

(ii) Department of Tourism.

8-9 Ministry of Civil Supplies, Consumer Affairs and Public Distribution :

(i) Department of Civil Supplies.

(ii) Department of Consumer Affairs and Public Distribution System.

10. Ministry of Coal.

11-12 Ministry of Commerce :

(i) Department of Commerce.

(ii) Department of Supply.

13-14 Ministry of Communication :

(i) Department of Posts.

(ii) Department of Telecommunications.

15-17 Ministry of Defence :

(i) Department of Defence.

(ii) Department of Defence Production and Supplies.

(iii) Department of Defence Research and Development

18. Ministry of Environment and Forests.

19. Ministry of External Affairs.

20-22. Ministry of Finance :

(i) Department of Economic Affairs.

(ii) Department of Expenditure.

(iii) Department of Revenue.

23-24. Ministry of Food :

(i) Department of Food

(ii) Department of Food Procurement and Distribution.

25. Ministry of Food Processing Industries.

26-28. Ministry of Health and Family Welfare :

(i) Department of Health.

(ii) Department of Family Welfare.

(iii) Department of Indian Systems of Mediciens and Homeopathy.

29-32. Ministry of Home Affairs :

(i) Department of Internal Security.

(ii) Department of States.

(iii) Department of Official Languages.

(iv) Department of Home.

33-36. Ministry of Human Resource Development :

(i) Department of Education.

(ii) Department of Youth Affairs and Sports.

(iii) Department of Culture.

(iv) Department of Women and Child Development.

37-41. Ministry of Industry :

(i) Department of Industrial Development.

(ii) Department of Heavy Industry.

(iii) Department of Public Enterprises.

(iv) Department of Small Scale Industries and Agro and Rural Industries.

(v) Department of Industrial Policy and Promotion.

42. Ministry of Information and Broadcasting.

43. Ministry of Labour.

44-47. Ministry of Law and Justice and Company Affairs :

(i) Department of Legal Affairs.

(ii) Legislative Department.

(iii) Department of Justice.

(iv) Department of Company Affairs.

48. Ministry of Mines.

49. Ministry of Non-Conventional Energy Sources.

50. Ministry of Parliamentary Affairs.

51-53. Ministry of Personnel, Public Grievances and Pensions:

(i) Department of Personnel and Training.

(ii) Department of Administrative Reforms and Public Grievances.

(iii) Department of Pensions and Pensioners Welfare.

54. Ministry of Petroleum and Natural Gas.

55-57. Ministry of Planning and Programme Implementation :

(i) Department of Planning.

(ii) Department of Statistics.

(iii) Department of Programme Implementation.

58. Ministry of Power.

59. Ministry of Railways.

60-62. Ministry of Rural Areas and Employment :

(i) Department of Rural Development.

(ii) Department of Wastelands Development.

(iii) Department of Rural Employment and Poverty Alleviation.

63-65. Ministry of Science and Technology :

(i) Department of Science and Technology.

(ii) Department of Scientific and Industrial Research.

(iii) Department of Bio-Technology.

66. Ministry of Steel.

67. Ministry of Surface Transport.

68. Ministry of Taxtiles.

69-70. Ministry of Urban Affairs and Employment :

(i) Department of Urban Development.

(ii) Department of Urban Employment and Poverty Alleviation.

71. Ministry of Water Resources.

72. Ministry of Welfare.

73. Department of Atomic Energy.

74. Department of Electronics.

75. Department of Jammu & Kashmir Affairs.

76. Department of Ocean Development.

77. Department of Space.

78. Cabinet Secretariat.

79 President's Secretariat.

80. Prime Minister's Office.

81. Planning Commission.

COMPOSITION OF UNION COUNCIL OF MINISTERS

Article 76, of the Constitution of India provides that there shall be a Council of Ministers with the Prime Minister as its head to aid and advice the President in the exercise of his functions. Article 75(1), postulates the following procedure for the formation of the Council of Ministers. Thus the first step in the process of forming the Council of Ministers is the appointment of the Prime Minister. The P.M. is appointed by the President but his choice in the matter is limited. He must select the leader of the majority party in the Parliament and if there is no single party commanding the majority, then he must select such a person who is his opinion can form a stable government. After the Prime Minister has been selected, the ministers are appointed by the President on the recommendation of the Prime Minister. The President must accept the recommendations of the Prime Minister choose other Ministers. Thus, the discretion of the President in the choice of the Prime Minister and other Ministers is limited. A member of the Rajya Sabha also can be appointed the Prime Minister. For example Mrs. Indira Gandhi was from Rajya Sabha when she was appointed the Prime Minister on the death of Shri Lal Bahadur Shastri. Shri Narashimha Rao our P.M. contested Lok Sabha by elections and got elected thought he was tipped for Prime Ministership when he was not a member of Parliament. The Constitution does not lay down any limit as regard to the number of ministers. It is for the Prime Minister the determine the size of the Council and the categories minister. At present there are three types of ministers *(i)* Cabinet Minister *(ii)* Minister of State, and *(iii)* Deputy Minister. The 1992, Council of Ministers consisting of 58 members with Narasimha Rao as the Prime Minister is a three tier ministry cabinet ministers, minister of state—a few holding independent charge of the departments and a few working under Cabinet Minister and Deputy Ministers. Still representative to some state like Haryana is to be accorded.

Not does the Constitution prescribe any qualification for holding the office of minister. It only says that the minister must be a member of either. House of the Parliament though for a period of six months a non-member also may be appointed the minister. The minister holds office during the pleasure of the President which in fact means the pleasure of the Prime Minister.

FUNCTIONS OF THE CABINET

The Cabinet holds a pivotal position in the Union Government. All the powers of the President are in the fact the powers of the Cabinet. The functions of the Cabinet may be considered under the following heads :

1. Executive Functions. The Cabinet is the real executive in the country. It discusses and desides all sorts of national and international problems and decides the policy as regard to them. After the policy has been approved the appropriate department carries it out. If an individual minister does not agree with the policy, the proper course for him is to resign. One cannot remain in the Council of Ministers and yet disagree wih the policy determined by the Cabinet. The Cabinet usually meets once a week. Generally all the major appointments are palced before the cabinet for its approval.

2. Legislative Functions. The Cabinet plans the legisiative programme at the beginning of each parliamentary session and introduces the Government Bills. No minister can introduce a bill without the approaval of the Cabinet. It is for the Cabient to decide what bill will be introduced in a session. The control of the Cabinet over legislation is so complete that it will not be an exaggeration to say that the Cabinet legislates with the approval of the Parliament. The power of delegates legislation has further increased the legislative authority of the Cabinet. The Parliament passes the bill in skeleton form with power to the Cabinet to fill in the details. The rule making by the Cabient has added vastly to the powers of the cabinets in the moden democracies.

3. Co-ordinating Functions. To ensure the proper working of the different departments the Cabient department the Cabient co-ordinates their activities. The department have to abide by the decisions of the Cabinet. The Cabinet may appoint Cabinet Committee to look into a disputed matter between the different departments.

4. Financial Functions. The Cabinet is the main body to decide what expenditure is to be incurred on the affairs of the Union and how that money is to be raised and which taxes are to be levied for the purpose. No money bill can be introduced in the Parliament by a private member. At the beginning of every financial year the Cabinet places the budget before the Parliament. No change in the budget may be effected unless the Cabinet agrees to it. Thus the control of the Cabinet over the finances of the country is complete.

All the above powers and functions have given the cabinet the place of the steering wheel of the ship of the State. Its powers are enormous is the executive, legisltive and financial fields. In short, the Cabinet is the Government. It has been rightly described as the Keystone of Constitutional arch.

INDIAN CABINET FROM BRITISH RULE

Before the Indian Independence Act, 1947, all the executive authority in India was vested in the Governor

Gerneral-in-Council. The Independence Act fransferred the executive authority to the Council of Ministers and transformed the earlier Executive Council of the Governor-General into a Cabinet with the Prime Minister at its head.

The Executive Council. Before we study the position of the Cabinet in India's Administration today, it would be better to preface our study with a brief description of the Executive Council and its position in the country's administration during British rule in India. At the very outset it may be noted that the Exectutive Council was not a cabinet in the real sense of the term. By the term 'Cabinet' we understand a homogeneously constituted council marked by unity of purpose and responsible to the constituted legislature. The Executive Council of the Governor-General could not be called a Cabinet as it was neither responsible to, nor representative of the constitued legislature. It was subject to the Control of the Secretary of State and carried out faithfully his orders and directives even if these were in conflict with the views of the Council. It did not have a common outlook or unity of purpose.

With the inauguration of limited provincial responsibility and introduction of the rudiments of a responsible form of Government for provincial administration in 1918, the provincial Executive Councils were relieved of the responsibility for the subjects which were grouped as 'transferred' under the Government of India Act, 1919. These subject called 'tansferred subjects' were put under the charge of the ministers responsible to the legislatures. These ministes could remain in office only so long so they enjoyed the confidence of the legislatures. It may be noted that the Ministers did not replace the Governors-in-Council who continued to the responsible to the British Parliament through the Government of India and he Secretary of State.

The pace of provincial autonomy started by the Government of India Act, 1919 was accelerted by the

Government of India Act, 1935. This Act gave the provinces full autonomy, abolished the distinction between 'Reserved' and 'Transferred' subejcts and transferred all administrative responsibility to the Councl of Ministers responsible to the Legislature. However, the Governor was charged with certain special responsibilities in regard to which he was to act according to his individul judgement and discretion.

At the Centre, a federation of the autonomous provinces and with princely States was envisaged. The executive authority of the Federation was vested the Governor-General to be assisted by a Council, some coucillors to assist him in the exercise of his powers relating to defence, foreign affairs, ecclesiastical and tribal affairs. The Governor-General was also given certain special responsibilities.

But as the federal provisions of the Govoernment of India Act, 1935 did not come into operation due to the failure of the Princes to agree in the required minimum number to execute individual instruments of assertion, the Executive Council continued to be accountable to British Parliament through the Secretary of State. The Council at the time was composed of six members to which five more eminent non-party Indians were added in July, 1941. But the enlarged council was wholly unrepresentative of India political opinion. In 1942, the strength of the Council was raised to fifteen which was maintained until the formation of the Interim Government on September, 1946.

The Interim Government. The Interim Government formed in 1946, under the Cabnet Mission Plan was the first government at the Centre in India to function as a Cabinet. All the powers and functions of the Government were vested in the Interim Government. The Portfolios of War and External Affairs which were held by Commander-in-Chief and the Governor-General respectively were now held by the Ministers of the Interim Government. The Commander-in-Chief was no longer a member of the Government. There were eighteen department organized in fourteen portifolios, viz., External Affairs; War; Finance Home; Commonwealth Relations; Information and Broadcasting; Agriculture; Education; Legislation; Health; Food; Commerce; Industry and Supply; Labour; Works; Mines and Power; Transport; Communication and Railways. Some of these departments were brought together in one portfolio, for example, the Departments of External Affairs and Commonwealth Relations were amalgamated in one portfolio. Similarly, the Deparments of Home and Information and Broadcasting were brought together in one portifolio. On June 27, 1947, a Department of States was constituted to replace the Political Department, to be administered by the Viceroy.

But as the events turned the Interim Government could not function harmoniously and its cabinet character was lost. The Muslim League nominess in the Government formed a separate bloc with the result that the cabinet soon degenerated into an assembly of warring factions blocking in unity and purpose. The political difference between the Congress and Muslim League continued to widen and it became difficult to carry on the administration. The British Government tried to narrow down the political differences between the parties but could not succeed.

The Council of Ministers. With the Indian Independence Act coming into force the Council of Ministers began to function on a team basis. The Prime Minister nominated the members of the Council and functioned as its leader. This ensured harmony and a unity of purpose in a cabinet composed of the members from the same political party. There were fourteen members of Council including the Prime Minister and a Deputy Prime Minister. The existing arrangement of portfolios in the Interim Government was left undisturbed. The Departments were, however, now designated as the Ministeries. Shri Jawaharlal Nehru, who as the Prime Minister in the Interim Government continued to be the Prime Minister and retain the portfolio of External Affairs. Sardar Vallabhabhai Patel was named the Deputy Prime Minister and retained his old portfolios of Home. Information, Broadcasting and States. Shortly after the constitution of new government a Minister without Portfolio was added to the Council. In the second half of 1948; three Ministers of State and two Deputy Ministers were appointed. One of the Ministers of State was given the charge of the Department of Rehabilitations while the other one was to look after the portfolio of Information and Broadcasting relieving the Deputy Prime Minister of heavy responsibilities. The third Minister of State and two Deputy Ministers were attached to the Cabinet Ministers to assist them. In 1949, the Chief Whip was given the status of a Minister of State and named Minister of Parliamentary Affairs.

The Council, thus, now included three categories of Ministers i.e. the Cabinet Ministers, the Ministers of State and the Deputy Ministers. The appointment of Ministers of State to hold charge of portfolios independently was an innovation. In other countries there used to be a Minister of State but his status was different from the one given to him in India. In France he ranked higher than a Miniser and performed some special functions. In England he was a Minister of the second rank functioning as the principal assistant to a Cabinet Minister. He had a cabinet rank but his salary was lower than that of a Cabinet Minister. In India no such distinction existed. He was included in the Cabinet and was remunerated equally with the Cabinet Minister.

Gopalaswami Ayyangar's Report, 1949. The need for reorientating the structure of administration and infusing and developing fully a sense of collective responsibility in the members of the Council of Ministers was felt since the transfer of power in 1947. But due to communal disturbances and other disturbing situations it was not possible to give immediate attention to that task Gopalsawami Ayyangar, an ex-civil servant, who was a Minister without portfolio at the time, was charged with the responsibilities of formulating proposals for re-organizing the machinery of government. He also examined the structure of the Council of Ministers and made certain proposals.

Gopalaswami Ayyangar in his Report, 1949, proposed that the Council of Ministers should formally include all the three categories of Ministers. The Cabinet Ministers were to play the senior most role. They are not merely the departmental chiefs but their responsibilities extended to the entire field of central administration. A Minister of State, Gopalaswami Ayyangar proposed, should normally be place in charge of a department or specified items of work included in the portfolio of a Cabient Minister, under whose general guidance and supervision he should work. However, he could also be given independent charge of one of the minor ministers. He would attend cabinet meetings on invitation in an advisory capacity in relation to the department under his charge. But appointing a Minister of State to hold a partfolio should be an exception rather than the rule. So far as the Deputy Ministers were concerned. Mr. Ayyangar proposed that they should not be given independent charge of any portfolio, but, of course; should be given full opportunities to acquiant themselves with the organisation and train themselves for the actual exercise of administrative responsibilities, if and when appointed, as ministers. The duties would normally involve assisting the ministers in piloting Bills and answering qustions in Parliament on behalf of Ministers concerned; to expalin policies and programme to the general public and maintain liaison with Members of Parliament and perform the special tasks entrusted to them by the Ministers concerned.

Council of Ministers under the New Constitution. When the new constitution of India was enacted on November 26, 1949. The British conception of a Cabinet form of government was embodied in it. Curiously enough however, it did not see the term 'cabinet' but instead used the term 'Council of Ministers' in its provisions. Article 74, of the Constitution mentions this term for the first time which reads as follows :

'There shall be a Council of Ministers with the Prime Minister as the head of aid and advise the President in the exercise of his funcions.'

The Prime Minister is appointed by the President and usually the elected leader of the majority party in the House of the People. The other members to the Council of Ministers are appointed by the President on the recommendation by the Prime Minister who usually selects the members from his own party. The ministers are collectively responsible to the Lok Sabha. But all the members of the Council do not, however, meet together to decide any question of policy. It is the Cabinet, the inner Council, consisting of ministers of the first rank which takes decision in all such question. The Prime Minister is the link between the Prisident and the Council of Ministers. All communications to and from the President from and to the Ministers flow through the Prime Minister. No minister can as master of right, have an audience with the President.

Composition of the Council of Ministers. The Constitution does not fix the size of the Council of Ministers. It is for the Prime Minister to determine the size according to the requirements of the occasion. The Council of Ministers as constituted in 1962, consisted of 52 Ministers divided into three categories, i.e., Cabinet Ministers, Ministers of State and Deputy Ministers. The Cabinet Ministers were 18, the Ministers of State were 12 and the Deputy Ministers were 21 in number. In addition to them were 7 Parliamentary Secretaries. As told above, the appointment of Ministers of State, to take charge of independent portfolio was an innovation in our cabinet system which did not conferm to the practice in other Parliamentary democracies. After the first General Elections when the Council of Ministers was reconstituted, a change in the classification of Ministers was made, the Ministers of State being elevated to the Ministers of the Cabient rank. Bu this abolition of the designation of Ministers of State and their redesignation as Ministers of Cabinet rank created confusion as to relative functions and responsibilites of the Ministers concerned. The result was that when the second government was formed in 1957, after the General Election the old practice was reverted to and appointments were made in the three ranks of Cabinet Minister, Minister of State and Deputy Minister.

The Deputy Ministers do not hold charge of independent profolios. They assist the senior Ministers and perform such functions as are entrusted to them by the Ministers. There are no rigid rules defining the relations between the Ministers and Deputy Ministers. The extend to which a Deputy Minister can be made use of depends and the measure confidence which the former is prepared to give to the latter. Some enthusiastic Ministers are also not inclined to share authority and power with their deputies. It is necessary to make the Deputy Minister fulfil role that there must be established a relationship of understanding and confidence between the Minister and his Deputy.

Regarding the composition of the Council of Ministers it may also the remarked that there was a time when political offices were to be distributed as a reward to prominent political workers in the struggle for independence. But now the time has come, after fifteen years of independence, when political consderations should not be made to weigh much and appointment should be made on non-political considerations.

The Constitution (39th) Amendment Act, 1975 provides that Parliament may, by law regualted any matter realting to, or connected with, the election of a President or Vice-President including the grounds on which such elections may be questioned. The validity of any such law and the decision of any authority or body under such law shall not be called a question in any court. Thus, the 39th Amendment the Constitution placed beyond challenge in courts the election of the President or Vice-President and election to Parliament of a person holding, the office of Prime Minister or Speaker. These four offices have been declared to be high offices and matters relating to their election shall be regulated by a Parliamentary law may be by a Parliamentary forum other than a court. The President is not answerable to a Court of Law for anything done, while in office in the exercise of his powers. It was, therefore, provided that matters relating to his election should not be brought before a court of law but should be entrusted to a forum other than a court. The same reasoning applies equally to the incumbents of the office of Vice-President, Prime Minister and Speaker.

PRIME MINISTER'S OFFICE (PMO)

In a Parliamentary democracy the Prime Minister is the centre of power and responsibility. In crisis situations decisions are left to the Prime Minister. He, therefore, needs institutional help and assistance to take immediate decisions. There is no disagreement for such support to the Prime Minister but there were differences as to the way in which institutional support is to be provided. Some were in favour of using already existing administrative machinery within ministriers, while some favoured the Prime Minister's office to give direct assistance to the Prime Minister. There can be no question that every P.M. is entitled to have an office of his own manned by advisers loyal to him. This is the basic justification for the existence of the PM's office. This question was discussed by the ARC and its. Study Team recommended for setting up of such institutional support which will not duplicate the work of existing ministries and will deal with only overall issues.

The existing institutional support consists of the Cabinet Committees, the Secretaries Committees, Cabinet Secretariat and the Prime Minister's Office. Prime Minister's Secretariat/ Office occupies the status of a department of the Government of India under the Allocation of Buesiness Rules, 1961 without any attached and subordinate office under it. This office is not responsible for the Prime Minister functioning as head of the Cabinet. It is responsible for his functioning as Chariman of the Planning Commission. It is a official link between the PM and his Ministers, President. Governors, Chief Ministers and Foreign representatives. On the public side, it is concerned with party matters, personal correspondence and complaints from public, etc.

FUNCTIONS OF PM'S OFFICE

The functions of the P.M.'s Office are as following :

(a) To deal with all references, which under the rules of business, have to come to the Prime Minister.

(b) To help the PM in the discharge of his responsibilities as the Chairman of the Planning Commission.

(c) To help the Prime Minister in respect of his/her overall responsibilities as Head of Government. It includes liaison with the Union Ministries and the State Governments on matters in which the PM may be interested.

(d) To assist the P.M. in the examination of cases submitted to him for orders under prescribed rules.

(e) To deal with the public relations side of the PM's office, that is, relations with the press, public, etc.

The PM's office is not responsible for his functions as the head of the Cabinet, except the matters of personal correspondence between him and individual Ministers. Generally, the personality of the P.M. and his view of his own role would greatly influence the nature and span of functions of his office. Its activities may be broadly divided into four parts. One procssing a large number of cases submitted by various ministries and Cabinet Secretary for inforamtion, approaval and sanction etc. These are basically routine matter, but this is what bureaucracy enjoys doing the most, as such cases provide ample opportunity for nit-picking and exercise of effective power at the personal level. In actual fact, the PMO has little to contribute in this area, as the government operates within an elaborate frame-work of ruels and regulations, and the proper forum for their correct application is the ministry concerned and not the Prime Minister's Office. The second function of the PMO concerns with policy formulations. Most of the issues originate from ministers under the independent charge of Cabinet Ministers, and the basic input as also the policy frame is furnished by the administrative ministry. In more important cases the Cabinet Secretary and committee of Secretaries provide useful insights and offer a wider perspective. The third function is that the Prime Minister would certainly like to use his office to reveiw and monitor particular activities of some ministriers, keep a tab on developments on certain fronts and, at times, depute his staff officers to undertake sensitive assignments. This is a wholly unstructured and grey area of the PMO's work, and its nature and content would differ a great deal from one Prime Minister to another. The fourth, vital sphere of PMO's activity which has not been clearly recognised, defined or exploited. In the first instance the bright vision of the poll promises gets buried under mountains of routine and the cosy comforts of office. But it is imperative for a serious minded Prime Minister, who aspires to go before the electorate again, to pick on a few long-term policy issues or ameliorative measures right at the start of his term and then entrust a special cell in his office continuously to monitor, review and assist the implementation in respect of each issue. This arrangement would necessarily involve greater centralisation in one wing of the PMO. But it would be the right kind of centralisation, i.e., enhancing the Prime Minister's ability to push forward major policy initiatives taken by his government.

EVOLUTION OF PM'S OFFICE

Before independence the Executive Council of the Governor General was give secretariat assistance by the Secretary to the Governor General. The secretariat was very small one that worked for the Governor General in his capacity as the head of the government. After indepedence on 15 August, 1947 our first Prime Minister, Pandit Nehru set-up a personal secretariat known as the Prime Minister's Secretariat. He established PM's office as distinct from the Prime Minister. He was assisted by a long "Special Private Secretary", K. Ram during his 17 years period as Prime Minister. Nehru did a good part of his work through the Foreign Office which he himself headed. This ministry acquired an out of proportion prestige and importance but it was never a power focus. With Nehru's departure the situation changed. Lal Bahadur Shastri lacked Nehru's charisma. As Prime Minister he was indeed "first among equals". To established himself, and to make up for his comparative lack of familiarity with issues involving foreign policy, science and technlogy, he instinctively felt the need for a stronger office and appointed a full-fledged secretary level servant.

ROLE OF PMO

During Nehru's period decision making centre was Cabinet Secretariat and Cabinet Secretary was the head of the administration and Civil Service. But Lal Bahadur Shastri appointed L.K. Jha senior officer of the ICS Cadre, as his Secretary. His powerful and dynamic personality raised he status and stature of the secretariat. In his time the pattern emerged was that as the P.M. Coordinates the work of the Cabinet and his secretary has become the coordinator of Secretariat activity. This led to the "decline of the Cabinet Secretariat activity to the role of clearing house for cabient Papers." Not only this Shastri inspite of a Competent full-fledged Foreign Minister in Sardar Swaran Singh, appointed a high powered committee of six secretaries to deal with foreign affairs. The membership comprised, the Cabinet Secretary, two members from the Finance Ministery, the Defence Secretary the Foreign Secretary, and L.K. Jha Secretary to P.M. While other Secretaries in the Foreign Office were not included. As a result deep resentment arose among bureaucrats and the Secretary to P.M. emerged as the influential Civil Servant. There were instructions to the Ministers to keep the PM's Secretariat in picture in all matters of any importance and as Prime Minister's Secretary Jha would generally have the last word.

The appointment of Mrs. Indira Gandhi as Prime Minister was accompanied by significant changes in the economic and political environment. The economy was in a state of crists, economic plans had declerated to what was called a "plan holiday". The devaluation of the rupee, turned out to be a major political fiasco without doing much goods to the economy. The authority of the Central government had considerably eroded. Her cabinet did not consist of like minded persons. In such a situation the P.M. faced a two-fold challenge. The first was to establish her pre-eminence in the Cabinet and the second to forge a coherent set of policies and develop a credible political stance. To meet these challenges the PM needed aids who were not her colleagues and who could give her professional assistance and advice. Mrs. Gandhi gradually expanded its strength and authority. L.K. Jha continued to be Mrs. Gandhi's Secretary and he accompanied PM on almost every foreign tour. The role of L.K. Jha provoked Hiren Mukherji to remark in the Lok Sabha that

PM. Mrs. Gandhi was surrounded by "political Up-starts and slimy bureaucrats." This created quite a stir in the labbies. This status was further raised when he was appointed a member of the Atomic Energy Commission, a position hitherto reserved for the Cabinet Secretary. When Jha was appointed as the Governor of Reserve Bank, P.N. Haksar succeeded him as the Secretary to the Prime Minister. Haksar took full charge of the Secretariat and made it the main focus of power. The entire intelligence set-up judicial appointments, Department of Personnel. Centre State relations and several other instruments of authority were under its charge. By the end of 1970, the PM's Secretariat under P.N. Haksar had acquired all the lustre and authority of a power centre. The politicians, bureaucrats and the industrial barons courted it for favours and patronage. It made and unmade the ministers and decided about the composition of the party high command and its various components.

After her Congress's landslide victory in the elections of 1971. Mrs. Gandhi expanded the authority of her Secretariat. After imposition of internal emergency on 25th June, 1975, the PM's Secretariat become the centre of all authority and its writs began to be obeyed by all central ministers, departments and all other executive agencies; and once powerful cabinet secretariat had to play a second fiddle. During emergency the PM's Secretariat was there but its powers and authority had been transferred to R.K. Dhawan who liaisoned closely with Sanjay Gandhi. "The PM's Secretariat in reality was reduced to a post office to obtain orders from the new power caucus and communicate it to the concerned Ministeries." In 1977, a big political change occurred, the Congress Party was badly defeated at the polls and new Janata Party government headed by Morarji Desai came to power. He was against the concentration of power in PM's Secretariat, therefore, he gratly reduced the authority of PM's Secretariat and its nomenclature was changed to the Prime Ministers's Office

(PMO). He declared that the desired to reduce the all powerful secretariat to the status of mere office of the Prime Minister, whose role will be to assist the PM in his task. Desai appointed V. Shankar, a retired ICS as his Secretary, the Cabinet Secretary, Nirmal Mukherji, dealt directly with the PM on most of the issues, without going through his Secretary. The prestige of the Cabient Secretary was restored. The functions of Ministeries of Home and Finance which were taken away from them, were assigned back to them. Mrs. Gandhi's return to power as a result of the elections of 1979-80, sanctified the role and status of Sanjay Gandhi. He was once again the power centre. P.C. Alexander was brought back from a UN job to head the PM's office—only its name was not changed but everything else was changed. The Minister of Home was once again denuded of its powerful instruments. Though the PM's office got back its status-quo ante-authority and acquired many additional hands, Sanjay Gandhi exercised his authority mainly through R.K. Dhawan who was now elevated to the rank of a Joint Secretary and designated as Private Secretary to the P.M.

Rajiv Gandhi's period begins from Nov., 1984 and he did not change what his mother had so firmly established. Only some more additions were made. R.K. Dhawan was banished and Fotedar stepped in. Mrs. Sarla Grewal took over from Alexander as PM's Secretary. Rajiv Gandhi fashioned the PM's Office into the kinds of instruments that it become interferring in the minutest of detail and duplicating the work of most departments of the Central Government. This extended even to External Affairs with a Joint Secretary of the PM's office belonging to the Foreign Service tendering independent advice. The size of the office grew enormously. Not only did all decisions get locked up there but a culture developed of even senior officers of ministeries not to mention ministers, trying to find out the "mind" of the PM's office before formulating the simplest of proposals. Rajiv Gandhi was keen to inject new ideas into the system and the PMO was tailor made for this, PMO was very active on the economic front as Rajiv Gandhi wanted to liberalise the economy. PM was keenly interested in technology, the PMO took lot of innovative steps in the field of science and technology. After 1989, elections V.P. Singh became the Prime Minister and his short term of nine months was full of social and political problems, but his PMO was subdued one so was the case during the four months PM's tenure of Chandra Shekhar. Neither V.P. Singh nor Chandra Shekhar allowed PMO to be treated as the virutal parallel government as it used to be prior to them.

But when Congress came to power in 1991, under the leadership of P.V. Narasimha Rao, he appointed A.N. Verma, IAS as his Principal Secretary and later Venugopal as Secretary PMO. By reasons of temperatment or because he wanted to distance himself from the Rajiv style, Narashimha Rao opted to begin with, for a greatly sobered down PMO. The Union Minister of State for Communications Rajesh Pilot commenting about the P.M.O. Said, "We do not get instructions from the P.M.O."

Meandwhile the PMO has made a comeback to the spolight, though still largely a faceless organisation. The man in it is fast acquiring the clout of a Gopi Arora or Vinod Pandey. Verma virtually runs the ministeries in Rao's control with every file being routed through him. The very busy Verma also handles the Foreign Investment Promotion Board which till last month had cleared proposals worth about Rs. 1,700 crores. But his real power, says a PMO official, lies in being Rao's "ears". In this capacity he played a crucial role for the Prime Minister in sounding out senior bureaucrats and important ministers for the selection process of new Cabient Secretary... In his second year in power, surrounded by men who share his belief in striking, but striking softly. Rao appears to have gained confidence and adapted to the rather tight fit of the Gandhi throne. Assertive even to the point of becoming irritable, his earlier image as the elderly almost a political statesman has been eroded.

Further, newspaper reports depicts that in the Narashimha Rao government, the principal secretary to the PM presided over the Inter-Ministerial Committee which gives the final nod to foreign investment proposals. Functionally, either the Ministry of Industry or the Ministery of Finance should fulfil this crucial role. The strong protest lodged by K. Karunakaran, the then Minister of Industries found mention in 'Business India' and Economic Times. There have also been several other occasions when some Central Government Ministries mildly pointed out that they had been over-ruled by the PMO.

The Prime Minister's office of Deve Gowda was, though a low profile one but the working of PMO remained the same as it was during his predecessor's time. The following examples support this point. First, the proposal of Union Coal Ministry to shift CKL headquarters from Calcutta to Ranchi (Bihar) has been blocked by the PMO. Second, the public revelation of the Home Minister, Indrajit Gupta that he was not kept informed about some of the major decisions taken by the Cabinet on behalf of his Ministry, be it the appointment of controversial UP Governor. The PMO is still functioning as an over-lord of the Ministry. Yet over the years ministers in most cases thankful for being where they are, have chosen to accept the PMO as a super-authority. Now it seems that a strong PMO is only salvation for any Indian Prime Minister, but concentration of power is a danger to a democratic soceity.

FUNCTIONS OF STATE SECRETARIAT

In a state administration the secretariat holds a very powerful and pivotal position. From here all the instructions flow. Since most of the work in the state is done in the field, one of the serious problems is as to what is the relationship of state with field administration.

Before we discuss the organisation of the State Secretariat, it is essential to discuss its important functions. Needless to say that most important function is to preserve data, facts and figures, which are needed from time to time by the Cabinet to frame state policies and programmes. The secretariat helps the Finance Minister in the preparation of budget and also other general policies and programmes. It is required to suggest measures which make the execution of the policies feasible and practical. It also ensures that policies are being implmented at all levels. Then another responsibility of the secretariat is that it should ensure that each item of expenditure has approved budget provision and it is to see that the expenditure does not exceed that. Where necessary, the state secretariat suggests measures for the revision and modification of the policies laid down by the legislature and makes them more acceptable to the people.

Since the execution of policies need officers at all levels it is the responsibility of the state secretariat to assess the requirements of staff. Prescribe qualifications and make recruitments. It prepares all drafts for introduction in the legislature and prepares replies to the questions and problems raised by the legislature or legislators. It also arranges for the meetings of both the Houses of legislature and also sends representaives for attending meetings both inside and outside the state.

Field Establishments. Such are in brief but main functions of the secretariat. But these days a controversy has arisen as to what should be the functions of the secretariat in relations to the field establishments or what is technically called executive department. This problem is very serious particularly because field establishments contribute a lot in the running of state administration. There is a strong section of scoeity which believes that secretariat should perform as few functions as possibly it can. They believe that the secretariat should confine itself to policy making only and leave implementation of decisions to the care of the field establishments. They argue that the secretariat should only perform house keeping activities leaving everthing else to the specialists in the fields. They put forth the argument that the generalists in the secretariat contribute nothing to the work of the specialists except delay.

Functions of the Field Establishments. We have already discussed some of the important functions of the secreariat. Now let us discuss the functions of the head of a field establishments. The field estabishments may be authorised to propsoe budget for the activities of its department for the ensuring years. A field establishment should be considered as technical adviser to the ministry and given considerable facilities for carrying out research programmes. He should have considerably liberty in making improvements in the techniques of working of his department. He may be authorised to train the officers of his department in these new techniques and inspect the district staff to ensure that the work is being smoothly run. Within the prescribed limits he should also be allowed to re-appropriate budget from one head of account to the other. In personnel management he should be authorised to make all appointments, confirmations, postings; transfers and promotions and also make officiating arrangements, of course within the rules. He should also be competent to exercise disciplinary powers over the subordinates working under him and in his jurisdictions.

Administrative Reforms Committee, Jaipur. The Administra-tive Reforms Committee set-up by the Government of Rajasthan submitted its report in 1963, and made some valuable suggestions about the functions to be allotted to the secretariat. The Committee divided these functions into a 3 categories namely :

(a) General matters

(b) Service matters

(c) Financial matters

In General matters the committee recommended that the state secretariat should be authorised to deal with all metters of general policy matters connected with :

(a) inter-departmental co-ordination;

(b) interpretation or relaxation of existing rules;

(c) Correspondence with other states and with the Government of India;

(d) preparation of plans;

(e) financial review of plans;

(f) conferences both inside and outside the state;

(g) committees of the legislature;

(h) delegation of powers;

(i) changes of headquartes; and

(j) appeals against state government.

While discussing financial mattters the committee was of he view that the state secretariat should deal with scrutiny of budget proposals and major re-appropriation from one head of account to the other. It should also deal with matters connected with :

(a) new items of expenditure;

(b) sanction of expenditure from contingent grant;

(c) writing-off certain amounts and so on.

About service matters the committee recommended that it should deal with approval of service rules; papers relating to senior appointments/promotion etc. of senior officers; initial appointments of officers belonging to state serviecs and cases relating to awarding major punishments to them and also matters connected with creation of new posts, their extension, special pay and re-employment etc

Present Position. The problems connected with relationship of field establishment with state secretariat are of course very delicate and tender. Of course too much concentration of authority in the hands of states in not very desirable but at the same time too much decentralisation is impracticable. It is primarily because in our present set-up the secretariat is the store house of information for the minister. He draws all information from it before replying to the criticism made by the members on the floor of the legislature. Decentralisation beyond a certain limit will make the system of ministerial responsibility to the legislatures impracticable and almost impossible and our whole present set-up of parliamentary system of government will collapse. Therefore, decentralisation to the extent demended by its propagandists is not possible in Indian State but at the same time present style of too much concentration of authority in the secretariat is also unwanted.

MUNICIPAL ADMINISTRATION AFTER, 1947

The Municipal Corporation, the Municipal Council notified area Committee, and Cantonment Boards constitute the urban local bodies.

Corporation. The Municipal Corporation which are found in metropolitan cities possess wider powers and enjoy more autonomy than other Municipal Councils. In an Indian Corporation there is a statutary distribution of powers among the Corporation Council, the Commssioner and the standing committees. The Council is composed of popularly elected representatives. The Commissioner who is at the apex of the administration is appointment by the State Government. The standing committees derive their powers either from the Act or through delegation by the Council.

The Mayor is the only ceremonial head of the corporation having no executive powers. The Commissioner—the Chief Executive Officer of the corporation supervises the day-to-day administration of the corporation.

The bigger corporations like Calcutta, Madras and Delhi have sub-municipal units *viz.*, borough Committees in Calcutta, Zonal Committees in Delhi and Circle Committees in Madras. Many purely local functions like vaccination improvement works registration of births and deaths are earmarked for them. The corporation system in a way bifurcates the beliberative and executive functions. The Council constitutes deliberative wing and the Commissioner functions as the Chief Executive. The Municipal Corporations enjoy uniformity in this respect. At present, there are even seventy corporations in India.

Municipal Councils, Notified Area Committees. The municipal councils which are commonly formed in urban areas have an integrated structure. The Chairman leading the council—the deliberative wing happens to be the chief executives as well. In almost all states the office of the Executive Officer has been provided. The Executive Officer is responsible for day to day administration. At present there are 1493 Municipal Councils in India and 202 Notified area committees and 385 town area committees.

Cantonment Boards. Besides there are 62 Cantonment Boards in India. In addition to the above local bodies some specialised bodies like Improvement Trusts, Port Trust and Development Authority have been provided. All these urban bodies aim at the development of urban area under their purview.

However, despite a rapid growth of urban local bodies after the attainment of Independence general impression is that the urban local bodies in India have failed to come up the expectations of the people. Dodwell is of the view, "The advent of freedom even has not very materially, substantially improved matters in the field of local self-government which does not at all measures up in efficiency and honesty to either the central or state government standards."

Role of the Local Bodies in General. Local bodies from a substantial step towards centralisation of power and promotion of democratic value. Their contribution to the efficiency of government is also substantial as they share the burden of the bigger district officials so far as performance of local tasks are concerned. The locally elected representatives of these bodies and local officials perform these tasks. They are more effective instruments of social and cultural development of urbanites as they inculcate in civic sense and neighbourhood consciousness among them.

Organization and Management. The urban local bodies are subject to state legislation. Hence the local bodies in different states vary as regards their organization powers, functions and resources. Adult franchise has been adopted. Joint electorate system has been introduced. Single membered constitutencies have been substituted for multi-membered constitutencies. In some of the towns it has resulted in the rise of communal and caste considerations. However, it is suggested that multi-membered constituencies may also be adopted at the local level of foster integration between different castes and communities and for according representation to weaker sections of community.

Term of the Municipal Council. Till recently the tenure has been three years. Some state governments enhanced it to 4 to 5 years. The third conference of the Municipal Corporation held in 1962, proposed a 5 years term from the Municipal

Corporations if they did not conflict with Parliament and State Legislature elections. The local urban relationship committee also proposed that the tenure of corporation and municipal councils should be 5 years.

Mayor/Chairman. The Mayor is the Chairman of Corporation whereas president is that of the municipal council. The mayor does not possess executive powers though chairman of the counil is vested with such as authority. Dichotomy of deliberative and executive functions exists in corporation but such a bifurcation is not possible in small councils. The medium sized municipalities must opt for a full time paid Executive Officer to help the elected Chief Executive.

Alderman. In some corporations Alderman who have been extended the privileges of elected councillors are selected. They are specialists who are equipped with the technicalities of the local administration. Apart from this women and special interests not represented on the Council hitherto are given representation on the council. The corporation of Bombay and Madras are enamoured of this institution.

Mode of Election. In U.P. and M.P. Chairman was directly elected but it proved to be a failure. There have been mutual bickering among the councillors. This resulted in the rise of the weak President/Chairman which adversely affected to the efficiency and continuity of administration. There is in fact a great use of opting for a mechanism of legislative accountability to ensure stability to the officer of the Chief Executive without depriving council of its authority of control.

Executive. The Chief Executive is at the highest rung of the ladder. He implements the policies formulated by the popular representatives. He possess disciplinary authority over the departmental heads and the subordinate staff. He coordinates their activities as well to effect efficiency. It is threfore, expected that the Chief Executive must be an official enjoying community from functional politics and not a victim of undue interference. He must however, be faithful to the deliberative organ and execute its decisions un-reluctantly.

Committees and the Councils. Both the corporations and councils have adopted committee systems. These committees handle relatively less important matters. In certain cases they play advisory role to the council whereas in certain cases they themselves have to arrive at decisions in which the committee system in the municipal councils has not been successful because the latter have been reluctant to entrust powers to the committees.

Personnel Administration. There has been an imbalance between the people's aspirations and needs on the one hand and the actual conduct of municipal administration on the other hand. The paucity of finances added to the gravity of the problem. Non-utilization of available sources properly also made things worse. Rapid urbanization and the emergence of developmental tasks necessitated high degree of administrative and technical skills.

The Municipal personnel with the Executive Officer at the apex are categoriesed as technical and non-technical. Both these categories are further classified as top, and middle managements and rank and file. The middle level are further divided into upper and middle classes—upper comprises supervisory staff and lower middle class consists of clerical staff and their equivalents. Municipal Medical Officer of Health, Municipal Engineer Secretary comprise top management heads of branches viz., Accountant, Tax Supdt., Octroi Supdt. Office Supdt.., Chief Sanitary Inspector. Fire Supdt. are included in this category. The lower middle class comprise assistant Octroi Supdt. Octroi Inspectors, Sanitary Inspectors, clerks, drivers, firemen.

As regards their appointments process, different practices prevail in different states. In general employees getting Certain amount of salary are appointment by the Municipal Councils.

The top management are appointment through State Public Service Commission. The executive officers in certain states like Haryana are appointment by 5/8 majority of their respective councils. The lower category of employees getting less than Rs. 160/- p.m. are also appointment by the majority of the council. However, the names of the candidates are to be entertained through employment exchange.

In order to have effective and rational personnel system a balance may have to be struck between local autonomy and government control. The synthesis of a unified local government service a separate municipal personnel system and an integrated system can help in having proper personnel system for urban local bodies.

CHIEF SECRETARY

In state administration Chief Secretary enjoys a unique position. He is the guiding force and a very powerful personality. His Status in the state aministration is very high. He is head of general administration.

Status of Chief Secretary. In state administration Chief Secretary has been called as the 'King pin' of administration. He is head of all the Secretaries in the state. He works under the control of Chief Minister. Normally senior most civil servant is appointed to this post. He is the leader of administrative set-up of the State. He enjoys the confidence of the Chief Minister. Usually only that person is appointed as Chief Secretary whose appointment is approved by the Chief Minister. Tenure system does not apply in his case. His high status can be imagined from the fact that in the state government threr is no person of his equivalent rank and there are only few posts in the central government which are of his equivalent rank. Rajasthan Administrative Reforms Committee while discussing his position said, "By virtue of his unique position as the head of official machinery and adviser to the Council of Ministers the Chief Secretary has an extremely important role to play in the state administration. Apart from the attending to the work of the departments which are directly under him, he should be in a position to effectively co-ordinate the work of different secretaries and ensure that there is certain degree of uniformity in the policies adopted by the state government with respect of different departments." The Committee was of the view that he should be consulted by the Minister-in-charge of a department before taking any major policy decision.

Functions of Chief Secretary. The Chief Secretary has following important functions to perform :

1. He advises of Chief Minister on all matters.
2. He prepares papers for cabinet meetings and takes steps for the execution of their decisions.
3. He exercises control over the whole secretariat.
4. He makes appointements, postings and transfers of state service personnel.
5. He represents state in the Zonal Council.
6. He controls staff of the ministers.
7. He presides over all high level committee meetings.
8. During crisis he acts as a balancing wheel in the state administration and ensures that the state administration does not bow under the pressure of emergency.
9. He acts as a spokesman of the state government.
10. He looks after such matters which have not been specifically allotted to a Secretary.

His Rank. Chief Secretary enjoys a very high rank in the state. There is no other parallel rank in the state. In the central government his rank has been equated with that of the Cabinet Secretary. Sometimes Cabinet Secretary convenes the meeting of Chief Secretaries of the States, thereby providing a forum where they can discuss problems of mutual interest and find means for co-ordinating their common plans.

Recognition of Services. Since 1973, the post of Chief Secretary is a tenure post and a senior most civil servant, can be appointed to this post. Increasingly it is felt that with the change of ministry. Chief Secretary should not be disturbed. His services are being appreciated and there is a suggestion that our rules should be suitably amended so that Chief Secretary, after his retirement becomes a member of the Legislative Council of the State to which he has served. It is realised that his work is very important and that is gaining recognition.

SOME IMPORTANT DEPARTMENTS OF STATE

In an Indian state, organisation and working of state secretariat is almost on the same pattern as in the central secretariat. The official hierarchy is almost the same both in the centre as well as the state. The difference broadly is on two basis. Firstly there are field establishments in the states and secondly the states are more in contact with the people than the secretariat of Central government.

Departments of the State Secretariat. As already pointed out there is no scientific basis for the organisation of departments in the state secretariat. It is all a matter of convenience, as to which department should be created or abolished. A state secretariat usually has such departments as :

1. General administraion,
2. Health,
3. Finance,
4. Education,

5. Co-operation,
6. Animal Husbandry,
7. Agriculture,
8. Power and Irrigation,
9. Food,
10. Banking,
11. Roadways,
12. Forests,
13. Development,
14. Housing,
15. Industries,
16. Jails,
17. Planning,
18. Excise,
19. Labour and Employment,
20. Legislative,
21. Local Self-Government,
22. Social Welfare,
23. Police,
24. Panchayats,
25. Public Works,
26. Vigilance.

It is very difficult to enumerate the list of departments which the different states have but the above mentioned departments usually function in every state. Similarly it is difficult to discuss the organisation of all these departments.

Education Department. Each state has an Education Department. It is headed by Education Minister who is political head of the department. He decides about educational policy of the State. Then comes the Secretary of the Department of Education, who is the administrative head of the department. Each Education Department has a Director of public Instructions who is assisted by many officers in the department. Usually each Education Department has three wings namely *(a)* School Wing *(b)* College Wing *(c)* General Administration and Planning Wing. Each wing is headed by a Senior Officer usually of the rank of the Joint Director. Each Joint Director is assisted by Deputy and Assistant Director who has sufficiently large administrative and financial powers.

Then the state is divided into circles in education matters. Each Circle Education Officer belongs to State Education service. His main responsibility is to supervise the working of Direct Officers under his control. Some administrative and financial powers have been delegated to him. He has also been given powers to punish clerical staff. He is usually helped by a male and a female Deputy Circle Education Officer each.

Each circle is divided into districts and each districts is headed by District Education Officer and assisted by number of Deputy Education Officers. The number of these deputies depends on the strength of the District. A District Education Officer enjoy considerably large administrative and financial powers. Deputy Education Officers are mainly inspecting officers and inspect the schools falling with in their jurisdictions.

The Education Commission in its Report has recommended that the State Education Department should look after the development and implementation of a programme of school education. It should help in improving standards of education of both the teachers and the taught. It should carry out an extensive programme of supervision and inspection and also maintain quality institutions.

Health Department. Health is another important department in a state secretariat. The department is headed by a minister, who as usual is political boss and gives guidance regarding health policies. The main responsibility of the department is that it should take both preventive and precautionary measures to check the spread and out break of diseases. There is separate Director of Health Services who looks after the working of Public Health Department. There are many Deputy and Assistant Directors General of Health Services who assist him in the discharge of his duties.

In each State there is also Department of Medical Relief which is under the administrative control of Inspector General of Civil Hospitals. He also get directions from the Minister of Health. Each civil hospital is controlled by a Civil Surgeon who supervises the work of all the employees working in the hospital. He advises the District Officers in health matters.

In each state there are many charitable hospitals and their work is also supervised by the Inspector General, Civil Hospitals.

State Medical Councils. Each State has a medical council. Each such council maintains a register of qualified practitioners. It also reviews the system of medical education and the manner is which examinations are be conducted. It exercises disciplinary powers over medical practitioners.

This is brief to the organisation of the education and health departments which are two important departments of the state. It is just to give broad outlines as it is just impossible to discuss the organisation of all departments within the limited available space. •

CABINET SECRETARIAT

The Cabinet Secretariat play a very important role as its very name implies. It serves as the coordinating body of the cabinet. Its main functions are :

(i) to provide secretariat machinery for effectively transacting the routine business of the Cabinet;

(ii) to work at the Secretariat for the various Cabinet Committees;

(iii) to keep the President, the Vice President and all the Ministers in touch with the major activities of all the ministers of Government; and

(iv) to co-ordinate the important Central-State Conferences convened by the various Central Ministries.

Organisation of Cabinet Secretariat. The Cabinet Secretariat is headed by the Prime Minister and consists of a Secretariat and an attached Office, namely the Central Statistical organisation. The Secretariat Organisation comprises:

1. Main Secretariat. The main Secretariat, which consists of branches like cabinet Coordination. Administration and General Section, is responsible for the Secretariat work connected with the meeting of the Cabinet and its Sub-Committees.

2. O and M Division. O and M stands for Organisation and Methods. The O and M Division was created in March, 1954 and was attached to the Cabinet Secretariat. It functions directly under the Prime Minister. The primary objectives of the Division are :

(a) to supply the leadership and drive, and

(b) to build-up a common fund of information by a cooperative effort experience in O and M Work.

It stands for paying intelligent and critical attention not only to what is done but also to how it is done and at what cost in time, labour and money and also paying attention to the design of the machine and its working processes and not merely to its end products. In a vast and diversified organisation like that of the Central Government, it was felt necessary to devise a system which could spread efficiency and economy over as wide an area as possible.

The work of O and M Division is carried through the O and M units set-up in each Ministry, each unit being under the charge of a Deputy Secretary functioning as O and M officer in addition to his own duties. The Director O and M Division, exchanges ideas and experience with the O and M officers of various ministrier, from time by holding joint meetings. The Deputy Director, O and M Division pays informal visits to the various ministers from time to time and make random checks to see how far the prescribed procedures are being followed and also tenders advice of various problems of O and M work.

3. Military Wing. The Military Wing is responsible for all Secreatriat work connected with the meetings of the Defence Committee of the Cabinet, the Defence Minister's Committee the Chief or Staff Committee, the Joint Planning Committee, the Joint Intelligence Committee, etc.

4. Economic Wing. The Economic Wing is responsible for all secretariat work connected with the Economic Committee of the Cabinet, the Committee of Economic Secretaries and the supply Committee.

Central Statistical Organisation. The Central Statistical Organisation was established in May, 1951. The main functions of the organisation are :

(i) to prepare and publish the Annual Statistics Abstract, of Statistics and Weekly Bulletin of Statistics and Guide to Current Official Statistics;

(ii) to attend to work relating to the United Nations Statistical Organisation;

(iii) to present in graphic form the current statistics with a view of throwing light on the developing economic situation;

(iv) to undertake special work for the Central Government Ministers or the State Government, including provision of facilities for training of officers in the day-to-day statistical work;

(v) to co-ordinate the statistical work of the Ministries and other Government Agencies;

(vi) to keep continuous touch with National Statistical Organisations in other countries of the world particularly with regard to the latest development in methodology and organisation;

(vii) to develop definition and standards for improving national and international comparability and the quality of information required by Government.

The Organisation functions under the guidance of an Honorary Statistical Adviser to the Cabinet and is headed by a Statistician, who is assisted by various technical and Secretariat staff.

Cabinet Secretary. The Cabinet Secretariat functions under a Cabinet Secreatry. He is a very senior bureaucrat who has seen the tides of time gained rich experience by holding variety of administrative posts before reaching the highest wing the ladder. He is almost the pivot of the Cabinet System. He is entrusted with the positive functions of securing co-ordination as well as timely and effective action by all the Ministries in all these matters in which the Cabinet as whole is interested. He convenes meetings of secretaries and senior officers whenever necessary. He is a sort of adviser to all the permanent officials. He guides and advises them whenever they come to him for advice in the departmental difficulties. In short he is their-friend, philosopher and guide.

Gopalaswami Ayyanger explaining on the role of Cabinet Secretary in his Report on Re-organisation of the Machinery of Government said, "The status and functions of the Cabinet Secretary should be clearly understood. He should be an Administrative Officer of the highest rank selected for the office for his special qualities of tact, energy, initiative and efficiency and he should be entrusted as head of the Cabinet Secretariat, with the positive function of securing co-ordination as well as timely and effective action by all departments of the Government of India in all matters in which the cabinet as whole or the Prime Minister is interested. He should be a person commanding respect and confidence of all ranks of the permanent services... While not laying on the Cabinet Secretary any specific function which would impair the initiative and responsibility of head of departments, I think it would be desirable to establish the convention that he should be a sufficiently senior officer so as to command the confidence and respect of all Heads of Departments. His status should be such as to entitle him to be regarded as the first number of the Public Services under the control of the Central Government, and one in whose judgment and impartiality the Government, as well as the services, could rely implicity."

Thus, it is obvious that the Cabinet Secretary is an official to top ranking category of whom high quality of work is expected. As a head of the Cabinet Secretariat his duties are arduous and authority onerous. He is required to bring about co-ordination and secure timely and effective action by all Ministries and Departments in all matters. Hence, it is imperative that the Cabinet Secretary must be a senior officer of ripe experience, high talents and wide imagination.

●●

2

Performance of Public Enterprises

Despite growing world-wide interest in the privatisation of public enterprises, it is clear that public enterprises will continue to feature prominently in the organisational landscapes of developing countries. It is therefore important to be able to improve their performance. Estimates of the costs of foregone social welfare arising from public enterprise inefficiencies drive home the significance of the point.

According to Jones, for example, an improvement to the operating efficiency of the public enterprise sector of 5 per cent, without additional investment or adjusted prices, would yield: in Egypt, resources equivalent to 5 per cent of GDP, 75 per cent of direct taxes, or three times government expenditures on education; in Pakistan, resources equivalent to 1 per cent of GDP, or half of direct taxes, or 50 per cent of government expenditures on education; in the Republic of Korea, resources amounting to 1.7 per cent of GDP, or more than 1 billion dollars in 1981; in the People's Republic of China, resources worth 11 billion dollars, or enough to increase government expenditures on culture, education, health, and science by 150 per cent.

Many problems of public enterprise performance can be traced to difficulties with goal clarity and measurement, and the different views regarding goals and their priority held by take holders. It is easy to see why an organisation with no goals or goals that are only poorly specified or not widely shared will have difficulty maintaining reasonable levels of efficiency and effectiveness. Without clear objectives and a means of keeping score, a structured, purposeful, goal-directed organisation can quickly be reduced to a disjointed, uncommitted rabble.

Goal specification in public enterprises is complicated by the necessity for both commercial and non-commercial objectives because non-commercial objectives are more difficult to describe and measure accurately than commercial objectives. The possibility of explaining away poor commercial performance by referring to noncommercial objectives undermines any benefits-to motivation, control, direction-that might accrue from having in place measurable, clearly specified commercial objectives. This has the effect of turning the public enterprise into a government department rather than a hybrid public/private organisation.

The market-based solution is to make public enterprises more like private enterprises and to place strong emphasis on profitability as the major criterion of performance. In command economies in transition, performance problems arise primarily from insufficient autonomy and authority for managers at the level of the firm, particularly in relation to pricing, procurement, staffing, performance management, and marketing; from the absence of clearly formulated sets of attainable and measurable commercial and non-commercial objectives; and from the state's unwillingness to create owners who can protect the capital employed.

Modern market-based approaches to enterprise reform in such settings might entail all or some combination of:

- transforming all state enterprises into joint-stock companies whose shares would be held by portfolio management agencies acting on the owners' behalf;

- transforming the enterprise into a profitmaximising commercial entity and having this policy communicated unequivocally by the owners;
- terminating government subsidies to the enterprise;
- imposing strict budgetary constraints at the same time as prices are allowed to adjust to the market;
- compensating firms that are required to provide such services because of the absence of better, cheaper alternatives;
- appraising and rewarding the performance of individuals and groups in relation to their achievement of organisational goals, not as a result of performance improvements stemming from changes in exogenous variables over which they have little or no control;
- significantly curtailing the number of non-commercial functions fulfilled by the firm, meaning that the provision of such services as health care, education, housing, and subsidised consumer goods would cease or be minimised;
- establishing enterprise boards of directors composed primarily of members drawn from the private/ sector who have thorough product or industry knowledge, have represented clients, creditors, or suppliers, or have expertise in such fields as law, banking, and finance;
- assigning enterprise management the power to hire and fire workers and evaluate their performance, set product prices, and decide on product lines and output;
- allowing the owners to have control over board membership, and giving boards the power to appoint, dismiss, and reward enterprise management;

- empowering boards to dismiss managers who fail to perform satisfactorily; and
- empowering owners to dismiss boards that fail to perform satisfactorily. These measures would shift power away from state bureaus to the portfolio management agencies, banks, and boards of directors.

Very similar reforms have recently been applied successfully in New Zealand. Nevertheless, these proposals would clearly be difficult for some government bureaus and many enterprise managers in socialist countries to comprehend, let alone implement. A major impediment to reform in these countries is that most managers have simply been unused to making decisions or taking initiatives in the past and display bewilderment at the conceptual magnitude and speed of the changes they are being asked to contemplate and enact.

A key reform issue therefore becomes one of finding ways of transforming passive civil servants into proactive managers. In Poland these problems have been addressed in part by the use of a 'company doctor' programme. In cooperation with a private management consulting firm, the Polish government trains teams of analysts whose job it is to categorise state enterprises as 'healthy', 'salvageable', or 'hopeless'. Another possible tool would be drawing up management contracts that would hire management teams and systems from abroad.

Privatisation

Privatisation lies at the heart of the market based approach to public management. It is a central feature of most structural adjustment programmes in developing countries and countries transforming from planned to market economies. The World Bank is unequivocal in its support for privatisation: "Privatisation, when correctly conceived and implemented, fosters efficiency, encourages investment, and frees public resources for investment in infrastructure and social programmes". UNDP has also embraced the idea and has set up a special division for the private sector and the Inter regional Network on Privatisation to disseminate information and experience about privatisation.

Advocates of privatisation assert that "private ownership itself makes a difference... government ownership seldom permits sustained good performance over more than a few years"... According to the World Bank, more than eighty countries are in the process of privatising their state-owned enterprises (SOEs). They have done so for a variety of reasons or in the hope that: weak private sectors could be strengthened; higher investment ratios could be produced so that capital surpluses could be invested in the economy; technology could be transferred to strategic sectors of the economy; greater efficiencies and effectiveness would result; in the long-term, jobs would be created; and the costs of goods and services would fall as quality rose.

However, privatisation can be extremely difficult to achieve, as in the case of Sri Lanka where privatisation has been on the agenda since 1977. To date, only eleven enterprises have been sold and five management contracts concluded in that country. Formidable resistance to privatization—mainly from labour unions, political parties, and senior management of state enterprises—has also been encountered in India.

In India, as in other developing countries, "some public enterprises have social and other non-commercial objectives, such as improved income distribution, increased job opportunities, and the development of backward areas. Affected populations resent any roll back of concessions given them earlier". Severe problems have also been encountered in Argentina where the privatisation of the national airline and the national telephone company has resulted in worsening services and higher prices.

The Argentine experience demonstrates dearly the dangers of creating private monopolies without first having in place a solid regulatory framework to protect consumers. Likewise, in the former Eastern Block countries, privatisation has been far from straightforward. In these settings a major obstacle has been the reactive mind sets of managers and confusion concerning the purposes, processes, and outcomes of privatisation. In Poland, for example:

> Privatisation has been much more complex and difficult than originally envisaged when the privatisation law was passed in July 1990. There was no clear ideological orientation. Some important people saw it as simply a legal transformation of certain enterprises rather than a radical metamorphosis of the entire economy. The law calls for the transformation of enterprises from centrally controlled to market-driven, but builds in the maintenance of certain social goals, for example, by requiring that companies offer 20 per cent of their equity to employees at preferential rates.

Similar problems to those set out above have been encountered in the former East Germany and the former Soviet Union. In the former Soviet Union, the attitudes and expectations of managers appear to be particularly problematic:

> Every one of the managers met saw that the rules of the game had been altered. But rather than take steps to position themselves and their enterprises to deal with or take advantage of the changed set of rules, many were waiting to be told—by the ministry, by other central authorities, by anybody—what to do

> next. Management trainers interviewed said that a wait-to-be-told attitude typified Soviet managers, who were previously not expected and are now generally not prepared to make decisions, to seize opportunities, and to be self-reliant.

Nevertheless, the proponents of privatisation assert that SOEs are not a good idea because even where they can be made to work well, the effort required to bring about good performance is considerable, and reasonable performance cannot be sustained for more than a few years. Two factors are seen as being crucial to the success of privatisation. First, the enterprise should be divested into an open market: privatisation is easier and outcomes are more likely to be positive when markets are competitive. Second, overall macroeconomic conditions and policy frameworks should be 'market-friendly'. Where privatisation is contemplated in non-competitive markets, legal and regulatory devices to protect consumers must be established—examples where this would be necessary include water, power, and telecommunications.

A final set of considerations that needs to borne in mind concern the possible hidden costs of privatisation. These costs arise from difficulties associated with measuring and controlling the quality of private enterprise performance in certain spheres and the resistance of such enterprises to external assessment. This is particularly important in poor countries and economies in transition where regulatory mechanisms may not exist, or if they do, tend not to be as well established or enforced as they are in other parts of the world.

A second example involves garbage disposal and the disposal of toxic wastes more generally. Many government authorities in the industrialised countries contract out garbage disposal to private companies. Rich consumer societies produce mountains of garbage, so garbage disposal is big business. A major problem with garbage disposal is that it contains many different kinds of toxic wastes that are difficult, and therefore expensive, to dispose of safely or to contain.

Over time, toxic wastes seep into the water table and surrounding ecosystems and pollute land, drinking water, and water used for irrigation. It is extremely difficult for government—even in the rich countries—to ensure that contractors who undertake this kind of work are disposing of waste products safely. This is because it is difficult to determine whether chemicals and toxic wastes from a garbage dump are in fact leaking into the ecosystem.

Many years can go by before the effects of any leakage are detected in human and animal diseases and mortality rates. Further, the private companies concerned resist government attempts to investigate this aspect of their performance. It therefore requires extraordinary levels of capacity and commitment on the parts of governments to be able to regulate effectively in this domain. Where government regulation has been relatively successful, it has often forced the problem off-shore, leading to dumping in poor countries:

"During 1988 virtually every country from Morocco to the Congo, received offers from companies seeking cheap sites for dumping wastes". In 1988, for example, Guinea-Bissau agreed to bury 15 million tons of toxic waste from Europe. The government was paid $120 million, only slightly less than the country's GNP. Developing countries must acquire the expertise to make judgements about whether, or to what extent, to privatise so that they can enter into constructive dialogue with outside agencies. At present, the weight of ideology rather than hard evidence seems to hold sway.

Private Enterprises

A healthy private sector is a crucial component of any sound economy. Private enterprises generate large economic returns for the economy as a whole as well as for individual investors, particularly in a free market characterised by relatively open access to inputs, autonomy in investment and operating decisions, and incentives that are applied fairly and consistently to all participants.

Recent empirical research in developing countries confirms that there is a strong positive correlation between private sector activity and economic growth. It has also been shown that productivity growth is closely associated with private investment. Moreover, the presence of strong private sector growth in Ghana, Guinea, and the Gambia has been found to make a considerable—perhaps essential—difference to civil service reform programmes in those countries.

First, the granting of monopolies to state enterprises clearly impedes private sector development. Examples of inefficiencies and misuse of funds abound in state monopolies in agricultural marketing, urban transport, mining, manufacturing, and public utilities. Such barriers to entry deprive developing countries of local and foreign private investment, and the skills, knowledge, and technology that would accompany such investment.

Second, where legal barriers to entry do not exist, bureaucratic impediments often do. Such impediments include price controls, restrictions on the employment of expatriate staff and geographical location, requirements to use local supplies of variable quality, uncertainties regarding legislative change after a project has been implemented, slow and arbitrary decision-making, and circumstances conducive to corruption. Availability of finance is also an inhibiting factor in the growth of the private sector, particularly for small and medium-sized enterprises. Major problems have to do with financial market regulations that tend to discourage banks from lending to small enterprises; the absence of stock markets and merchant banks; foreign exchange controls; excessive borrowing by government, which crowds out private enterprises from financial markets; heavy taxation, which restricts the private sector's capacity for generating internal funds for investment; and the monopolisation by public investment programmes of foreign loans and grants.

A fourth consideration is labour policies that in some instances provide insufficient flexibility to employers, especially in relation to wage negotiation, productivity bargaining, and the laying off of unproductive workers. Price controls can disadvantage local producers by squeezing profits. The effects of such controls are particularly evident in the agricultural sector. In addition, overvalued currencies make it difficult for local producers to compete in international markets and reduce returns from exports. They also keep down the relative price of imports, which discourages import substitution.

Lastly, excessive tariff rates for products with low value-added may restrict competition and depress levels of efficiency and product quality. Quantitative restrictions on imports can promote corruption. As In an increasing number of developing countries these issues are being addressed by government. Certainly, there is no shortage of entrepreneurial spirit in most developing countries.

Contingency-based Mechanisms

The evidence supports the market-based approach, even in its milder forms. The biggest challenge posed to the dominant paradigm comes from East Asia where, in the past 25 years, per capita incomes have nearly quadrupled, a record of achievement unsurpassed in economic history. Few, if any, economists foresaw the East Asian economic miracle.

Thirty years ago many economists thought that a number of countries in Latin America had much better prospects for development than any in East Asia. This lack of foresight is understandable.

The extent of state intervention in the rapidly growing economies of East and Southeast Asia—the so-called 'tigers' of Hong Kong, Singapore, the Republic of Korea, and Taiwan and 'cubs' of Indonesia, Malaysia, and Thailand—varies considerably, suggesting a contingency approach to questions of economic management, which may be superior to market-based mechanisms entailing state minimalism. The evidence demonstrates:

(1) that Taiwan and the Republic of Korea did not have particularly liberal trade regimes;

(2) that in certain respects their public sectors were quite large;

(3) that both states tightly controlled the financial system; and

(4) that both states employed policies to promote particular industries, including fiscal concessions, special credit facilities, and protection.

Evaluation of the East and Southeast Asian experience is currently being undertaken by the World Bank, partly on the insistence of Japan, which is the Bank's second largest shareholder. Japan has long criticised the state minimalist approach of the World Bank:

> In 1991 Japan's Overseas Economic Cooperation Fund told the bank it was putting too much emphasis on deregulation and privatisation and made a case for selective import protection in developing countriesand for the use of subsidised credits as a tool in industrial policy.

So far there is relatively little evidence from developing countries undergoing market-oriented reforms to suggest that the approach is working as well or as quickly as development theorists had hoped. This makes the Asian experience, and Japanese advice regarding development strategies, all the more noteworthy. If present trends continue, per capita incomes in East and Southeast Asia could well overtake those of many of the industrialised countries by the early twenty-first century.

Even after allowing for such desirable conditions as macroeconomic stability, high rates of investment, and export-led development, it is still difficult to explain the very high rates of productivity growth, which are the region's main distinguishing feature. The puzzle is complicated by the region's lack of homogeneity. Among the successful economies, the extent of state intervention varies enormously. Hong Kong follows a minimalist approach, while at the other extreme, the Republic of Korea and Japan have intervened heavily. The extent of state intervention, therefore, seems to be contingent upon political, social, and cultural circumstances rather than being predetermined, as in the state minimalist approach.

The World Bank is reported as referring to this as a "strategic growth" model that favours the rapid accumulation of capital, the efficient allocation of resources, and technological sophistication but makes no prescriptions about responsibilities, whether public or private. The over-riding concern is the achievement of rapid economic growth through whatever means seem best suited to the task rather than the predetermination of governmental roles and responsibilities. East and Southeast Asian economies employ a mixture of market incentives and state intervention. For example, in order to ensure a reliable supply of low-cost capital, the financial sectors have been heavily regulated. Moreover, close links—including cross-share holdings—between financial institutions and conglomerates are encouraged.

Governments in the region have also intervened strongly in labour markets in order to ensure flexibility and that wages reflect supply and demand. Trade unions have been suppressed. The focus on exporting has exerted pressure on domestic prices for industrial inputs, keeping them in line with world prices. Many governments have used import controls to protect key sectors of the local economy and provided subsidies to export industries. In most of the rapidly expanding East and Southeast Asian economies, state—owned enterprises have played an important role—and ways have been found to maintain the competitiveness of such enterprises.

In the Republic of Korea, for example, performance appraisals of the management of public enterprises are sometimes carried out by external review panels consisting of experts from universities and government officials. If their enterprise receives a good rating, managers can receive annual bonuses of up to three months salary. Rankings of SOEs are published in the press. There is strong evidence from the Republic of Korea and, more recently, from Pakistan that such measures lead to significant improvements in efficiency and effectiveness.

In many respects, the Republic of Korea's success can be attributed to state intervention: From the early 1960s the government carefully planned and orchestrated the country's development... (it) used the financial sector to steer credits to preferred sectors and promoted individual firms to achieve national objectives... (it) socialised risk, created large conglomerates(chaebols), created state enterprises when necessary, and moulded a public-private partnership that rivalled Japan's.

A clear dilemma is created for external contributors by the East and Southeast Asian experience, particularly in relation to former communist countries but possibly in relation to all developing countries. That is, should donors continue to advocate shock therapy measures involving the deregulation and privatisation of everything as quickly as possible or advocate a more gradual, state-managed transition? The answer to this question should not depend on whether state intervention in all circumstances has worked, because it clearly has not. Rather, it should depend on a careful analysis of the nature of failed state intervention and the circumstances surrounding such failure.

The main lesson of the Asian experience must surely be that the nature and extent of state intervention was managed skillfully to suit the economic, cultural, and political circumstances of the different economies of the region at different stages in their development. In some cases, such as that of the Republic of Korea, governments adapted very quickly to changing circumstances. Strong or determined government is therefore far from always being a bad thing.

Public management strategies may have to be revised accordingly. While the prospects in developing countries for replicating the East and Southeast Asian economic miracle are not good, valuable lessons can still be learned, particularly at the level of institutional design. They include the following:

- **Industrial Promotion.** The cases of the Republic of Korea, Taiwan, and Japan demonstrate that state involvement in the promotion of certain industries is not detrimental to development. State intervention in these countries involved both leading and following the market. In most environments, however, industrial promotion on the part of the state should involve followership, with export performance being a necessary condition for continuing assistance.

- **Education.** State involvement in education, which increases the ratios of skilled to unskilled people in the work force, is a critical feature of the East and Southeast Asian experience.

- **State-society Links.** In the countries mentioned, the state was highly autonomous.

- **Pilot Agencies.** Core government agencies, such as MITI in Japan, the Industrial Development Bureau in Taiwan, and the Economic Planning Board in the Republic of Korea, provided strategic planning and lobbying capabilities far beyond the reach of individual entrepreneurs. Although relatively little is known about the organisation and management of these agencies, their central government location and the high calibre of personnel employed made them extremely influential.

●●

3

Development Administration

The end of colonialism in the post World War II period transformed the basic character of public administration. Hitherto, public administration was oriented towards law and order and was regulatory in nature. It was now called upon to become Development Administration, that is, an administrative system the primary goal of which is to initiate and step up plans and programmes to raise people's living standards. Writing as early as in 1946, R. Tottenham in his famous report on the reorganisation of the Indian administration articulated the new concern:

> State was to renounce the old conception of Government as a regulatory, policing and taxing mechanism, and openly to adopt the conception of Government as the nation's common instrument for expanding its social and economic welfare in all those spheres where individuals and private associations cannot achieve effective results.

Similarly the Bengal Administration Enquiry Committee under the chairmanship of Sir Archibald Rowlands announced the goals of post-war Indian administration thus: 'The main emphasis in the activities of Government henceforward will be in the development field and directed to the full utilisation of the material and human resources of the province'.

India was thus moving towards development administration. Independence in 1947 converted such an orientation into firm ideological commitment. When the colonies emerged to full Statehood, the new rulers who had pledged themselves to the goals of development during the days of the freedom movement systematically initiated bold plans of economic betterment of their people. The term 'development administration' was coined in the post-war period to emphasise this new focus.

The advent of development administration, however, does not imply that development did not take place hitherto and had remained frozen. Developmental efforts—the so-called 'nation-building' activities—were consciously stepped up with the introduction of dyarchy in the provinces under the Government of India Act, 1919.

The term 'development administration' first appears in an article by an Indian civil servant, V.L. Goswami (of the ICS). In his article, 'The Structure of Development Administration in India', published in The Indian Journal of Public Administration (vol. I, 1955, pp 110-18), Goswami gives a formal description of the administrative machinery of the community development programmes in India. George F. Gant, who was intimately associated with the Tennessee Valley Authority and later with the Ford Foundation, is however considered the father of the concept. In his book, Development Administration: Concepts, Goals, Methods, first published in 1979, Gant says that he, along with another scholar Egbert de Vries, had started using the term 'development administration' in 1955 or 1956. The term originated in the Gontext of rural development though in the course of time it encompassed much more and thus transcended that limited concern. Edward W. Weidner, Fred W. Riggs, Ferrel Heady, John D. Montgomery, Milton J. Esman, LucianPye, Merle Fainsod, Irving Swerdlow, William J. Siffin—all of them Americans—are among the more prominent scholars who have contributed to the development of the concept of development administration. The former colonies were receiving massive American technical assistance, to administer which American personnel were coming to the do-nee countries of Asia and Africa.

One may here say a word about comparative public administration, which emerged sharply after the end of the colonial era. The newly decolonised countries, now called developing societies, attracted the attention of western, mostly American scholars. The researches sponsored or undertaken to study them were intended to promote development, the evident concern of these countries. This explains the sustained interest taken in them by funding organisations whether of the United States or the United Nations. In short, development administration became the direct concern of comparative public administration.

Development administration does not suffer from dearth of definitions even though the concept is relatively young. Donald Stone defines it as 'the blending of all the elements and resources (human and physical) ... into a concerted effort to achieve agreed upon goals'. He further observes: 'It [development administration] is the continuous cycle of formulating, evaluating and implementing interrelated plans, policies, programmes, projects, activities and other measures to reach established development objectives in a scheduled time sequence.' George Gant observes:

> Development is the term used to denote the complex of agencies, management systems and processes a government establishes to achieve its development goals. It is the public mechanism set up to relate the several components' of development in order to articulate and accomplish national social and economic objectives. It is the adjustment of the bureaucracy to the vastly increased functions required to respond to public demands for development. Development

> administration is the administration of policies, programmes and projects to serve development purposes.

A.U.N. publication of 1975 even goes to the extent of opting for the term 'development administration' in place of traditional public administration. It observes that the term 'development administration' emphasises that 'the focus of attention is on the building and improvement of a public administration system as part of the total effort of national development'. It continues: 'It covers both the administration of development (i.e., public administration as an instrument of national development) and the development of administration (i.e., measures to enhance the administrative capacity for development).

The content of development administration is still evolving. The first and foremost concern of poverty is with bread. In the initial period of independence, the concern of development administration was economic, that is, raising the people's standard of living. The foremost concern was to promote economic growth and to increase production. During the 1950s and 1960s, development was virtually identified with economic growth with the increase in GNP. The exclusive emphasis on economic growth, however, gave birth to imbalances and other hardships in the developing countries. The evaluation of these growth-oriented plans disclosed that economic growth increased alongside increasing poverty and unemployment among the masses. The inequalities between the rich and the poor were increasing. In recognition of such anomalies, the goal of development came to be redefined as growth-with-justice.

Development administration had to wrestle with many other problems as well. Some suggested that transfer of technology would solve the problem of poverty in developing countries. Others wanted these countries to change their attitudes and traditions as part of the discipline of development, forgetting to ask themselves: if traditions .are to be banished, what would ultimately remain in the societies? Sometimes, the Indian family system was viewed as unfriendly to development. These are facile, erroneous observations. The strength of the joint family system is now being realised when one looks at the top level industrial houses in India: a joint family is a supporting asset of development, not its enemy.

Nor was development to overlook the task of nation building *i.e.*, to achieve national unity and to weld together people with diverse cultural and racial backgrounds so that they feel one with a commonly shared destiny. A sense of nationhood was to be developed. Getting India independent was not enough: the task has been to make Indians out of us, who are basically Punjabis. Bengalis, Biharis etc. Today, the concept of development has become more encompassing and humanistic. The latest concept is Sustainable Development. In the words of the World Commission on Environment and Development (1987) which coined this phrase, sustainable development is 'development that meets the needs of the present without compromising the ability of future generations to meet their own needs'.

There is, thus, a broadening of the concept of development. In the 1950s and even the 1960s, development was interpreted in purely economic (GNP) terms. This definition proved sadly insufficient and inadequate. Economic growth was then supplemented by social justice. Other dimensions were also gradually added. Development is now to take care of the total human being, who has his social and cultural dimensions too. No longer is mother Earth to be plundered in the name of development. Pollution must be controlled; forests must be preserved, wildlife is to be promoted. In other words, development must be environment-friendly.

At one time, a dichotomy used to be maintained between development administration and traditional or regulatory administration. Development administration was concerned with, say agriculture, education etc. Administration of law and order, on the other hand, was part of the traditional or regulatory administration. Indian planners are still in the habit of classifying public activities into 'Plan activities' and 'Non-plan activities'. Police, for instance, is a non-Plan item. Nevertheless, the dichotomy between development administration and so-called regulatory administration was evidently senseless. Development cannot occur without firm law and order in society. What is more, development itself is a tension7generating process: its successes inevitably beget new social problems, demanding the attention of development administration. In this light, we may consider as the most acceptable and practical the definition of development administration given by Irving Swerdlow.

The activities coming under the broad purview of development administration may be called 'discrete' and 'diffuse'. A fertiliser factory or a steel plant, where the completion time is more or less firmly estimated, is a discrete activity. But many activities in public administration are not amenable to any time estimation. One cannot, for instance, determine the terminal date for rural development or community development. A vast area claiming the attention of development administration deals with diffuse operations. Activities in this category are complex and .intricate, and cannot be subject to PERT/CPM.

The accent of development administration is on change—or on planned change. John Montgomery defines development administration as carrying out planned change both in the economy and in the social services. Harry Friedman's definition includes two elements—'the implementation of programmes designed to bring about modernity and the changes within the administrative system which increase its capacity to implement such programmes'. Fred W. Riggs views development administration as 'a process leading to an increasing ability to make collective decisions, especially decisions that involve long term environmental changes'. The emphasis on change becomes transparent in the following observation, which was made regarding the intensive agricultural developmental programme, which was but a part of the developmental programmes of India:

> The main objective of the intensive agricultural development programme is to accelerate the rate of growth by bringing about a basic change in the situation in which it operates. The main purpose of the administrative system that India has inherited is on the other hand, to ensure security and hence allow only the minimum possible change. The intensive agricultural development programme puts a premium on the technician who is the harbinger of change. The Indian administrative system gives primacy to the administrator whose main function is to lay down and administer the rules designed to ensure conformity. The basic idea of intensive agricultural development programme is that it should be a tailor-made programme to suit the needs of a particular area which can be adjusted by the local authorities promptly and effectively as and when the situation changes.

The general tone of the above quotation, it should be obvious, is that the established administrative machinery is not the best suited to development administration. Change being inherent in development administration, the acquired administrative machinery, procedures, personnel policies and relations with the environment—all these have to be retuned and harnessed to the new and novel goals and processes of development.

Developing countries had hardly any choice but to make the career bureaucracy the instrument of development administration in the absence of an alternative institution available and ready to take up these activities. Bureaucracy had acquired the reputation for delivering the goods, however complex the nature of the tasks. It commanded the highest respect as embodying the cream of the country's intelligent youth who had been tempered in the school of experience. When India began to prepare developmental plans in the mid-1940s, and the question arose as to who should coordinate these plans, even specialists at that time thought that the generalist District Collector as a rule habitually carried legendary respect and influence which they lacked. The specialists themselves, therefore, showed preference for the generalist administrators. Development administration employs an army of specialists of diverse types, but top management vests in the generalist administrators.

An important dimension of development administration concerns the people's participation in the development process. Today's government is a big government with increasing range and scale of developmental functions. The latter's success crucially hinges on people's active involvement in both their planning and implementation processes. India's panchayati raj, introduced since the early 1960s, is a bold governmental effort to seek citizen participation in developmental effort. This makes developmental planning realistic to suit local needs. What is even more, it opens up grass roots source of politics, which is essential for sound democracy.

Problems

The experience in executing development administration now extends to five decades. Over these decades, the following have been experienced as the problems in its optimum execution: centralisation, lack of coordination, corruption, redtapism and rigidity. Centralisation is perhaps the foremost problem. There is excessive concentration of power and decision-making at the top levels of government, particularly in matters of allocating financial and other resources. Those who hold the reins of power are unwilling to delegate powers to the theatres of action—the field offices. The result is excessive consultation, delays and cost overruns.

Lack of coordination between the ministries and departments concerned is another major problem. The present practice is to entrust developmental functions to various departments, which are organised on a sectoral basis. Thus, there are departments of agriculture, animal husbandry, public cooperation, public health, education, 'public works etc. Each department routinely maintains its field agencies to implement its respective programme. There is hardly any coordination between them. Agricultural development, for example, requires supplies, in proper sequence and on time, of fertiliser, seed, water, credit and arrangement for storing and marketing. Involved in these various tasks are the Departments of Agriculture, Irrigation, Husbandry, Cooperation, Electricity, etc. Failure of even one department is liable to retard the achievement of targets.

Corruption. Because development administration necessarily entails massive spending of public funds, corruption is rampant and has so far defied an effective solution. According to some knowledgeable sources, 80 per cent of the financial resources in rural development, which accounts for a large chunk of development administration in India, is siphoned off to line private pockets. Prolonged inattention to the problems of corruption, one must note, has brought down many regimes in the third world. Along with widespread graft is the problem of lack of commitment of development bureaucracy to their task. This is a grave problem.

Red-tapismand inflexibility are the other serious problems. Modern public administration is based on hierarchy, recruitment on the basis of merit, strict observance of rules, regulations and procedures. These are the well known attributes of bureaucracy designed to maximise efficiency and objectivity. In development administration, however, these traits lead to red tape and inflexibility and thus frustrate development goals. Developmental needs are poorly served by insistence on public tenders, approval of contracts, procurement of equipment, disbursement of funds etc., all of which cause delay in decision-making and implementation.

Issues in Development Administration

Development administration poses a number of issues for the national policy-makers. The first is the exact balance between centralisation and decentralisation. Advocates of centralisation speak of the need for unity of vision, comprehensiveness of planning, society-wide coordination of effort, rational allocation of resources, and speed in policy making. Conversely, proponents of decentralisation invoke the virtues of local initiative, effort and social responsibility—all of which demand decentralisation. Centralisation and decentralisation are two alternatives; and an acceptable distribution of power need not remain valid for ever. An appropriate solution lies in how much of both. The question partly relates also to the proper allocation of functions and resol1rces between the central and lower levels of government.

A second issue concerns the limitations and shortcomings of the career bureaucracy as the chosen instrument of development administration. Development administration calls for administrators who, besides possessing managerial skills, are good in forging external linkages, i.e., enlisting the support and cooperation of people and agencies whose participation is essential to the success of such programmes. They must equally possess understanding of the dynamics of development process and the socio-cultural environment.

Alternatives are being tried out to escape the cumbersome rules and procedures of the Weberian bureaucracy. These have included the use, for planning and implementation, of ad hoc bodies, task forces, public enterprise, and voluntary organisations. Attention is also being given to adapting bureaucracy to the new needs and make it responsive to local needs. An internal restructuring of the career bureaucracy is inescapable to fit it to the challenges of development administration. Development administration necessarily employs specialists of diverse backgrounds, and in much larger numbers. Historically, public administration in developing countries has been generalist-dominated, in which the specialist is at the tap and never on top. A readjustment of the generalist-specialist relationship is the crying need of development administration. This, naturally, implies enhancing the role and status of the specialists, who are the harbingers of progress in society.

Another issue posed by Fred Riggs, is that the existence of weak extra-bureaucratic political institutions in developing countries poses a serious handicap to development administration. The expansion of administrative agencies has outpaced the development of parliamentary and political institutions, according to him. The resultant heavy-weight position of the bureaucracy impedes development. An essential piece of administrative reform in developing countries is, therefore, a conscious strengthening of political institutions, including parliamentary institutions.

Strategies of Development Administration

The accent of development administration being on change, it is primarily concerned with application, with practice, with execution. Yet the question remains: what, in a society, brings about social change, which is the essence of development administration? Two broad theories prevail on this question, and within each, two alternative strategies have emerged.

These are, the 'administrative systems approach' and the 'Social systems approach'. Fig. 1 presents these approaches and their strategic offshoots.

The administrative systems approach is evidently the dominant one. It assumes that some societies are more capable than others in producing goods and services to meet changing demands. Their public sector is marked by particular forms of organisation, processes of allocating resources, modes of management, etc. It also assumes that developing countries have definite advantages in their late commitment to productivity. What has been developed elsewhere can be adapted.

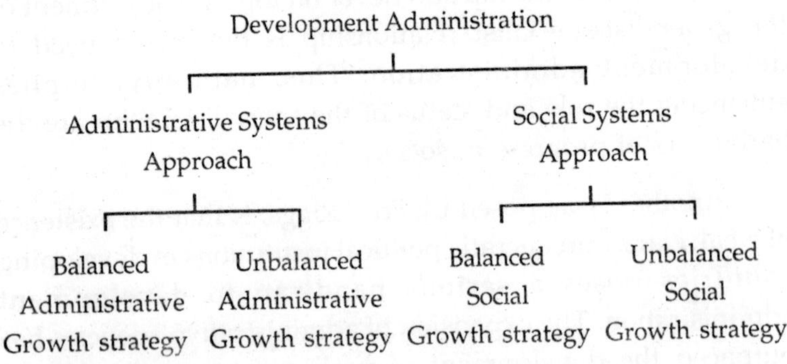

Fig. 1. Strategies of development administration

The administrative systems approach has two alternative strategies. One is the 'balanced administrative growth' strategy, which argues that piecemeal changes in public administration are inadequate and even self-defeating. What is needed are extensive and complementary centres of productive rationality—personnel systems, budgetary and fiscal procedures, planning processes, etc. They are complementary in the sense that they 'buy' each other's products and take advantage of each other's external economies.

The second strategy, which may be called 'unbalanced administrative growth' strategy, argues that if a country has the skills and resources to, build a modern administration (which is the recommendation of the balanced administrative growth strategy) it would not remain underdeveloped at all. What developing countries lack most is the capacity to make rational, productivity-oriented decisions, Scholars of the 'unbalanced administrative growth' school thus recommend increasing the rational capacities of the administrators. They recommend improving decision-making, planning, and management practices in public administration, and establishment of enclaves of administrative efficiency.

The administrative systems approach assumes that public administration is autonomous and lays emphasis on streamlining the processes of administration. Improved administration is thus assumed to be successful administration, and the content of programmes is not of direct concern to it.

The agonising slowness of change, especially economic, in developing countries has made some development administrators enunciate the social systems approach. The impetus also partly comes from the kind of impact of administered programmes on social behaviour. The social systems approach examines the interrelationship of factors in the social systems to find the source of higher productivity. A society is composed of interdependent subsystems, collectively engaged in functions such as social stratification, socialisation, planning and execution of goals, etc. A change in some subsystems inevitably generates change in others, ultimately bringing out a change in the entire social system. Often, the concept of 'stages' is employed to highlight major changes which have taken place in society historically. The terms commonly used for the stages are traditional. transitional, modern, agrarian, industrial, fused, prismatic, and diffracted. The different stages of social interaction give birth to different administrative systems.

The social systems approach claims two strategies—namely the 'balanced social growth' strategy and unbalanced social growth' strategy. The former strategy· argues that effective administration demands the existence of autonomous yet interdependent centres of power in society. These provide resources for, and obtain performance from, each other. In other words, administrative reform depends on healthy quasi—independent economic subsystems, a strong political subsystem, and functionally specific interest groups. Without them, bureaucracy misallocates resources, usually to its own name. If power is concentrated in the bureaucracy, other subsystems become weak and dependent, unable to perform their interest articulation and aggregation functions.

The 'unbalanced social growth' strategy assumes the interrelationship of various subsystems of society. But it seeks empirically and inductively to discover how different configurations affect the type and functions of bureaucracy. It. therefore, believes that there are situations where bureaucracy may develop autonomous yet interdependent centres of power. In other words, bureaucracy may be a catalytic agent to development also—it can devise ways to produce steel, fertiliser, to generate electricity and to induct more children and teachers into schools. This strategy is thus less pessimistic than its alternative.

●●

4

Public Service Ethics

The view that public servants merely execute policies and decisions made by the political executive is an anachronism. There is no such thing as policy-administration dichotomy. Public servants not only administer; they also provide policy advice. Also, in the course of administering policies and programmes, they make policy by enunciating rules and regulations and by making precedent-setting decisions.

The extent of the citizens' dependence on public officials in a developing country like India is not well understood in western societies. More often than not, the citizen approaches the public servant as a supplicant, without resources. The relationship is, therefore, one of dependence, not of equality. Moreover, public officials in India do not operate within the kind of legal framework that is common to many societies in the West where citizens may sue public servants for acts of either omission or commission. In India, the public official enjoys a wide area of immunity.

As a result of the 'information revolution', however, ordinary citizens have acquired much more knowledge about the activities of public officials; this has led to growing public demand that these officials exercise their power in accordance with the highest standards of ethical conduct. Indeed, ethically upright behaviour among public officials is an increasingly important facet of the legitimacy of government in the eyes of the public.

India has a set formal and elaborate list of ethical rules for public servants, with accompanying penalties for violation. Many of these rules date back to the early days of British colonialism. Their development was a pragmatic, piecemeal response to particular ethical problems. The ethical rules for public servants in the state governments are very similar to those in the central government. It is notable, however, that at both levels of government the rules of public servants are much more comprehensive and restrictive than those for elected officials.

In India, as in most countries around the world, the best known ethical rule is that no public servant should engage in corrupt practices. A public servant in India is also expected to maintain absolute devotion to duty. He must be - and must appear to be—honest and impartial in the discharge of his duties. He is also required to observe a high standard of conduct in his private life so as not to bring discredit upon the public service. For example, a public servant is liable to action if he neglects his wife and family or acts in an unbecoming manner. Thus, the expectation of good behaviour runs through both the public and private lives of government employees. In this respect, the Supreme Court of India stated in 1967 that:

> If Government were to sit back and permit its officials to commit any outrage in their private life provided it falls short of a criminal offence the result may very well be a catastrophic fall in the moral prestige of the administration. If the contention that a government servant is not answerable for the misconduct committed in his private life is correct, the result would be that, however reprehensible or abominable a government servant's conduct in his life may be, the Government would be powerless to dispense with his services unless and until he commits a criminal offence or commits an act which is specifically prohibited by

> Government Servants' Conduct Rules. This, would clothe the government servant with an impunity which would place the Government in a position worse than that of a private employer.'

Several forms of conflict of interest are also prohibited. A public servant is instructed to avoid accepting lavish or frequent hospitality from any individual having official dealings with him or from industrial or commercial houses who wish to be close to him so as to promote their pecuniary interests. There are numerous restrictions on a public servant's acceptance of gifts and favours. Even when a near relative gives him a gift worth more than Rs 500 he must as a rule report this to the government. He must also report a gift from personal friends who have no official dealings with him if the value of the gift exceeds Rs 200. In all other cases, he cannot accept a gift without the government's approval if it is worth more than Rs 75. In addition, a public servant is urged to avoid the familiarity which arises from private hospitality, especially hospitality provided by business houses. When he is in doubt as to the propriety of accepting an invitation, he should decline it. He must also refuse invitations from persons who have cases pending before him.

A public servant is not permitted to accept part-time employment, whether it is with the Government or elsewhere, even if it is after office hours. Moreover, he is prohibited from negotiating with private firms to secure commercial employment while he is still in government service. This restriction flows from the view that a government servant is under an obligation to devote his energies wholeheartedly to the performance of his duties and not to divide his attention and effort in search of employment elsewhere.

Still another rule designed to avoid conflict of interest in the public service provides that: 'No member of the services shall, except with the previous sanction of the Government, permit his son, daughter or dependent to accept employment with private firms with which he has official dealings, or with other firms having official dealings with Government.' This rule is similar to those rules preventing retired High Court judges from practising before the same court, the Supreme Court judges from practising before any court, or the Comptroller and Auditor-General of India from accepting any government post after retirement.

A public servant may be found guilty of corruption if he cannot account satisfactorily for the possession by himself or by any other person on his behalf of money or property disproportionate to his known sources of income. The underlying presumption is that one who cannot account for a large accretion of wealth, which he could not possibly have saved from his known sources of income, has necessarily abused his official position and indulged in corruption. There are detailed rules regulating the buying of (and addition to) immovable property. One such rule, for instance, lays down that a public servant 'shall on first appointment to government service and thereafter at intervals of twelve months, submit a return of immovable property owned, acquired or inherited by him or held by him on lease or mortgage, either in his own name or in the name of any other person.' This means, among others, that a public servant should report to, and seek the permission of, the Government before commencing the construction of or addition to, any building.

Despite the comprehensive coverage and far-reaching implications of ethical rules in India, there are many areas of administrative conduct in general that are not covered by these rules (*e.g.* lackadaisical performance, intellectual dishonesty, inadequate commitment to serving the public, etc.). Moreover, the codification of even specifically ethical rules does not mean that all public servants will conduct themselves according to the rules. The disturbing fact is that although India has an elaborately drawn code of ethics for its public officials, unethical conduct is often accepted and even rewarded.

Changing Profile of Administrative Ethics

Independent India inherited a high level of public ethics from Mahatma Gandhi and of administrative ethics from the British Raj. During the period when India was governed by Jawaharal Nehru, who was Prime Minister until his death in 1964, unethical activities existed but were generally considered to be aberrations. But as early as India's second five year plan (1956-61), which was oriented toward industry and increased levels of public expenditure, there emerged serious ethical problems involving both politicians and public servants. A succession of inquiries into corrupt practices was held. The most publicised of these inquiries focused on the activities of Pratap Singh Kairon, K.D. Malviya, Biju Patnaik, and Biren Mitra, all of whom were subsequently forced to resign. In an effort to stem the tide of corruption, the Santhanam Committee on Prevention of Corruption was established in 1962. This was followed by the setting up of the Central Vigilance Commission, the strengthening of the Central Bureau of Investigation and the tightening of the conduct rules of the public service.

The mid-1960s is the great divide in the history of public ethics in India. It marks the complete fading away of the Gandhi-trained era and the emergence of new politics the keynote of which is amorality. Mahatma Gandhi resolutely held that ends and means were inseparable but the new political leadership showed little concern about means. Moreover, even the ends have become increasingly personalised while being camouflaged in populism and demagoguery.

Political opportunism became rampant. In the pursuit of personal or political gain, including Cabinet posts, many legislators changed their loyalties as easily and quickly as they changed their shirts. 'Big money' became an integral part of new politics and a parallel economy has been allowed to grow with impunity. Today, the black money is estimated to amount to 50 per cent of India's GNP. No punitive action has been taken to eliminate this menacing parallel economy. On the contrary, those engaged in it are continually rewarded. The Voluntary Disclosure Schemes of 1951, 1965 and 1975 merely converted black money into white. So did the Special Bearer Bonds scheme of 1981. The political leadership, which has the power to remedy the situation, is itself the beneficiary of this ill-gotten wealth.

Similar developments have been taking place in all walks of life. Many of those who are in seats of power and influence today have benefited from unethical and corrupt practices. Both politicians and public servants have been involved in these practices. A finding which is common to the twenty-three commissions of inquiry into the conduct of highly placed persons is that public servants have, in varying degrees, subordinated themselves to the will of their ministers even when clearly improper and illegal activities were involved. Public servants have often been, if not accomplices, at least privy to the wrongs committed by their political masters in pursuit of their sordid interests. Ethical rules for public servants, which have been so sedulously codified over the years have become largely irrelevant as a motivating force for a sizable segment of the bureaucracy.

In India, as in many other developing countries, corruption has reached such a high level that it almost appears to have become a way of life. Yet corruption is only one form admittedly the major form - of unethical conduct among public officials. Certainly many public servants interpret to their personal advantage the 'grey area' which lies between formal statutes and regulations on the one hand and guidelines and unwritten rules on the other. Just because a public servant does not accept bribes does not mean that he is ethically upright. He acts unethically when he devotes minimal effort to carrying out his responsibilities, when he curries favour with his minister by giving him the advice he wants to hear, when he wastes public funds and, in general, when he ignores the public interest. Many public officials justify their questionable behaviour by providing an overly sophisticated interpretation of the rules with the result that contrived legality submerges morality. Some of the rules themselves are of dubious morality because they are designed to serve the personal desires of the rule-makers; the result is legalised corruption.

Examples of legalised corruption are legion. In most public organisations in India, the 'staff car is in practice monopolised by the most senior official, even for purely personal purposes. Also, many public officials prepare their travel or tour itineraries so that they can visit their favourite places regularly. Especially regrettable is the fat that new recruits to the administrative services become easily socialised to accept and expect such practices without feeling any tinge of conscience. Another, more subtle, form of unethical behaviour is 'playing safe'. The success of a public servant is often assessed on the basis of how peacefully and noiselessly he can perform the responsibilities of a particular position. As a result, he runs no risks, turns a blind eye to malpractices in his area of jurisdiction and makes sure that he adheres to formal rules and regulations. This has spawned the 'babu raj' (rule by petty clerks) in India under which many higher officials have rendered themselves ineffectual. It is, however, unethical to function like 'babu's babu' (clerk's subordinate) while occupying a senior position and drawing a high salary.

Today India is burdened with a huge non-operating infrastructure which is nothing short of institutionalised immorality. The electricity boards are overstaffed and their personnel are busy making overtime allowances but they still provide electricity to consumers for barely twelve hours per day. Telephones which have been installed do not function properly but the public sector employees involved are apparently unconcerned. Ethical erosion on a large scale begins with such seemingly small matters.

Remedies for Unethical Conduct

One effective means by which political and bureaucratic leaders can promote high ethical performance among public servants is to set a good example. In practice, however, government leaders and their subordinates have moved a long way from the ideas of Mahatma Gandhi, and of distinguished former public administrators like Mokshagundam Visvesvaraya, whose life was a model of proper ethical behaviour. Visvesvaraya always put professionalism above everything else and possessed intellectual and moral integrity of the highest order. He never wasted public resources or sought self-interest from public office. When writing personal letters, he would use his personal stationery and even kept with him a pack of candles which he would light when doing private work.

It is important also that leaders of society outside government provide a model of high ethical standards for both public officials and citizens in general to follow. Public officials are unlikely to worry about being ethical if there is not strong support among the population at large for high ethical performance in government. Watchdog organisations are needed to monitor the activities of people in positions of power and to subject them to a social audit. The mass media must also be conscious of its educational role in the search for administrative morality. Finally, public service ethics could be significantly enhanced if both students and practitioners of public administration were exposed to more formal training on public service ethics.

What is urgently required to improve the level of public service ethics in India is the implementation of a package of reforms firmly supported by top political and bureaucratic leaders. Reform of the country's political system is most urgently required and in this sphere nothing is more important than reform of the electoral system. The cost of seeking political office must be reduced. In addition, there is a need for reform in the management of the political parties so as to bring them under greater public scrutiny and control. Elections are fought at an extremely high pitch because the stakes are so high. Increasingly, the government's powers of regulation (*e.g.*, granting licences and permits) are being used for blatantly partisan purposes. This abuse must be stopped. Moreover, the laws of the land, especially those on taxation, must be enforced with uniform strictness so that Indian society is spared the shame of having a parallel economy thriving on black money.

There is a need for appropriate reforms in the machinery and procedures of government. Administrative procedures in many areas are very cumbersome and often incomprehensible, with the result that a citizen frequently has no choice but to bribe an official even to get lawful work done. No less important is the deliberate promotion of openness in administration so that the public knows, what government employees are doing and can therefore better hold them to account. An open government is a valuable safeguard against unethical practices by both politicians and bureaucrats. It is important also that senior public servants exercise effective supervision over lower -level employees having dealings with the public and to ensure that unethical practices are dealt with swiftly and firmly. Furthermore, India must set up a permanent machinery to check on political and bureaucratic corruption.

●●

5

District Administration

The pattern of district administration in India is continuing since the times of Manu. In Manu's time, about a thousand villages formed as district and was in the charge of a separate official. Even today the number of villages in a district is almost the same. During the periods of Hindu rulers of North India such as Mauryans, Guptas and others the kingdoms were divdied into provinces and provinces were divided into districts. The provinces were under the charge of Governors and districts were under Sthanikas or Rajjukas during the Mauryan period and under Vishvapatis during the Guptas. They were assisted by other subordinate officers as incharge of small parts/divisions of a district.

THE DISTRICT COLLECTOR

The district is the basic unit of administration below State level in India. A district is placed under under the charge of a district officer called the District Collector or Deputy Commissioner, the king-pins of our administration. The district is also the unit of administration for the various other Government departments like police, industries, agriculture, education, medical and health, public-health, electricity, etc. However, the position of the Collector is different from that of the officers of other departments functioning in the district. He is supposed to be the Chief representative of the Government in the district. His office corresponds directly with the government.

EVOLUTION OF THE OFFICE OF COLLECTOR

The present institution of the Collector may be directly derived from the East Indian Company got the diwani rights and decided to take upon themselves the administration of revenue. At the same time, they decided that the Collector is to supervise the revenue collection and to preside over the courts. At that time revenue collection was a major and very important function, hence, the Collector came to occupy a very important position. In 1872, Sir George Compbell, at the time, Lt. Governor of Bengal said that the Collector is the general controlling authority over all the the Departments in the district. He said the District Magistrate/Collector should be supreme in his area, except in matters of courts of justice.

After independence, the circumstances changed and the functions and powers and position of the Collector also changed. Democracy and specialisation in post-independence period had affected the powers and prestige of the District Officer. The separation of judiciary from executive and advent of Panchayati Raj and growing resentment of technical departments and their officers towards the Collector's dominant position in the district have some of the potent factors which have adversely affected the position of the Collector. But he is still a chief coordinator of all the functionaries in the district and representative of the Government as a whole at the district level.

The District Officer is known as Collector in Rajasthan, Gujarat, M.P., Maharashtra and Andhra Pradesh etc. In Punjab, Haryana, Assam, J and K and Karnataka the Deputy Commissioner and District Magistrate (DM) in U.P. and West Bengal, is the head of district administration. He is a generalist, IAS Officer direct recruit or a promotee from State Civil Service. He performs more undefined than defined functions.

FUNCTIONS OF DISTRICT COLLECTOR

The District Collector is the ultimate boss of the district, responsible for every single event which happens in his jurisdictional area. Inspite of the size of the districts, attendant lethargy and complexity and corruption, the institution of the District Collector is one of the most powerful ones in the country. Even today, despite Panchayati Raj and the Mandal, the Collector is still perceived as being above petty politics, and truly for the people. First we will discuss his most important functions, namely, land Revenue. Law and Order and developmental functions and others.

Land Revenue. The office of Collector was created to collect revenue. The first Governor-General of India, Warren Hastings had created the office for the dual purpose of collecting revenue and dispensing justice. He is he head of the revenue department of the district. In this capacity he exercises the power of general supervision and control of the land records and their staff. He functions concerning land revenue are of serveral types such as collection of land revenue, canal dues and other Government dues; distribution of *'taccavi* loans and recovery of these dues; distribution distress *'taccavi'* due to losses to crops caused by natural calamities/disasters, relief to fire sufferers; payment of *'Zmindari'* abolition compensation and rehabilitation grant; relief to the fire sufferers, assessment of loss of crops due to floods, drought or locusts in the harvest season for recommendation of relief given to the affected farmers, control over land records, land acquisition and all matters relating to land records; inspection of mutation work, hears appeals against the orders of the lower consolidation authorities, relief measures in cases of scarcity conditions caused by natural calamities like fire, drought, flood, water logging and excessive rains, etc.; assessment and realisation of agricultural tax; collecting and furnishing multifarious agrarian statistics concerning rain fall, crops etc; supervision of the Treasury and Sub-treasuries, enforcement of Stamp Act; ensuring proper administration of land and proper sale and mortages of land; submission of periodical reports to higher authorities and seeing that the rights in land are held and enjoyed and passed from one party to another according to law in a peaceful manner. For the proper performance of revenue functions the Collector is assisted by other revenue officers. The district is divided into sub-divisions, tehsils, Kanungo circle and patwari circles; and the officer incharge of these are SDO. Tehsildar. Kanungo, Patwari and Village headman, *Patel* of Chowkidar to assist the Collector.

Maintenance of Law and Order. At the district level, according to the Police Act, 1860, and the Police Regulations of different Staters police functions are under the overall supervision and control of the District Magistrate. He is responsible for maintenance of law and order. The district police under the Superintendent of Police, is his main instrument to maintain law and order. As a District Magistrate he promulgates orders if there is any danger of breach of peace and public order. He can inspect police station and ask for any information record, statement and register dealing with crime. He grants licenses for explosives and fire arms. He can order enquiry into an accident caused by explosion; can also issue warrants for the arrest of a suspected offender on apprehension of breach of peace, a person may be detained by him. In 1993, thousands of workers of BJP were arrested to prevent them from participating in the rally at Boat Club. New Delhi by the district administration.

In serious cases of breach of peace. DM can seek the assistance of Special Armed Forces or the Provincial Armed Constabulary (PAC) maintain peace. Home Guards can also be called at a short notice in case of need. In case of widespread disturbances CRPF battalions may be requisitioned by him. Central government, can ask the other States Governments to send their armed forces. He may impose curfew in a particular area if situation demands. He has power to dispense unlawful assemblies and issues orders under Section 144 of Cr. P.C.

In case the civil police is not able to control the law and order situation the D.M. can seek the assistance of the army. The Criminal Procedure Code provides power to the DM to order the Military officers to assist in the maintenance of law and order. There are liasion officers in the army from whom assistance can be sought in times of need. The DM has to hand over the situation to the army which then tackles it on its own under their own command and commanders. It means that army can open fire on its own without seeking the approval of the Magistrate in each case. If at any time DM feels that the situation is under control, he can ask the army to withdraw.

The general consensus is that the army should be called only in extreme situations to assist civil authorities in the maintenance of law and order and as far as possible state police and the central paramilitary forces should control the situation.

The Collector conducts inspection of jail, disposes the cases of undertrial prisoners, grants superior class to prisoners, orders premature relase of prisoners, release of prisoners on Parole, deals with mercy petitions of prisoners, submits annual criminal report to the government, appoints village chowkidars, deals with labour problems, strikes etc. He takes neceesary action for eviction under public Premises (Eviction) Act and Rent Control Act. He hears general complaints of the people against any matter relating to the disrict administration. He makes necessary arrangements for the holding of fairs and exhibition in order to ensure peace.

Maintenance of law and order is impossible without proper intelligence system. The area which is known for mischiefmongering needs special attention on the basis of intelligence gathered. In the district activities of student organisations, particularly of bigger ones; activities of communal organisations, of political organisations, they might be planning political agitations, and activities of such persons who are known for creating law and order problems; needs constant watch and intelligence.

The intelligence system is organised by the Special Branch of the State Government. It has a small unit at the district level, which supplies information to the State and keeps informed of these developments to the S.P. and D.M. at district level. But S.P. and D.M. do not solely depend on this official information, they also develop their own sources and check and cross-check the intelligence gathered by the official unit. Timely information is a great help in maintaining law and order. The police acts on the orders of the Magistrate.

The relationship between the DM and Superintendent of Police is full of tension. The SP feels that his position has unnecessarily been subordinated to that of the DM, but the control of law and order by DM has stood the test of times since its inception. He being the head of district administration, has wider resources to gather information and much broader view of administration compared to S.P. Many arguments have been given on both sides but the controversy is continuing.

Developmental Function. Since independence the nature and scope of governmental fucntions have increased. The government is striving to achieve socio-economic justice. The realisation of these two-fold objectives has led the government to perform developmental functions. With the increasing activities undertaken by the Government, this function of the Collector has been gaining more and more importance.

To perform developmental functions, two types of patterns have emerged in different states. One is Maharashtra, Gujarat and Gujarat pattern in which all the developmental functions have been brought under the control of the Zila Parishad and all district level officers of development department have been placed under the administrative control of Zila Parishad. A separate IAS officer has been appointed as Chief Executive Officer of the Zila Parishad, who exercises control on all officials of Zila Parishad.

The second Pattern is found in Tamil Nadu and other States. The Collector looks after both the regulatory as well as developmental functions. Both the patterns have worked satisfactorily. Prior to the introduction of Panchayati Raj in 1959, on the recommendations of Balwant Rai Mehta Committee, 1957, the Collector was connected with all the developmental activities in the district, including community development. After the introduction of Panchayati Raj, developmental activities have been handed over to the elected bodies and the role of Collector in this respect differs from stae to state. Balwant Rai Mehta Committee had suggested "at the district level, the Collector or the Deputy Commissioner should be the captain of the team of officers of all development departments and should be made fully responsible for securing the necessary coordination and cooperation in the preparation and execution of the district plans for community development.

The prevailing practice in many States at present is to make the district collector the coordinator of developmental functions and appoint an officer Additional District Collector and Chief Executive officer of the Zila Parishad. The Collector being the final authority in the district and is in a better position to get the cooperation of all district functionaries, therefore, he is in a better position to look after the developmental functions in the district. In agriculture development programmes and even in other development programmes a large number of agencies were required to supply inputs wisely. Therefore, coordinaion is required to make sure that the necessary inputs are available to the farmers at proper time. Moreover, there are number of special programmes like, Integrated Rural Development Programme (IRDP), Drought Prone Areas Programme (DPAP), Desert Development Programme (DDP), Rural Landless Employment Guarantee Programme, National Rural Empoyment Programme. Training and Visit System. JRY, Prime Minister's Employment Programme, etc. There is hardly any programme which does not involve the land acquisition, land management, regularisation of sale and purchase of land, etc. A number of coordination committees are functioning for implementation of various programmes under the District Collector to ensure successful implementation of different development programmes.

Other Functions. In addition to these above discussed functions, he performs many other functions of various natures:

(1) The Collector is the Returning Officer for elections to Parliament and Vidhan Sabha constituencies and has responsibility for coordination of election work at the district level.

(2) Grant of old age pension, grant of house-building loans.

(3) He conducts census operation every ten years.

(4) Acts as protocol officer in the district and issues tour programmes of Ministers and VIPs and makes arrangement for stay of VIP at Circuit Houses.

(5) Preparation of district gazetteers and protection of ancient monuments.

(6) He is the responsible for National Saving or the State Loans floated from time to time and contributions to the National Defence Fund.

(7) Supervision and control over municipalities in the district.

(8) He is the chairman of seveal committees such as the Soldiers and Sailors Welfare Fund, Staff Committee. Public Grievances Committee, Family Planning Committee, etc.

(9) Controlling, drawing and disbursing officer of the district staff.

(10) Management of Government estates.

(11) Enforcement of Press Act.

(12) Attending to character verificaion, issue cerificate of domicile, Scheduled Castes and Backward Classes, Political sufferers etc.

(13) Training junior officers in official procedures and administrative work.

(14) Postings, transfer and leave of the leand revenue officers working under his control.

(15) Superintendence over all other branches of district administration.

Position and Role of Collector. The role of the Collector is changing at a fast pace due to various welfare schemes. The Collectors as the head of the district administration, is closely connected with the development programmes and has acquired a key position working as a guide and philosopher.

The District Officer, as chief agent and the representative of the State, serves as a channel of communication between the Government and the residents of the district. The District Collectors is an overburdened officer due to the expansion and increasing developmental activities.

Other District Level Officers. The other district level officers are the District and Sessions Judge, Civil Surgeon or Chief Medical Officer, Superintendent of Police, Executive Engineer PWD and PHEd., District Education Officer. District

Food and Supply Officer. District Social Welfare Officers and District Development Officer etc. They are important officers of their concerned departments.

All these officers have technical control and supervision over their own deparments, the District Collector supervires and coordinates their work who should keep him informed of their activities and report to him on any serious thing likely to disturb law and order.

LOCAL GOVERNMENT

Literally, local government means the administration of a locality. Had we been living in the times of the city States of ancient Greece or Rome, this simple, plain definition would have been sufficient enough to bring home to us the full meaning and significance of the term local government. This definition seems to be too simple and inadequate to cope with our needs and requirements. Thus, we must take into account the total perspective of the situation. However, different scholars have defined the term 'Local Government' differently.

In general local government as opined by W.A. Robson may be said to involve the conception of territorial, non-sovereign community possessing the legal right and the necessary organisation to regulate its own affairs. This is turn pre-supposes the existence of local authority with power to act independently of external control as well as the participation of the local community in the administrative of its own affairs. This definition leads us to say that there is inevitably an ultimate limit to the freedom of action of the local authority. Otherwise, it would occupy the position of a sovereign state; while it is likewise obviously impossible for all the citizens to participate at all times in the acts of local authority. It should also be borne in mind that insistence on moden electoral system and decision by majority votes as the only valid criteria of autonomy would exclude many signficant phenomenon. G. Monlagn Harris defines the local government as government by the people themselves through freely elected reprsntatives. However, he has given the contrary German view regarding self-government put forward by M. Goetz that 'Self-government implies merely a form of communal administration'. In other words the self-government is something less than self-administration. He goes so far as to say that, while it is necessary to local self-government that the power to frame a policy vests in some organ, "it is immaterial what from this policy framing organ takes. The power may be vested in an individual." Local government is at the bottom of a pyramid of governmental institutions with the national government at the top and inermediate government, i.e., state regions and provinces, occupying the middle range.

Some of the Indian scholars too have attempted to define local government. B.K. Gokhale uses the term 'Local Self-Government'. To him, "Local Self-government is the government of a specified locality by the local people through the representatives elected by them. However, K. Venkatarangaiya goes further when he says that local self-government is the administration of a locality - a village, a city or any other area smaller than the state—by a body representing the local inhabitants possessing a fairly large amount of autonomy, raising at least a part of its revenue through local taxation and spending its income on services which are regarded as local and therefore, distinct from state and central services.

The analysis of the views of the various scholars indicates that some of the definitions take only the limited view of the concept of local government because they fail to embrace all the aspects. John Clarke has attempted to give a comprehensive definition, but fails to appreciate the elements of locally chosen and controlled councils and of local finance. Sigwick has suggested the legal status of local bodies. Similarly

Jennings' definition too suggests the legal status. However, W.A. Robson and K. Venkatarangaiya have given the most satisfactory and acceptable definitions.

Concept of Local Government

The concept of local government thus, is multi-dimensional. It has been pointed out that it is basically an organised social entity with a feeling of oneness. The local government is an integral part of the political mechanism for governance in a country. As a body corporate with juristic person, it represents a legal concept. Further Local Government is an administrative concept, not known to other levels of Government, with its councillors involved in making, unmaking and remaking administrative decisions in council and its committees with direct bearing on civil services to the local people, and now in nation building activities. Not only this, but also environment contributes to its birth, growth and development.

Some Examples :

(a) A small group of human settlement with agriculture as a major profession of the people and inadequate means of communication is characterised as a rural local authority.

(b) A human settlement with diverse professionals i.e., agriculturalists and non-agriculturalists co-existing along with some means of communication is often classified in India, as a municipality.

Political. The political dimensions of Local Government presents to us the most important of its conepts, which is however, different from other forms of public agencies, in spite of the fact that they have some common characteristics.

Since the operational freedom to fulfil local needs and aspirations with necessary popular mandate is the hall-mark of local government, it is, thus, a variant of democracy, in spite of its variance in form. To be more specific, because of its democratic character, it imparts political education to the local people.

Economic. The concept of Local Government has an economic dimension of much significance. A local body can prove to be efficient and effective without much effect if the locality is economically sound. It has been pointed out that the economic base of different classes of the community determines the local politics. In India, for instance, a rural local authority is dominated by the farmers, while an urban authority has professionally diversified composition. The economic dimension in nutshell highlights the facts of the local authorities: one, with a bearing on their very existence as units for self-governance; and the other, their legitimate place in the national development.

Administrative. In fact, the local government is operationally an administrative organisation with the confluence of politics, administration and technology. The local authorities have been placed in such a way that both, a units of local self-government and as agents of government, they may succeed in achieving the optimum results without sacrificing the basic norms of democracy. This is so because they conform to the two cardinal objectives of Public Administration : efficient performance and responsible performance. Initially local government may face some problems, but, with the attainment of maturity, local government may produce results that may combine the best of the two worlds, democratic and bureaucratic.

Legal. The legal dimensions of the Local Government presents two things: one, *it is the agent of State* and as such, represents public interest. In the capacity of the agent of State, it exercises a part of the sovereignty of the state delegated to it within its geographical boundaries. Two, *it is self-governing institution.*

In nut-shell, it can be pointed out that legally, the local authorities can be described as creatures of government. Not only this, but the contention that local self-government is an inherent right of local people is not longer held valid. The developing countries, that lack strong traditions for grass root democracy, do not present a happy picture. In India, the local bodies have been dissolved or superseded frequently. This shows the tendency of the higher level of government to destroy its own creatures. Over the years, the scholars have been stressing time and again for providing some constitutional safeguards until favourable democratic traditions strike roots. This will facilitate in arresting the unhealthy tendency. In this regard, Ashok Mehta Committee on Panchayati Raj Institutions, favoured similar constitutional stipulation. However, this view point for providing constitutional Satus to Local Civil Institutions has materialised by the enactment of 73rd and 74th Constitutional Amendment Acts of 1992.

Geographical. With territorial jurisdiction over a particular human habitation, the Local Government may be conceptualised in geographical terms.

The geographic includes, the features like

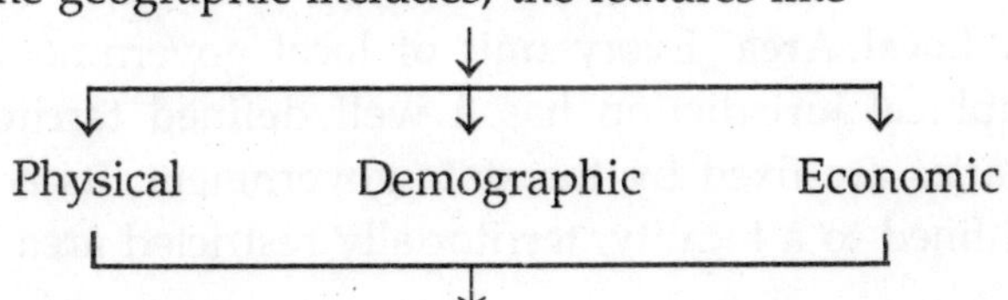

These features in turn affect the policy formulation, implementation and law pertaining to local government.

As we are very much aware, the local government stems from the concept that among the inhabitants of a given area, there is a consciousness different from the inhabitants of other areas within the same country. For example, consciousness of the inhabitants of Jalandhar Municipal

Corporation in Punjab will differ from the people of Hyderabad. This is called the concept of neighbourhood, which makes the inhabitants of an area automatically aware of the interests which infringe upon them more directly than upon others. Thus, for rendering meaningful services to the local people, the decision makers need to have adequate knowledge of the geo-demographic conditions/variants.

CHARACTERISTICS OF LOCAL GOVERNMENT

From the above discussions on the meaning and dimensions of the concept of local government, it is clear that a system of local government has some special features. On this count D. Lokarel has opined that five features thus characterise a system of local self-government and these are—*(i)* a local body; *(ii)* local inhabitants; electing and ultimately controlling the body; *(iii)* autonomy of the body of the sense of freedom from the control of higher authorities within at least a limited sphere, a recongnition of distinction between local and non-local services and taxation. In this, one more can be added, *i.e.*, local area. However, the most essential attribute of local-government is its representativeness and responsible nature.

1. Local Area. Every unit of local government in its geographical jurisdiction has a well defined territory. Its boundaries are fixed by the state government. Its activities are confined to a locality, territorially restricted area.

It may be a city, a town, a village or a group of villages or even a district. One significant principle guiding the area is that inhabitants of an area have a community of social and civic problems which require a solution.

2. Local Authority. We have already pointed out that Local government represents a particular set of local views, conditions, needs and problems which are administered by a local authority—a Council or a Board. It is elected by and responsible to the people for the locality. The local authority is empowered to raise the necessary revenue and administers the money for promoting social welfare. However, each local authority will not have the same approach in respect of every service. This sets the tone of administration. To be more specific, the pattern of administration, the personnel, the finance and the methods and procedures may vary from one local authority to another, from city corporation to municipality, from urban to rural body.

3. Local Inhabitants. The main object of a local government is to discharge those functions which are primarily of benefit to the local population. These benefits relate to the provision of civic amenities, health facilitis, roads, prevention of epidemics, etc. In other words all those amenities which make living better, physically, economically socially and culturally should be assigned to the local inhabitants. Not only this, but, also the benefits effected by the local authority cannot be assigned to any one community. It has been rightly observed that the functions and services covered by the expression 'Local Government' are considered of local rather than of national importance.

4. Local Autonomy. This characteristic of local authorities, coupled with democratic character, constitutes the real essence of local government. In fact, the scope of local functions has a direct bearing on the scope of local autonomy. But to determine the extent of local autonomy seems to be a difficult exercise because local jurisdiction varies from one pattern to another, one country to another, and within the same country, from one local authority to another. For example, in India, in the Panchayati Raj System, higher levels enjoy more autonomy than the lower levels. Similarly, bigger local authorities, like the municipal corporations, enjoy greater degree of autonomy as against the municipalities. In a similar fashion, urban bodies may be more autonomous than the rural ones depending on their political maturity, financial strength and the nature of problems they face.

The concept of 'Autonomy' is a multi-dimensional concept. It has been subjected to the forces of constancy and change. Historically, the concept of autonomy is ancient one, but, in its modern sense, signifies the legal self-sufficiency of a social body and its actual independence. Conceptually, local autonomy tends to become a synonym of the freedom of a locality for self-determination or local democracy. According to Dimock and Dimock the autonomy is a privilege of being left alone. Autonomy has legal, politcial, administrative and financial dimensions. However, among the modern local governments, political freedom with broad based legal foundation, provides, the essence of local autonomy because the political autonomy in the wider perspective includes local administrative and financial freedom.

In nutshell, the core of local autonomy comprises the following things :

(a) The local government is a body corporate.

(b) It has a legal personality of its own. That is in the eyes of law, it has free will and power of action of its own.

(c) The inhabitants of a local area have a legal right to choose their government.

(d) It has legal jurisdiction over its locality and people.

(e) The local government is bestowed by a law a sort of immortality, a continuous life. The people may come or go, population may increase or decrease, the form of government and the extent of powers may be changed yet its legal entity will continue. Thus, its perpetual seccession will also continue indefinitely.

(f) The elected element of a body enjoys supremacy over other elements of local government.

(g) To local affairs are regulated by bye-laws framed by the body.

(h) The local government guides, supervises and controls local administration.

The above mentioned facts do represent the core of local autonomy, but it must be understood that autonomy is manifestation of sovereignty. Sovereignty and the various facts of autonomy discussed above are wheels within wheels. The outer wheel is sovereignty, while politcial, administrative and financial aspects of autonomy are the inner wheels. However, the authorities which have been given the responsibility to run the local government are neither sovereign, nor self-created entities. The complete sovereign status is impossible.

5. Local Finances. It is necessary for any institution to have some sources of revenue because "revenue is the first essential of a government. No administration can be carried on without it. Balwant Rai Mehta team on Panchayati Raj rightly remarked that local finance, in many respects, the key to successful local government, assumes an important place. The local government services are financed, wholy or largely, out of locally raised funds. The local revenue is derived from local enterprises, local services or the wealth of local citizens located within the limits of local bodies. The local government is clothed with authority to levy and collect taxes.

It is this authorty of local government that accords it a unique position among corporate bodies. However, unlike other levels of government, its levying authority has legal and constitutional basis. In fact, the local government possesses revenue raising and spending authority only to the extent that the State/Central government grants to them.

RURAL DEVELOPMENT

Conceptually rural development is taken as development of the rural areas. Among other things, rural development in India includes increase in agriculture production, extension of irrigation facilities, improvement in the techniques of cultivation, provision of educational facilities, construction of link roads, health care etc. For years, it has been emphasised that immediate industrialization is a cure for the problems of less developed countries. In the sixties, agriculture became the nucleus of all development activities resulting in the comparative neglect of other sectors. It took us many years to realise that rural development is not the same as agriculture development, although the latter is an important part of it. Exclusive concern with agriculture development has, at times, created disparities and inequalities which run counter to the basic objectives of rural development.

Today, rural development is described as a "process aimed at improving the well-being of people living outside the urbanised areas." These non-urbanised areas, however, are not a separate entity but are part of a far flung sysem of spatial and economic linkages, Rural development, therefore, takes into account the forward and backward linkages between the rural and urban areas.

EFFORTS TOWARDS RURAL DEVELOPMENT

Before independence Britishers made to direct or significant attempt towards rural development in India. A few voluntary efforts here and there could not make a dent in the rural scene. It was only during the period of the Second World War when the increase in food production was required, rural development received some attention. But even during that period, rural development was a minor symphony in the governmental orchestra of the time. Some voluntary efforts were, however, made long before independence.

At the time of independence, the country was in the grip of illiteracy, hunger and backwardness. The situation in rural areas having more than 80 per cent of the country's population was more severe. After independence rural development acquired a high level of priority in the hands of the new leaders. A realisation has been there since the very beginning of the planning process that no matter how fast is the progress in the field of industry, power, transport etc., unless the rural areas progress with equal speed, the country cannot make a real headway. As all aspects of rural life are inter-related, lasting results could be achieved only by handling them simultaneously. A comperehensive country side Community Development Programme covering agriculture, rural industries, education, housing, health, recreation etc., was launched as Gandhiji's birthday in 1952, to tackle the problem of rural areas in their entirely in a concerted and coordinated manner. It was intended to bring a change in the mental outlook of the people and to instill in them the spirit to strive for better living conditions. The main objects of the programme were identified as :

(a) the proper utilization of the vast unexploited resources lying dormant in the countryside;

(b) to infuse a spirit of self-help amongst the rural population by organising developmental work through representative institutions like the panchayats and cooperative scieties;

(c) to encourage village people to become self-reliant, responsible citizens, capable of and willing to participate effectively with knowledge and understanding in the building of the nation;

(d) to put continued and heavy emphasis on improving and modernising agriculture production;

(e) to utilise the free time of the villagers for the benefit of the community as a whole;

(f) to eradicate hunger, disease, squalor, ignorance and idleness;

(g) to extend full benefits of the cooperative movement to rural families;

(h) to upgrade the social status of the village teacher to enable him to participate in these programmes. Thus the programme aimed at bringing about an integrated development of rural India covering the social, cultural and economic aspect of community life. The programme accorded the highest priority to agriculture but also included the improvement of other important sectors viz., communications, health, sanitation, housing, education, welfare of women and children and cottage and small scale industries.

Accepting the recommendations of Grow More Food Committee (1952), the Community Development Programme was supplemented by National Extension Service on Gandhiji's birthday, in 1953. For implementing the programme, the country was divided into blocks of 100 villages each, comprising a population of 60 to 70 thousands and covering an area of roughly 250 sq miles. A block had two active stages of operation, Stage I of five years followed by Stage II of another five years. At every block, the Block Development Officer was made the Chief Coordinator and chief executive officer and had been provided with a team of experts (extension officers) in various fields such as agriculture, animal husbandry, cooperation, education, cottage industries, works, health etc. The Community Development Programme and National Extension Service thus formed the rural dimension of India's development planning.

Initially, the programme worked well. However, within a few years it lost its initial momentum and participation and involvement of people showed a considerable decline. The village panchayats, the block advisory committees, he district planning committees, the project advisory committee—all lacked capacity, vitality and power to represent people's view point, thus proved powerless and ineffective. The failure of the CDP provided the basis for the appointment of Balwant Rai Mehta Committee in January, 1957. The Committee observed that the popular participation of the CDP enlisted through advisory bodies was not adequate. Accordingly the committee observed: "So long as we do not discover or create a representative and democratic institution which will supply, the 'local interest', supervision and care necessary to ensure that expenditure of money upon local objects conforms with the needs and wishes of the locality, invest it with adequate power and assign to it approprivate finances, we will never be able to evoke local interest and excite local initiative in the field of development." On the recommendations of he committee, a three-tier organisation of Panchayati Raj was created in 1959, for effective rural development through people's participation. According to the Third Five Year Plan, "The establishment of these democratic institutions at the district and block levels and the role assigned to the Gram Sabha and the village panchayat constitute fundamental and far reaching changes in the pattern of rural development The primary object of Panchyayati Raj is to enable the people of each area to achieve intensive and continuous development in the interest of entire population."

Ever sicne the failure of CDP and having been handicapped by a backlog of rural poverty and backwardness, India has been continuously experimenting with various programmes in one form or the other. Considerations of equality and justice, coupled with a desire to increase productivity, have prompted the government to initiate several programmes for the weaker sections of rural society. Some prominent programmes were : Intensive Agriculture District Programme, Small and Marginal Farmers and Agricultural Labourers Development Agencies, Minimum Needs

Programme, Applied Nutrition Programme, Drought Prone Areas Programme, Hill Area Development Programme, Command Area Development Programme, Crash Scheme for Rural Employement, Pilot Intensive Rural Employment Project, Food for Work Programme.

The Intensive Agricultural District Programme, popularly known as the 'package programme', was started on a pilot basis in 1961, in seven selected disricts and subsequently extended to some other disricts. The programme aimed at combining technical known-how, credit and production facilities for stepping up agricultural production and the utilisation of maximum possible land for this purpose. The operation of the programme contributed to a significant improvement in the use of critical inputs like improved seeds, fertilizers and plant protection measures.

Applied Nutrition Programme was launched in 1961, in collaboration with UNICEF, FAO and WHO. It was started to make a systematic attempt on a significant scale to develop a coordinated and comprehensive programme of nutrition, education and training in production, preservation and consumption of nutritionally valuable food.

On the basis of the recommendations of the All India Rural Credit Reform Committee (1969), during the Fourth Five Year Plan welfare schemes for small and marginal farmers and agricultural labourers were introduced. Small and Marginal Farmers and Agricultural Labourers Development Agencies (SFDA/MFAL) were initiated because small farmers were suffering a number of hardships due to fragmentation of holdings, insecurity of tenure, inadequate and untimely supply of inputs, lack of credit facilities, unsatisfactory arrangements for marketing and storage. The functions of the agencies are to identify the participants according to norms laid down, draw up suitable programmes for improved agriculture and subsidiary occupations, arrange credit through institutional sources and get the programmes executed through the existing development and extension agencies in the project areas. Each SFDA/MFAL agency was expected to study the problems of target groups in its area, to raise their earning capacity and acoordingly evolve appropriate programmes and devise the necessary institutional financial and administrative arrangements for their execution.

The Drought Prone Areas Programme aims at long-term development of areas frequently affected by drought through integrated development of local resources in agriculure and allied sectors. The programme seeks to raised the productive capacity of these areas in order to ensure sustained income and employment particularly to the vulnerable sections of the rural society.

Unemployment retards all the efforts towards rural uplift and increases the problem of rural poverty. Apart from the rural development programmes which brought benfits to some of the unemployed, some special programmes for rural employment were taken. To provide employment to at least 100 jobless persons in each block, an ad hoc scheme known as Crash Scheme for Rural Employment was launched during the Fourth Plan. Subsequently another scheme known as the Pilot Intensive Rural Employment Project was started in 15 selected blocks, a type of an action-cum-study project aiming at finding out suitable models for rural employment. Another scheme in this category, the National Scheme of Training of Rural Youth for Self-Employment (TRYSEM), was initiated from August, 1979. The main thrust of the scheme is on equipping rural youth with necessary skills and technology to enable them to seek self-employment. It was proposed to train about two lakh rural youth every year in various skills. These programmes have been further supplemented by National Rural Employment Programme (1980), and Rural Landless Employment Guarantee Programme (1983).

It is seen that there has been no death of rural development programmes and these can be broadly classified as : Those which cater to the needs of the village community and areas development as a whole; those serving the interests of the landowning class; and satisfying the requirements of the landless agricultural labourers and artisans. Most of these programmes have been designed in one way or the other for the disadvantaged group. Also there has been fairly heavy investment under these programmes both by centre and the states considering the overall resources of the country.

A number of studies brought out the fact that the process of rural development so far had been mainly benefiting the richer sections of the rural society. The big farmers were reaping the benefits of the massive investments in rural areas. The net result was that the rich were becoming richer and the poorer were becoming poor. Such a situation forced our planners to have a second look at the entire philosophy of developmental effort. It ws realised that all the schemes meant for alleviation of poverty are organised in unplanned and unintegrated manner. Instead of comprehensive planning, the various schemes were carried on ad hoc basis. The resource and income develoment programmes were not well integrated with the availability of supporting inputs and services or outlets like marketing etc. A careful planning was, therefore, required towards achieving coordination and consoiidation in order to remove the confusion arising out of a multiplicity of programmes and agencies through the process funnelling diverse programmes into a single stand.

PLAN SCHEMES FOR URBAN DEVELOPMENT

During the last three plan periods, a number of central schemes covering different aspects of urban development have been launched. The administrative agencies for implementing these schemes are the state governments and municipal authorities and other local bodies. The schemes cover water supply and sanitation, urban housing and related activities, preparation of master plans for cities and regions, and urban community development. For improving water supply the Sanitation Programme (Urban) was lauched in 1954. Urban husing and related activities are covered by size different schemes of subsidized industrial low income group housing, slum clearance and improvement, middle income group housing, rental housing for State government employees, and land acquisition and development. An additional housing scheme for economically weaker sections was also operated for a few years, but this was ultimately marged with the industrial housing scheme. All these schemes came into operation between 1952, and 1962. The last two schemes on urban community development were started in 1962, and 1965, respectively.

These urban development schemes have been formulated in great detail, specifying purpose, coverage, operating agencies, methods of financing and the like. Two Central Ministries—Health and Family Planning; and Works, Housing and Urban Development—between them look after the schemes, Only two schemes, *viz.*, the National Water Supply and Sanitation Programme and the Urban Community Development Scheme, are in the charge of the Ministry of Health and Family Planning, while the Ministry of Works, Housing and Urban Development is responsible for all the housing and related schemes and the scheme for the preparation of Master Plans for cities and regions.

For projects costing more than Rs. 10 lacks under the National Water Supply and Sanitation Programme, central secrutiny and approval is necessary. The schemes on Urban Community Development and on Master Plans lay down staffing patterns and pay scales. The financing patterns of the schemes are also not uniform. For instance, the Water Supply and Sanitations Scheme offers 100 per cent loans, while the

Master Plans Scheme provides for 100 per cent subsidy. Between these extremes, there are two schemes—Slum Clearance and Improvement, and Subsidized Housing—providing a mixture of loan and subsidy. Again, two schemes, Slum Clearance and Improvement, and Urban Community Development, require matching contributions. Three other schemes for middle income group housing, land acquisition and development, and rental housing for State government employees are entirely financed from non-plan sources—by the Life Insurance Corporation of India. There are also two examples of schemes for water supply and sanitation, and for low-income group housing which are jointly financed from plan and non-plan sources by the Central Government and the Life Insurance Corporation.

Agencies of Town Planning and Implementation. The manner in which these schemes are being operated results in the State governments and local authorities being reduced to mere agencies of the Centre and has led to the 'vertical integration' of the various layers of government.

Moreover, the mixture of grants and loans in the plans schemes is usually arbitrary not based on a careful examination of the relative productivities of the schemes. The variations in the nature of the financing of the schemes results in their unnecessary proliferation, restiveness in their execution, and a fragmented approach towards urban development. The only way to remedy these defects is to abolish the existing scheme-wise approach and introduce broad heads of conditional Central plan assistance, combining all the closely related activities under a broad head, such as Urban Development.

Legal Hurdles. The legal hurdles standing in the way of regulated and planned urban development are of two types : *(i)* absence of suitable legislation for town and country planning; and *(ii)* procedural obstacles in the law for land acquisition.

Town and Country Planning Legislation. The first town and country planning law was passed in Bombay as early as in 1915. It was followed by similar legislation in Madras in 1920. The 1915, Bombay Act was later suspended by the Bombay Town Planning Act, 1954, and again by the Maharashtra Regional and Town Planning Act, 1966. The shortcoming of the earlier acts was that town improvement was conceived in parts and not for an entire town. Essentially, therefore, these acts followed the improvement trust approach to town planning and were not concerned with comprehensive urban planning.

The Bombay Town Planning Act, 1954, was the first comprehensive town planning legislation in India. This was followed by similar legislations in Assam in 1960 and Karnataka in 1961. In Uttar Pradesh, the Nagar Mahapalika Adhiniyam, 1959, is a law both for plan preparation and for is implementation.

The Bombay Act of 1954, empowered the local authorities to plan within their respective jurisdictions. Under the Madras Act of 1920, the local authorities may plan within their areas and in the vicinity, while the municipal corporations in Uttar Pradesh can exercise their planning functions for areas as far as two miles from their city limits. In Karnataka, the local authorities are responsible for planning within their jurisdictions, although the State government may create a single planning authority for a city and neighbouring areas beyond its limits. Such an authority may also be set-up for a group of rural and urban local bodies. The Assam Act empowers the State department of town planning to prepare plans for any urban area and constitute special authorties to implement these plans.

We thus see that all the States have comprehensive town and country planning legislation, the urban local authorities being also the planning agencies. The extent of the responsibility of local bodies for planning outside city limits is not uniform, but there is a clear recognition of the need for such planning and its implementation. If the local government authorities are chosen as development agencies as well, there is no reason why their planning jurisdictions cannot be extended suitably beyond city limits.

In quite a few States there is legislation for the purpose of controlling land use. The U.P. Regulation of Building Operations Act, the Bihar Restriction of Uses of Land Act, the Madhya Pradesh Town Periphery Control Order, the Punjab Capital Regulation Act, the Chandigarh Periphery control Act, and the Calcutta Metropolitan Area (use and development of land) Control Act are examples of limited planning legislation. These acts are only mesures of negative control.

●●

6

Structure of Personnel Administration

The development of scientific administration and the awakened sence of social responsibility evinced in the countries of the West at the end of 19th century gave rise to the problem of how the available labour resources could be engaged to work effectively to minimise the cost and maximise the production and profits of the organisation by reducing the cost of wastage and implementing the new techniques and methods in men, materials and machines. The problems relating to personnel also increased with the increase in the size of the industrial units. At that time the condition of workers was not satisfactory. They were regarded as slaves. But now there is a great change in the attitude of industrialists towards labour since the beginning of the twentieth century. They have now realised that labour is a partner in the functioning of the industry. On the other hand workers are also skilled, educated and united. The sense of social responsibility has developed among workers. Moreover, Government also came forward and took various steps in improving the conditions of the labour force since then. The mounting pressure of labour problems, rise of labour union, changed attitude of administration towards labour and the lenient view of various governments towards the work force were some of the developments which were responsible for the growth and development of personnel administration. The following are some of the factors which may be held responsible for the growth of personnel administration:

1. Technical Factors. The following factors were responsible for the growth of personnel administration:

(i) **Industrial Revolution.** Industrial Revolution played an important role in the development of industries. It brought in revolutionary changes in the methods and techniques of industrial production. The industries were shifted from the former workship to new mills and factories. Steam and power supplemented or were substituted for the efforts and energy of people. Though production processes were simplified by the use of new and new developed machineries and techniques, but on the other hand, other problems relating to men, materials and machines were emerged. In order to reconcile the situation, the existing principles of administration were suitably changed or amended or new principles were developed.

(ii) **Experiments in other Social Sciences.** New experiments and research in other social sciences also contributed to the growth of personnel administration. Hawthorn experiment field of psychology affected the attitudes of the employers to a great extent. Researches in behavioural science also subscribed to the development of personnel administration. These experiements developed new techniques and methods which are being used in selecting the right person on the right job and developing them very scientifically by introducing new methods of training.

(iii) **Use of Science in Industries.** With the advent of science new and new products, methods, techniques and processes were developed in the fields of production, communication and marketing which affected the industrial development and the personnel relations. To cope with the problems of industrial development, new offices were created such as engineers, production manager etc.

2. Government Attitude. The Government attitude towards labour, administration and business had changed considerably. The change in Government attitude was mainly due to:

(i) The change in the concept of labour from the commodity concept to the human concept was given a wide recognition. He is now regarded as a human being and master of all the industrial activities. The idea of workers participation in administration has been recognised by almost all the Governments of the world.

(ii) Widespread acceptance of physiocratic or laissez-faire view-point which was popularised by Roussean, Bentham and Hobbes and was further advanced by Malthus, Adam Smith and other so-called classical school of economists. This view point proposed a minimum of public intervention in economic activities. But the political interests of the countries could not be safeguarded by this policy in World War I, hence the protection policy was introduced by nearly all the countries in the world. Businessmen could get an opportunity to earn huge profits as the rescue of the employees in getting them ride of exploitation by the employers.

(iii) Establishment of welfare states in most of the countries of earth which enacted various labour laws for the welfare of the industrial force.

Thus the Government attitude was one of the factors in the development of personnel administration or industrial relations.

3. Awakening Among Workers. After World War I, workers began to become united and a new industrial labour movement soon became an important element in this structure. The unions emerged in the early stages of industrialisation as means of protesting the changing careers—opportunities open to employees and questioning the concentration of power and authority in the hands of owners. They expressed the concern of industrial employees about working conditions—levels of wages, stability of employment and status in the new industrial society of work. At later stages some other factors also subscribed to their causes. They were: *(i)* Economic hardship to workers due to inflation after World War I; *(ii)* Political movements and success of Russian Revolution in 1917; *(iii)* Emergence of International Labour Organisation in 1919. The union movement succeeded in improving the labour relations in industries.

4. Cultural and Social Changes. The following cultural and social changes also contributed to the development of industrial relations:

(a) Education. Education brought the change in the attitude of labour towards their work. They realised that work is worship and they would be more benefited if they worked hard. They could very easily understand what was right and what was against their interest. They could no longer be exploited.

(b) Change in Social Value of the Labour. Social values of workers affect the efficiency of worker on the job. If a worker is given due regard in the society or by his fellow workers, he will be the most contented man in the society and his efficiency will be increased thereby. Large-scale production and advanced means of transportation and communication increased the social value of labour. Personnel problems have increased thereby. Therefore, new personnel principles were developed.

(c) Population Problem. Population problem also had impact to the problem of personnel administration. The problem of active utilisation of men arises most in the countries having a vast population like China and India. Problems of unemployment and wage fixation had their direct link with the population.

5. Change in the Attitude of Administration. Development of scientific administration, Industrial Revolution, awakening of workers, favourable attitude of Government towards labour and change in the social value of workers were some of the factors which compelled the administration to make a change in its attitude towards labour. The workers which were regarded as slave in earlier years, are now regarded as partners in the administration.

6. Problem of Co-ordination and Control. Large scale production created the problem of control over the thousands of persons working in unit. The need of co-ordination betwen personnel objectives, developed methods and techniques and overall objectives of the organisation was realised. New structural relationship were developed. The problems of control and co-ordination cannot be solved unless an intensified study is made in the nature of working personnel.

7. Change in Size of the Business. Industrial Revolution and technical changes in methods and machines proposed the large-scale production. By the use of technically-developed machines and simplification of methods, large-scale production became possible. Division of labour and specialisation functions were developed requiring a large number of technical and non-technical works. In order to get the work done by these people efficiently the need of personnel administration was felt.

8. Change in the Form of Business Organisation. In earlier years business was carried on under sole proprietorship. With the advent of joint stock companies as a form of business organisation, the size of the business has increased exhorbitantly. So new administration techniques were developed to cope with the problems of personnel in large industrial houses.

The present day scene on personnel relations is the result of these technical, social and scientific changes in the field of industrial economy.

SCOPE OF PERSONNEL ADMINISTRATION

At the initial stage of development, the scope of Personnel Administration was very limited. With the growth and development of business and industrial enterprise, the activities of these enterprises became more and more complicated and diversified. With this, the scope of Personnel Administration also continued to increase.

Indian Institute of Personnel Management (I.I.P.M.) has described the scope of Personnel Management as follows : *(i)* To dertmine personnel policies. *(ii)* To determine the methods of recruitment, training, placement and promotion etc. *(iii)* To determine the wage system and the conditions of employment. *(iv)* To provide good working conditions and facilities to the workers and employees. *(v)* To establish harmonious relations between labour and capital.

Strauss and Sayels have described the following functions in the scope of Personnel Administration : *(i)* Recruitment selection and placement of employees. *(ii)* Specialised services, such as safety, supervision and control etc. *(iii)* Job analysis, job description and job evaluation. *(iv)* Scheme of compensation payable to the employees. *(v)* Maintenance of Personnel

Accounts. *(vi)* Personnel welfare programmes. *(vii)* Programmes of workers education and training. *(viii)* Labour relations. *(ix)* Public relations. *(x)* Personnel planning and evaluation.

On the basis of above study, it can be said that following are the functions included in the Scope of Personnel Administration :

1. To adopt Suitable Wage System. An important function of Personnel Administration is to adopt a suitable wage system to remunerate the employees so that they may be motivated to extend their full co-operation in the achievement of objectives of the organisation. The wage system must be of the nature that may motivate them to work more and more.

2. Recruitment, Selection and Job Determination for the Employees. The Workers are motivated to apply for jobs in the organisation with the help of advertisement and other measures. The best workers and employees are selected through written test and interview. After selecting them, they are placed on a suitable job.

3. Labour Welfare Activities. Personnel Administration has to perform many activities for the sake of the labour welfare. It includes health and safety programmes, recreation facilities and educational activities etc. These activities increase efficiency and ability of employees.

4. Education and Training of Employees. Another very important function of Personnel Administration is to provide the best possible facilities of education and training to the employees. The programmes of education and training may be started for the benefit of both the old and new employees. During training period employees are paid an allowance at a fixed rate. After completing training they are placed on a job according to their ability.

5. Job Analysis, Job Distribution and Job Evaluation. All the works to be done in business and industrial enterprise are critically analysed so that it may be determined that which job should be assigned to an individual employee.

6. Public Relations. Personnel Administration has to perform some activities for public relations also. These activities include to maintain contacts with social welfare organisations, to provide necessary information about the organisation to publish magazines etc.

7. Personnel Accounts. Personnel Administration has to maintain all the relevant accounts regarding employees of the organisation, such as the number of workers, absenteeism, work done by employees, wage roll etc.

8. Personnel Planning and Evaluation. It includes following activities to determine personnel policies and programmes, to evaluate these policies and programmes, to conduct personnel audit etc.

CLASSIFICATION OF SERVICES

India is a federal polity in which central govt. has certain responsibilites to discharge. Similarly in our federal set-up there are states which hae their own constitutional and legal obligations to discharge towards the citizens. For proper discharging of these obligations in the country there is a strong bureaucracy, which is steel frame work of our administration. In bureaucracy there are persons belonging to—*(1)* All India Services *(2)* State Services and *(3)* Those working in the ex-cader posts. All these services are manned by the Central Government.

Characteristics of All India Services. All India services have the following characteristics :

(a) Each member of the All India Serviuces is allotted to a particular state. Thus a person belonging to All

India Services has a dual control, namely that of the central government as well as that of the State to which he has been allotted.

(b) They enjoy more social prestige and are given more emoluments as compared with the persons belonging to other services.

(c) All India Services are common both to the centre as well as the states and thus can be employed both at the centre as well as in the state to which he belongs.

(d) The members of these Services can be posted at any higher level position.

(e) With the passage of time they have become a class among themselves and are not maintaining any contracts with the people.

(f) Both in the centre as well as the states they are treated as policy makers.

Case for All India Services. In India we have already many All India Services, which among others include :

1. Indian Administrative Services.
2. Indian Police Services.
3. Indian Foreign Services.
4. Indian Railway Services.
5. Indian Audit and Account Services.
6. Indian Forest Services.
7. Indian Economic and Statistical Services.
8. Indian Income Tax Services.
9. Indian Postal Services.
10. Indian Information Services.
11. Central Secretariat Service etc.

But inspite of these services there is an increasing demand than more All India Services should be created. Some of the Arguemnts advanced in favour of creation of these services are as :

1. Efficiency. It is essential that in the public services there should be a minimum standard of efficiency. This standard must always be observed. It is argued that the candidates selected on All India basis will be fare more efficient than those selected on regional basis. For the sake of efficiency it is essential that All India Services should be created.

2. National Integration. It is hoped that the members of All India Services will view every problem from national and not from regional point of view and as such the concept of nation as a whole will grow.

3. Sense of Impartiality. It is also argued in favour of All India Services that the people belonging to these services will not easily bow to the local pressure. They will also resist the state government from doing anything wrong. In this way a sense of impartiality in services comes, which is still more essential because of increasing influence of politicians in running the administration.

4. Uniformity. If there are no all India Services, then the States will recruit their own personnel. While making recruitment it is impossible to have uniform standards. For uniformity of standards, it is better to have All India Services.

5. Rich Experience. People belonging to all India Services can be assigned any responsibility and can also be posted in any part of the country, therefore, they gain rich experience. They will become leaders of the nation in the real sense of the term.

Case Against All India Services. But there are critics who are opposed to the idea of All India Services. Some of the arguments advanced against the creation of such servcies are :

(a) It is said that the creation of All India Services is opposed to the idea of federal system. In our federal policy there is a pre-supposition that each State will have a separate and self-contained administrative sphere. All India Services will be opposed to this idea.

(b) In Indian polity centre is supposed to lead, assist and set-up standards. But All India Service will mean imposition and not guidance.

(c) An All India Services will mean provocative direct involvement of the centre in the affairs of the state which will, in actual practice means, undermining the authority of the state governments.

(d) In an All India competition, the person belonging to developed states will come more successful as compared with those belonging to less developed states and thus former will dominate the later.

(e) The people belonging to All India Services will be required to the paid more by the state on whose strength they are borne as compared with the officers belonging to state services.

(f) In the system there is every danger that local candidates will be ousted and thus employment problem in these states will be aggrevated.

(g) It is also argued that in this system less developed states will almost remain un-represented or less represented. In the words of S. Hukam Singh. "Therefore, my submission is that some consideration for regional recruitment must be provided so that backward areas also have opportunities to develop side by side till a stage comes when their youngmen can stand in competition with other provinces.

(h) Increasing switch over to regional languages it is feared, is likely to result in making the idea of All India Services unworkable.

But it is argued that the disadvantages of All India Services are more due to regional considerations rather than with a view to broader national outlook. The need of the hour is not to promote regional but to develop all India outlook. That is why the idea of having more and more All India Services is developing. Today the trend is in favour of All India Services.

RECRUITMENT

In view of ever increasin role of civil service personnel, every nation has begun to pay more and more attention to the problem of recruitment of these personnel. There is a constant desire that only intellgent and vigorous persons with initiative and far sightedness should be picked up with this end in view different tests are being applied. Recruitments are made either on the basis of oral or written tests or both. Different methods which are being applied aim at only one thing, namely picking up the intelligentia and cream of the nation for the services.

According to Stahl recruitment means securing right people for particular jobs and it may take the form of advertising for large groups of employees.

The method of selection is the central point of interest in a public personnel programme. It is the focal point of the complete public personnel programme. Hence first rate recruitment policy is needed to the building up of a superior staff. Under the career service system no element requires so much care and importance as the recruitment policy.

Hence recruitment requires the first preference on the build-up of the administrative set-up. On this element much more depends the efficiency of Public Service. In this way recruitment is most important for the determination of the public service. A defective recruitment policy may result in the downfall of the entire administrative structure and to prevent it from such deterioration entry of incompetent persons to the office of responsibility, necessitates adoption of sound requirement policy. If the recruitment policy is defective, we may impart the personnel any training in in-services it will not help improving the standard of personnel. This makes it clear that there is the necessity of sound and well-to-do scientific recruitment policy that should be methodical and should follow the constitutional necessity with political outlook.

Recruitment Method. For the recruitment of the personnel two methods are followed: *(i)* recruitment from within and *(ii)* recruitment from without. As far as the first recruitment from within is concerned it is mostly by the promotions of the personnel. According to seniority and efficiency the personnel are promoted to the upper grades. The second method of recruitment can be said to be real method of recruitment. Here the question arises as to which method should be given preference over the other. It should be kept in mind that the question concerns mostly with the higher and middle positions only. In the personnel recruitment generally the lowest personnel's positions are filled or recruitment from without. As such there exists no lower class of personnel to be promoted. Here, we can say it clearly that neither of the two methods is complete in itself and they have their advantages and disadvantages. It is better to have at their pros and cons to understand them better.

Advantages of Recruitment from within or from Promotion. After careful study we find that the following advantages exist for the recruitment from within :

(a) Experienced persons are promoted tc upward positions. Through the experience they are able to discharge their responsibilities to upward positions nicely.

(b) Employees have got enough chance to advancement and promotion.

(c) If the recruitment is from without government will have to impart special prolonged training to such persons and to avoid such botherations they will adopt the promotion method of appointment from 'within'.

(d) Those personnel appointed in lower grades work most conscientiously so that they will be promoted soon to higher positions. Here their working efficiency, holds them good in their higher officers opinion.

(e) Public Service Commissions are relieved from the unnecessary botherations are recruiting authorities.

(f) This method of recruitment from within renders the public service more attractive. Personnel are attracted to such services with a future hope of promotion. People from 'without' know that there is promotion from low to high posts and hence they do not hesitate to join at lower ranks low grades.

(g) Recruitment from within or promotions is an unavoidable ingredient of career service. It can be said that career exists only 'if top positions are filled from within and not from outside, and if it is filled from outside, it can be said that there is a bar on the advancement of the employees for promotion.'

(h) Recruitment from within or promotions will allow the workers to work with contentment. This will boost the morale of the employees.

Advantages of Recruitment from without or Direct Recruitment

The following are the advantages from the direct recruitment or recruitment from without :

(a) This method of recruitment is a direct the most modern democratic method as everybody has a chance on equal footing to enter a public office.

(b) The best talented person can be appointed to the posts as area is too wide and open to all contestents throughout the country. But if the area is limited to the upgrading of the juniors to the senior office, then it is not possible to requisition the services of the best talent from the open market.

(c) The direct recruitment generates latest thinking in the personnel staff and effects the dynamic changes in the outlook of the service. Hence new ideas with changing situations come to rescue of the old traditional feelings in the field.

(d) The youth world is aware of the competitions and hence they know the current events uptodate, while they enter the personnel staff, they act according to the existing environment.

(e) Those new come ups of universities after their completion of the education would be jobless and feel utter frustration if these direct recruitments do not absorb them.

(f) As the public services absorb the newcomers directly, the services are always in tune with the tide of the time and know the tendencies of the present and so they try to mould the personnel to work accordingly.

(g) In the field of technical knowledge, outside or direct recruitment is found more useful because the newcomers bring new ideas, new techniques, new methods, and above all short cut expenses with development anew and hence they prove to be the best leaders of the day.

Disadvantages of Recruitment from Within

The recruitment from within or through promotion has the following disadvantages :

(a) The sphere of selection becomes narrower through the recruitment from within as this recruitment is limited to the persons already appointed in the services.

(b) If the recruitment is only open to the promotions or it from within then the public service is as such 'closed' to the new entrants in the line. It means no infusion fresh blood hence there comes the absence of new talents and new outlooks with fresh attitudes.

(c) Those in office prove to be most incapable and inefficient persons and their selection to the higher officers results in the continuing of the same things. This could be avoided if the recruitment is open to all. This will lead to the selection of efficient persons from the outside and more persons will be attracted to the post.

(d) Experience gains and brilliance goes out which was the result from the outside personnel appointment and we lose it as new energy becomes useless.

(e) Public serivces become based on conventions. They are not progressive. A person once occupying a junior office will march on his legs to the new office with the same attitudes and outlook and thus he becomes conservative and displays conservative outlook.

Demerits of the Recruitment from Without

(a) Personnel of new recruitment have no experience. They are quite fresh to the job. So it was thought over that they do not cover the ability to hold higher assignments of officers and if they are to be fit to the jobs they will be required to go on a long, expensive and intensive training. Hence, this will means a drain on state finances.

(b) If it is a decision that new recruitment is to be done from 'without', the employees 'within' the service feel no chance of promotion and they are averse to it and lose interest in the job and display inefficiency which impares the administrative capacity.

(c) Direct or recruitment from without brings the younger and inexperienced persons over the already working personnel in junior capacity though experienced. This arouses the feelings of hatred and jealousy among the older generation towards the new arrivals of personnel.

(d) If there is competition between inside and outside recruitments, it is conceived that new personnel will acquire more advantage over the older personnel due to fresh knowledge of the environment and current affairs. The older people within service do not get such opportunities for the studies of the latest material on the subjects concerned. Hence they lag behind.

(e) Direct recruitment is taken through examinations and interviews which are full of defects. Marking is subjective. Likewise interview is a matter of chance. A brilliant student may fail in viva if trend of interview disfavours him.

(f) Direct recruitment involves great number of candidates for the examinations while the posts are few. This adds to the problem of the U.P.S.C. to examine them. This causes in the end the delays in their results.

While elucidating the advantages and disadvantages of both these methods of recruitment, it is clear that both the methods do not fulfil the conditions satisfactorily required best for the services. Practically, both the methods are employed during recruitment. Neither of them could be left out completely. In our country we rely on both the methods. The proportion taken by each method varies according to the services. Some posts give weight to direct recruitment while other posts take recourse to inside recruitment. So also while filling the posts classwise and departmentwise selections are made while recruiting. Here, we may quote an observer who pointed out that, "An extensive outside recruitment at the highest grades is a reflection on the ability and talent available within the service and undermines the career idea, while complete absence of the direct recruitment for the higher positions is also a reflection on the service because it might be a symptom of self complacency."

PROCEDURE OF RECRUITMENT OF PERSONNEL

There must be a definite and well defined procedure for making the selection of employees in the enterprise. The procedure of selection in the series to steps through which the employees are finally selected for the enterprise. The selection procedure must be prepared in the manner that more and more information may be made available about the candidates so that the selection of best employees may be made. There cannot be any definite selection procedure applicable to all enterprises. However, the common steps of selection procedure are as follows :

1. Acceptance of Application Forms. First of all applications are invited from the prospective candidates. These applications may be invited through advertising the vacncies in News Paper, Magazine, Employment Exchange, Schools and Colleges, Training Centres, Labour Unions and other Educational Institutions etc. These applications may be invited on plain paper or on the prescribed forms which may be issued by the enterprise. The Candidates are advised to give the relevant information in these application forms. These applications provide a record of qualification, experience etc., of the candidates.

2. Analysis of Application Forms. A date is declared as the last date for submitting the application forms. After this date, all the applications received for a post are analysed in detail. The applications which are incompleted or which do not meet the requirement of post are set aside and the applicants of remaining applications are further invited for different tests and interviews etc.

3. Conducting Employment Tests. The selected candidates, which are selected on the basis of their applications, are called for employment tests. These tests may be of the following types :

(i) Intelligence Tests. Intelligence tests are meant to meausre the mental ability of an individual in terms of his memory, vocabulary, reasoning etc. These tests measure the power of understanding of the candidates. It is a very common test used in the selection procedure these days.

(ii) Personality Tests. Personality tests aim at testing the nature, habit, emotion, maturity and temperament of the candidates. These tests are helpful in deciding the spirit of groupism and feeling of mutual co-operation.

(iii) ***Aptitude Tests.*** Aptitude tests are the test which measure the capacity and potentiality for learning the skills required for the job. These tests are very helpful in forecasting the success of candidates on a particular job.

(iv) ***Job Tests.*** These tests measure the level of efficiency and skills of the candidates required for a particular job. For example, the candidates required for the posts of typist may be asked to type some material. By this test the speed of typing and accuracy in typing may be judged.

(v) ***Interest Tests.*** These tests are designed to evaluate the likings and dislikings of the candidates for different situations and different occupations. These tests are helpful in determining the jobs suitable to the individual candidates.

Employment tests are becoming very popular device of making the selection of best candidates for different posts. These tests help in measuring certain factors of the personality of the candidates.

4. Interview. The candidate selected in employment tests are invited for interview. The main object of interview is to find out of whether an individual candidate is suitable for a particular job or not. Face to face interview is the most important step of the selection procedure. It helps in judging the personality, ability, capability and the temperament of the candidates. It also provides an apportunity to check the information given by the candidates in their application forms. It provides the opportunity to the enterprise to understand the candidates thoroughly. It also provides the opportunity to the candidates to understand the organisation and the job. This way, it is a process of two way communication.

Interview must be conducted in a friendly, congenial atmosphere. Frank free, and friendly discussion must be held at the interview. The atmosphere of the interview must be such that the candidates may feel easy and may express their ideas and opinions freely and frankly. All the questions related to the educational qualifications, experience, general knowledge, attitude character, health, family background, hobby etc., must be asked from the candidates so that complete information may be obtained about them. On the other hand, complete information must be given to the candidates about the organisation also.

5. Medical Examination. After making the selection of the candidates they are checked by a reliable doctor or by a board of doctors to check their health. The main object of medical examination is to check whether the selected candidates are physically capable or not to perform the required job. The candidates which are declared medically unfit, are rejected.

6. Selection by the Supervisor. Candidates selected at the interview must be referred to the supervisor for final selection. If the supervisor feels satisfied, the candidates are selected. If the supervisor is a member of the interview board, this step of referring the candidates to the supervisor is not required.

7. Arrangement of Training. Necessary arrangements are made for providing training to the selected candidates, if necessary. The nature of training and the period of training depends upon the nature of job. Training increase the efficiency and morale of the selected candidates.

8. Issue of Appointment Letters. The candidates, who are approved in the medical examination also, are issued the appointment letters. These appointment letters must contain all the necessary information relating to their posts, period of probation, scale, terms of appointment etc. These letters must also mention the date by which the candidates should join the firm.

9. Follow Up. After making the allotment of the work to the employees, it is followed up. Under this process, the supervisor checks whether the employees are doing their work according to the instructions issued to them or not. It not, necessary instructions and directions are given to them.

RECRUITMENT AGENCIES

Every nation has one chief personnel agency whose work is to look after the personnel policy, related to all the employees under the government. However, it should be kept in mind that under a federal government, every individual federating state has its own chief personnel agency. The department of administrative reforms situated or centred in the Central Cabinet Secretariat is the chief personnel agency as far as India is concerned. The strucutre and function of the developments of personnel in India are given as follows:

The secretariat of cabinet has been divided into two departments *viz.*, *(i)* Cabinet Affairs department and *(ii)* Personnel and Administrative Reforms departments. As the head of these departments Prime Minister of India has the full and direct charge with supervisory powers. As such we can make it easy to understand in the following manner :

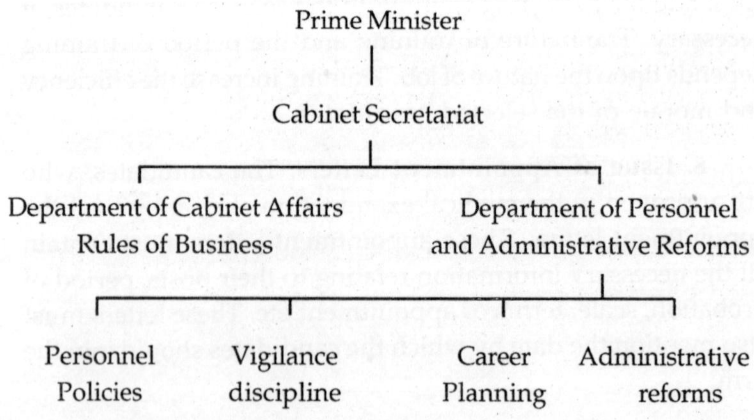

Administrative Reforms Commission (ARC) recommended on 1-8-70 to the government to create a separate department of Personnel and so this department came into existence from that date. By this creation the matters relating to Public Service were transferred from Home Affairs Ministry to Cabinet Secretariat. This came into effect from 7 Feburary, 1972 and the existing department of Personnel was renamed as the Department of Personnel and Administrative Reforms. This department again took over some subject from Finance Ministry. These were Revenue, Intelligence, Directorate of Enforcement. The Administrative Reforms wing of this department has only as far as its duty is concerned the improvement in administrative capacity. It devotes most of its time to the administration of services and not to the other works.

All service matters of general applicability are regulated by this department with full sense of responsibility. At the same time the department maintains for the recruitments to the services a common standard, while it looks after the training of the personnel. It formulates the principles by which it governs promotion, seniority, conduct and discipline with other conditions for services generally.

This department is also responsible for the regulation of matters that are generally applicable to all the services. It gives staff for the senior posts at the centre while other administrative posts for Central Secretariat Service are also considered for all India Services.

For all these services and purposes this department fulfils its responsibility towards *(i)* the creation of New All India Services. *(ii)* Rules and regulations under the All India Services Act *(iii)* all matters relating to the I.A.S. including the Indian Civil Service (I.C.S.).

As far as the duties of the department are considered, it formulates the policies and looks to their implementation. It also sees that the personnel for these various services are properly trained. At the same time they look for the career administration welfare of staff and their families.

Now out of the Personnel department, vigilance and discipline division co-ordinates the works of the ministries and departments of the Central Government to eradicate corruption from the public services. This department also does the work of supervision for the working of Central Bureau of Investigation (CBI). The Central Bureau of Investigation is responsible for investigation into cases of corruption including Government employees.

The functions which this department has to perform with responsibility are as follows :

(i) recruitment, promotion and moral of the services,

(ii) vigilance and discipline,

(iii) training,

(iv) adminstration of senior and middle officers,

(v) conditions of the service,

(vi) centralized aspect of managing I.A.S (Indian Administrative Services),

(vii) grievances and welfare of the staff,

(viii) Union Public Service Commission (U.P.S.C.),

(ix) planning of careers,

(x) allocation of personnel and integration of services due to the states reorganisation,

(xi) personnel administration agencies,

(xii) research in personnel matters,

(xiii) administrative reforms.

To this department five offices are attached. They are given here under :

(i) Central Bureau of Investigation (C.B.I), Sardar Patel Bhawan, New Delhi.

(ii) Institute of Secretariat Training and Administration, New Delhi.

(iii) Lal Bahadur National Academy of Administration, Mussoorie.

(iv) Directorate of Revenue Intelligence, New Delhi.

(v) Directorate of Enforcement, New Delhi.

Besides these each department of the Government of India and other federating state governments has a departmental personnel unit to tackle over all matters concerned with the personnel of that department. Indian Departmental Personnel units are only establishment units related only with the routine services similar to appointment, transfer and promotion. They require improvement on the lines of the department of Personnel and Administrative Reforms. They can be efficiently improved if they are fulfilled by competent and qualified personnel staff.

SOURCES OF RECRUITMENT

Once the manpower requirements are determined, the process of recruitment begins. Recruitment is the process of identifying the sources of potential employees and encouraging them to apply for jobs in the organisation. According to Dalton E. McFarland, "The term recruitment applies to the process of attracting potential employees to the company." The main purpose of recruitment is to create a pool of candidates from which personnel with required skills can be selected. Every organisation has to recruit personnel though the amount of recruitment may differ from organisation to organisation depending upon the size of the organisation, nature of job and the recruitment policy, etc.

The various sources of recruitment can be broadly classified into two categories : *(i)* internal recruitment, and *(ii)* external recruitment. Most organisations depend upon both the sources. The relative emphasis may differ from enterprise to enterprise depending upon the following factors:

(a) Training programme of the enterprise whether it prefers trained persons or wants fresh candidates to be trained by itself.

(b) Administration policy towards recruitment whether it prefers internal or external sources.

(c) The level of specialisation and training required for employees.

(d) The need for originality and initiative required from employees.

(e) Trade union's attitude towards administration's recruitment policy.

Internal Sources. Internal sources of recruitment consist of personnel already working in the enterprise. Many organisations fill job vacancies through promotions and transfer of existing staff.

Merits. Internal recruitment offers the following advantages :

(a) It keeps employees happy and in high morale.

(b) Employees know that they stand the chance of promotion to higher positions. This induces them to work harder so as to prove their worth.

(c) Internal recruitment ensures continuity of employment and organisational stability.

(d) It creates a sense of security among employees.

(e) Prospects of transfer to new posts inspire employees to keep on adding to thier knowledge and experience which leads to their development.

(f) Filling of vacancies from internal sources is quite economical and convenient. No time and money is to be spend on advertisement, test and interviews because the knowledge and skills of employees are already known. There is no need for orientation of employees for preparing them for the new job.

Demerits. Interal recruitment suffers from the following drawbacks :

(a) Existing employees may not be fully qualified for the new job. Required talent may not be available among the present staff.

(b) Internal candidates become accustomed to the company's work patterns and as such may lack originality and fresh outlook. Therefore, internal recruitment involves 'inbreeding' of ideas.

(c) All vacancies cannot be filled through internal sources. The enterprise has to depend upon outside sources for entry level jobs.

(d) This method narrows the choice and denies the outsiders an opportunity to prove their worth.

External Sources. The main sources of external recruitment are as follows :

1. Advertising. Advertising in newspapers and journals is the most popular source of recruitment from outside. It is a very convenient and economical method for different types of personnel. Detailed information can be given in the advertisement to facilitate self-screening by the candidates. If necessary, the enterprise can keep its identity secret by giving a post box number.

2. Educational Institutions. Universities, colleges and institutes of higher education have become a popular source of recruitment for engineers, scientists, adminstration trainees, technicians, etc. Business concerns may hold campus interviews and select students for final interview at their offices. Universities and institutes generally run placement bureaus to assist in recruiting students. But educational institutions provide only young and inexperienced candidates.

3. Employment Exchanges. Public employment exchanges are an important source of recruitment of personnel. Job seekers register their names with these exchanges. Employers notify job vacancies to these exchanges who pass on the names of suitable registered candidates to the employers.

4. Personnel Consultants. A consulting firm is a specialised agency which helps client companies in recruiting personnel. It serves as an intermediary between the enterprise and the job-seekers. On a requisition from a client company, it advertises the vacancy and receives applications. It may pass on the applications to the client company or may conduct tests and interviews of the candidates. It charges fee from the client company. This source is generally used for recruiting executives.

5. Jobbers and Contractors. These are a source of recruitment for unskilled and manual labour. They have close links with towns and villages for this purpose.

6. Unsolicited Applicants. Due to unemployment problem in India business concerns receive a large number of unsolicited candidates at the main gate or through mail. Such jobseekers may be considered for casual vacancies or for preparing a waiting list for future use.

7. Leasing. This method is often used by public sector organisations. Under it personnel from civil services, defence services and private sectors are employed for specific periods due to shortage of managerial personnel.

Merits. The main advantages of external recruitment are as follows :

(a) **Wide Choice.** The enterprise can choose the best personnel from among a large number of applicants.

(b) **Fresh Outlook.** Candidates recruited from external sources bring originality and fresh viewpoints. They are free from the in-built preferences and prejudices.

(c) **Broader Experience.** The enterprise can secure candidates with varies and broader experience.

Demerits. External sources of recruitment have the following disadvantages :

(a) **Danger of Maladjustment.** Some candidates chosen from outside may fail to adjust themselves to new environment. They may be irritable, quarrelsome or suspicious. They may have to be terminated and replaced.

(b) **Heart-Burning.** External recruitment creates heart-burning and demoralisation among the existing personnel.

(c) **Expensive.** Greater time and money have to be spent on advertising, test and interviews of external candidates. Cost of induction of new personnel is also higher.

(d) **Sense of Insecurity.** Recruitment from outside creates a sense of insecurity among the present staff. The staff may refuse to co-operate fully with the enterprise.

Evaluation of Alternative Sources. A company cannot fill all its vacancies from one single source. It must carefully combine some of these sources, weighting their cost and flexibility, the quality of men they supply, and their effect on the present work force. Following are some of the measures which can be used to assess how good or how poor various sources have proved to be :

1. Yield Ratios. These ratios tell us about the number of leads/contacts needed to generate a given number of hires in a given time. To take an example, suppose a company is contemplating expansion and needs 10 additional engineers in the next 6 months. On the basis of its past experience the company predicts as under : We must extend offers to 2 candidates to gain one acceptance. If we need 10 engineers we will have to extend 20 offers. Further, if the interview-to-offer ratio has been 3:2 then 30 interviews must be conducted and since the invitees to interview ratio is 4:3 then as many as 40 candidates must be invited. Finally, if contacts or leads required to find suitable candidates to invited are in 6:1 proportions then 240 contacts be made. These ratios are shown in this figure in the form of a pyramid.

2. Time Lag between Requisition and Placement. The basic statistics needed to estimate the time lag are the time-lapse data. To take an example, a company's past experience may show that the average number of days from application to interview is 15, from interview to offer is 5, from offer to acceptance is 7 and from acceptance to report for work is 21. Therefore, if the company begins its recruitment and selection process today, the best estimate is that it will be 48 days before the new employees is added to the pay-roll. With this information, the 'length' of the pipe-line for alternative sources of recruitment can be described and suitable recruiting sources chosen.

3. Gross Cost Per Line. This is arrived by dividing the total cost of recruitment by the number of individuals hired.

4. Employee Attitude Studies. These studies try to discover the reactions of present employees to both external and internal sources of recruitment.

5. Correlation Studies. These studies tell us about the extent of correlation which exists between different sources of recruitment and factors of success on the job.

6. Data on Turnover, Grievances, and Disciplinary Action Tabulated According to Different Sources of Recruitment. These figures throw light on the relatives merits of each source.

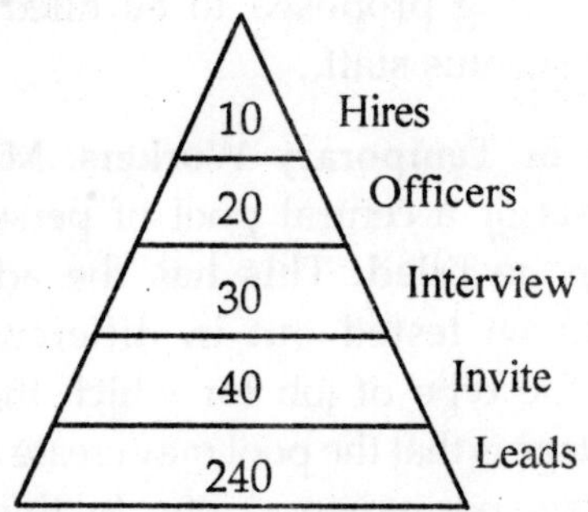

SOURCES OF RECRUITMENT IN INDIA

The different sources from which labour is recruited in our country are as follows :

Internal Sources

In many organisations in India at the time of new vacancies preference is given to people from within the organisation. Thus at the Tata Engineering and Locomotive Company, outside recruitment is resorted to only when recruitments for training personnel cannot be met from the resources generated by the company's training scheme or by internal promotion or when the vacancy has to be filled quickly. This ensures that in the company there is always a ladder by which men with the right qualities and merits can climb to higher levels qualities and merits can climb to higher levels.

External Sources

1. Employment Exchanges. The Employment Exchanges Act, 1959 which implies to all establishments including factories employing 25 or more persons casts an obligation on the employer to notify all vacancies but does not impose any obligation upon him to recruit any person through the Employment Exchange. Further, the Act does not apply to temporary vacancies of less than 3 months' duration and to vacancies involving proposed to be filled by promotion or absorption of surplus staff.

2. Badli or Temporary Workers. Many organisations keep badli lists or a central pool of personnel from which vacancies can be filled. This has the advantage that the personnel can be tested out in different jobs and listed according to the type of job for which they are best fitted. The disadvantage is that the pool may create disputes regarding wages, holiday, permanency, etc. In this connection it is significant to remember that any person employed for 240 days in a year is deemed to be in continuous employment for one full year which entitles him to claim compensation on being retrenched by the employer under Section 25-C of the Industrial Disputes Act.

3. Advertisement in Newspapers. Senior posts are largely filled by this method. Box number advertisements sometimes do not draw good candidates who feel that it is not worthwhile to apply without knowing employer's name. In ports and docks advertisement is the normal made for recruiting skilled and semi-skilled workers.

4. Technical and Other Institutes. Some establishments make arrangements with the I.T.I. (Industrial Training Institutes) of the Directorate General of Employment and

Training under which it supplies their trainees in accordance with the specifications of the employing agency. For managerial positions the practice of recruiting MBAs is increasing in India. The administration of several big organisations in India pay visits to these institutions for this purpose. Scouting for managerial talanet is done by D.C.M., Bajaj and other business houses among university and college students. Young persons showing promise are tapped with the help of faculty members.

5. Labour Contracts. Almost all the companies engaged in oil-processing including ONGC follow the contract labour method to carry out jobs which are of temporary and non-recurring nature. In mines of West Bengal, Bihar, Madhya Pradesh, Orissa and Andhra Pradesh recruitment through contractors is still very common. The system is, however, on the decline in the plantations.

6. Relations of Existing Employees. Some companies have agreements with recognised unions to give prior consideration to relatives of deceased, existing or retired employees if their qualifications and experience are suitable for vacancies. In Tata Iron and Steel Co. Ltd., the Standing Order of the Company clearly mentions the following order of priority recruitment :

(a) People of State;

(b) A dependent of an employee who has been permanently disabled, either totally or partially, by reason of an accident met with during the course of his employment, provided a job suitable to his qualification is available;

(c) A near-relation of an employee who has completed 25 years of continuous service if no other relation of that employee is in employment. The term 'relation' for this purpose is defined as husband, wife or wives, widow, son, daughter, brother, sister and son-in-law, in order of priority;

(d) In each category, members of Scheduled Castes and Scheduled Tribes should receive preference over others; and

(e) A relation of an employee who dies as a result of an accident should be given, on compassionate ground, top priority for permanent employment suited to his qualifications.

7. Bureau of Public Enterprises. One important agency in respect of first and second class employees of public sector undertakings is the Bureau of Public Enterprises which makes direct recruitment to various positions in these categories. Recruitment to class III and class IV positions is generally undertaken by the heads of concerned departments because centralised recruitment is difficult in view of the numbers involved.

The following table based on a study done by A.R. Negandhi and Barnard Estafen, in 1965 fo 36 Indian companies in 5 major industrial towns in India gives the different methods of recruitment of blue and white-collar workers and the number of companies using each method :

Table

Methods of Recruitment

	Number of companies using the method for				
Method of recruitment	*White Collar only*	*Blue Collar only*	*Both*	*Total*	*Number of Com- the method*
1	2	3	4	5	6
1. Public Employment Agency	—	—	36	3 (100)	—
2. Advertising	—	—	32	32 (89)	4 (11)

Contd.

1	2	3	4	5	6
3. Personal Application	1	—	29	30 (83)	6 (17)
4. Productivity Centres and Training Institutes	4	—	—	4 (11)	32 (89)
5. Direct hiring at the gate	—	22	—	22 (61)	14 (39)
6. Nomination by present employees	1	4	17	22 (61)	14 (39)
7. Colleges and Universities	7	—	—	7 (20)	29 (80)
8. Private employment agencies	6	—	—	6 (17)	30 (83)

Note : Figures within brackets denote percentages.

An analysis of the above table shows that :

1. The first three important sources of recruitment of white and blue-collar workers in India are Employment Exchanges, advertisements and personal applications in the order in which they are mentioned. The percentage of companies using these sources is 100, 89 and 83 respectively.
2. In case of recruitment of blue-collar workers the practice is to use informal and non-institutional sources, namely, nominations by present employees and hiring at the gate. In case of recruitment of white-collar workers the sources used are institutional.
3. Direct hiring at the gate is in respect of the blue-collar workers only and is practised by 61 per cent of the companies.
4. Recruitment of both white and blue-collar workers through nominations by present employees is

practised by 47 per cent of the companies. Eleven per cent of the companies use this method is respect of blue-collar workers only.

5. Sources exclusively used for recruiting white-collar workers are colleges and universities, private employment agencies and productivity centres and training institutes. These sources are still in their nascent stage of growth.

The study goes on to show that generally those seeking work as unskilled labourers are selected by the Personnel Officer or by his representative on the basis of experience and personnel judgment. In the selection of skilled and semi-skilled workers, majority of companies (29) use some kind of trade tests. The tests range from highly developed methods in a few foreign-owned companies to a mere testing of the employee on the machine to see whether he knows how to operate it. Indian organisations prefer to measure the applicant's performance on the job instead of relying on an indirect measurement of his skills through different kinds of tests. Psychological tests which are extensively used in the United States are rarely applied in India.

In one survey conducted in 1965, it was found that 50 per cent of the government and only 14 per cent of private units were making use of psychological tests to some extent.

Some important reasons which account for the unsatisfactory use of psychological tests in Indian industries are as under :

1. There being an unusually high number of applicants for every vacancy the main problem facing an employer in India is how to reject a majority of them without opening himself to the charge of favouritism. The raison d'etre of employing psychological tests in such cases is very often to have a device for

rejection rather than a device for scientific selection on the principle of the best man for the job. This emphasis on rejection has prevented an appreciation of the positive virtues of psychological tests.

2. There are still few tests in use in Indian industry which are standardised by Indian psychologists for Indian subjects with national or at least regional norms. Most of the tests used are foreign which have been adapted to Indian conditions on the basis of insufficient date. Several tests developed by Indian researchers at the Psychological Research Wing of the Ministry of Defence lie unpublished within the covers of the Ph.D. dissertations for which they had been submitted or in government files on grounds of secrecy.

3. Test are sometimes devised by persons who have inadequate knowledge of psychology. This always proves disastrous to the enterprise and deterimental to the subject. Administration's faith in the efficacy of test is lost.

4. The rise of trade unions and gradual realisation that for most skilled and semi-skilled jobs in factories group factors rather than variations in individual abilities and aptitudes are largely responsible for worker productivity, have given practically a death blow to the psychological selection procedure in India.

●●

7

Ecology of Public Enterprises

The ecology is complex and is unique to the public sector in some ways. Public sector managers face greater professional hazards than their counterparts in the private sector, where relationships are better defined and less in number. They are subject to political influence of a magnitude not experienced by the private sector. There is a larger focus on them in Parliament and even state legislatures have not hesitated in courting them. The ecological aspect is important for another reason also. Since the infrastructure for growth and development is under the control of the public enterprises in India the shortcoming of the latter become the problems of society as a whole, including the private sector. Electricity, transport, coal, etc. are under State ownership and their poor performance has an adverse effect all along the line.

The ecology of a public enterprise is an inclusive concept. It includes the Constitution, the political executive, the bureaucracy in the Secretariat, the Bureau of Public Enterprises, the parliamentary committees, the trade unions, the politicians, the officers' associations and the public. Fortunate is the manager who can manage the various ecological forces and factors to the advantage of his enterprise.

The Constitution

The Constitution is the ordering framework, and one may quickly recall the major constitutional parameters having a direct bearing on public enterprises:

1. India is a democracy of the parliamentary type, based on a system of periodic election held on the basis of universal adult franchise.

2. India is a union of states, the Constitution making both the centre and the constituent states autonomous in their respective areas of operation.

3. Irrespective of levels of political complexion, the government in the country is firmly committed to the directive principles of State policy enshrined in the Constitution itself, which direct it actively to work for the economic and social well-being of the people.

The federal character of the Constitution obliges the public enterprises to function within different political contexts, so to say. Though created and controlled by the central government, the public undertakings are necessarily located in various states, thus bringing them in contact with the state political systems also. The state governments may be under a party different from the one at the Centre. Even otherwise, different states have evolved their peculiar political cultures impinging more or less on all the institutions located within their boundaries. The ecology of public enterprises in eastern India is, for instance. somewhat different from the one prevailing in other parts, notwithstanding the existence of the industrial security forces and the central government's right, acquired under an amendment of the Constitution, to deploy the Central Reserve Police anywhere in the country on its own volition.

Ministers

A minister's control over a public enterprise flows in theory from his own accountability to Parliament. A public undertaking can never be viewed as a sovereign entity immune from any control. In a parliamentary democracy, the legislature obliges it to remain accountable to it, which determines the fundamental pattern of relationship between an enterprise and other organisations. The minister controlling a public enterprise is held accountable to Parliament, and the accountability of the enterprise to the minister is the obverse side of the coin.

In fact, the relationship is not simple or very innocent. A minister evinces a much larger interest in an enterprise than he is formally accountable for so far as Parliament is concerned. Before Parliament, he extols the sanctity of public sector autonomy; but while dealing with an enterprise he involves his ministerial accountability. He always ends up with a sizable 'unaccounted' jurisdiction which he is ever keen to extend; and in this heroic effort he is helped by his personal staff including the special assistant. He has an undoubted role in regard to an enterprise but it is in the area of policy making and guidance and, moreover, is of a general nature. In practice, he does not dwell within this field. Generally, a public enterprise remains torn between the ministerial indecision and ministerial interference. His main areas of interest, today, are individual postings, transfer, promotions, contract giving and like matters where personal patronage is involved. He is too closely involved in personnel matters, of individual staff members. Besides, he has even come to control what are purely internal matters of an enterprise such as award of contracts, procurement of supplies and the like. Indeed, the emerging operational philosophy governing the minister-enterprise relationship seems to be that the managers have to carry out the ministerial bidding, or quit—and quit unceremoniously. In 1980 the chairman of the Cochin Shipyard was abruptly transferred, allegedly because he would not toe the minister's line in the purchase of a ship engine. A little later, the chief manager of the Hindustan Steel met with a similar fate. There are many such instances of ministerial arbitrariness and such actions have created a climate of insecurity in public enterprise managers.

Bureaucracy

It is a maxim of parliamentary democracy that civil servants act in the name of the minister and are thus anonymous, but in practice they are a powerful institution commanding significant weight and influence in public decision making. Even if they are not exactly ruling servants they are not mere servants either. Public enterprises have an interface with the bureaucracy at several levels of operation. The civil servants in the controlling ministry of government exercise control over a public enterprise in a wide variety of matters although the nature and quantum of control varies with the form of organisation. They decide the policy matters, issue directives and instructions on various issues and supervise the working of an enterprise. They even undertake tours of the public undertakings under their administrative charge. Secondly, they are also nominated members of the board of directors and in this capacity exercise considerable influence and control over the enterprises. Thirdly, the civil servants are also seen to man a large number of middle level and senior level positions in the enterprise even though their professional knowledge about the enterprise is nothing to boast about. The practice of civil servants being on deputation to an enterprise was quite widely prevalent till recently, although it has not been entirely given up. At one time the public sector was almost a fiefdom of ICS/IAS. The IAS domination continues to be overwhelming in the state level public undertakings.

Bureau of Public Enterprises

The BPE came into existence in 1965, much after the conspicuous emergence of public enterprises in India. It was set up to become a central point of reference and consultation on important aspects of management, explore avenues of economy in capital costs, devise steps to improve productivity and profitability, review the working of public undertakings and to present reports and reviews of their working to Parliament. The Bureau publicly projected a rather low profile for itself, regarding itself as no more than a 'coordinating and servicing agency', but this modesty was more apparent than real. The fact is that it virtually acted like an 'overlord minister' in relation to the public enterprises, giving even an occasional impression of being the proverbial fifth wheel in the coach. It became yet another level of control and surveillance though its professional competence to engage in this role was questionable. The Bureau's personnel, usually drawn from the various services of the land, often projected themselves too far, in the process curbing the drive, initiative and innovative spirit of the enterprise managers. Besides, the bureau was itself a top heavy organisation, having more than doubled its strength within four years.

Parliamentary Committees

The Estimates Committee of Parliament used to examine, among others, the working of public enterprises until the setting up of the Committee on Public Undertakings in 1963. COPU seeks to examine whether the affairs of the public undertakings are being managed in accordance with sound business principles and prudent commercial practices, and presents its report to Parliament. Consisting of fifteen members drawn from both the Houses of Parliament, COPU makes known to Parliament, and to the larger public, how the public enterprises are operating. This is an educative, even corrective role but its limitations, too, should be readily recognised. Over the years, the control mechanisms at the disposal of Parliament have been discovered to be weak and inadequate and that august body is finding itself helpless in its relationship with the executive. It is also not very incorrect to say that some members, at least, of the parliamentary committee do not always resist the temptation of seeking small favours and benefits, and the public enterprise concerned does not much mind accommodating them in many ways. The resultant equilibrium may produce its own logic in the long term, but no one has bothered to analyse the consequences.

Politicians

The party system in India is characterised by one dominant party coexisting with many parties. As we have seen elsewhere, the single-party dominance system in India has had the effect of compromising, generally, the sense of impartiality and objectivity of public personnel. The political interference in administration, including public enterprises, is not inconsiderable in India, and this phenomenon owes itself to an ecology of shortages, unemployment, and political opportunism.

Many important decisions relating to an enterprise are sometimes politically determined, and are not based on professional and technical considerations. Not unoften, partisan, even personal factors lie beneath even crucial decisions like selection of sites, purchase of machinery, recruitment of senior level personnel, postings and promotion of personnel, and the list of irrationality can easily be lengthened.

But the politicians seek particularly to influence matters relating to personnel such as recruitment, postings, transfers, etc. Individual MPs and legislators are inclined to treat the public enterprise of their constituency as a kind of job bank; provider of employment and other benefits to their followers. Whether a politician may get a 'cut' for the service rendered is not very clear though the general feeling is that today an average politician does not much object to becoming an intermediary or a middle man working for a consideration. Many of them are thus seen to work for the 'sons of the soil' theory and fight for, so to say, a closer integration of the public enterprise with its surrounding region. Inevitably, even the work culture gets localised.

Trade Unions

Trade unions have a fairly long history in Indian industry and they entered the public enterprises almost naturally when the later began to emerge. Very quickly, however, they have risen as a powerful contextual component of public enterprises. Indeed. it may not be far off the mark if one were to describe them as a parallel hierarchy powerfully influencing the actions and behaviour of the blue collar and other lower level personnel in a large nation of public enterprises.

There are many factors behind such a phenomenon. The top management of a public enterprise is either not able or willing to adopt the approach of a private industrialist in its relationship with the workers: it has developed the habits of looking to the political leadership for getting cues and guidance whenever industrial peace is endangered. Most members of the top management have no permanent stake in the particular organisation they work in. and being essentially birds of passage they do not look at the problems in a long-range perspective. They prefer to pass their sojourn peacefully without raising anyone's hackles, which has an effect of weakening them in their relationship with the workers and the union leadership. The latter are well aware of the vulnerability of top management and taking full advantage of the situation, mount all sorts of demands in the sure hope of getting at least a part of them accepted. The union leadership is, as a rule, given to padding its demands. In such an environment militancy pays and over the years, unionism has become increasingly aggressive, intolerant, even norm less. The union leaders have emerged as a class by themselves and it would be very misleading to believe that they always and invariably work for the workers' interests only. They have on occasions even given an impression of using the employees as cannon fodder to satisfy their ego needs. The unions are not always wholesomely motivated at any rate, in a large number of organisations. 'I have yet to come across a union leader who is not corrupt', one senior railway officer bitterly commented when the writer was discussing this question with him. This may be a somewhat exaggerated view; nevertheless, the unions in public enterprises have generally become militant irresponsible, even violent, and the union leadership has low respect for the laws of the land, so much so that many labour leaders have begun to regard themselves as beyond the reach of the law, seeing themselves as immune from them. In the process, many unions have even begun to be run on thinly disguised mafia lines and union crime has come to be viewed very lightly. This has far reaching effect on the morale of officers in public enterprises, especially those in supervisory roles.

A noticeable feature of trade unions is their affiliation with the political parties of the land. Indeed, each party worth the name has its own trade union. Whether unions should become depoliticised is a moot point, but it is important that the parties at least promote and protect internal democracy n the unions so that they enjoy the spontaneous support of the workers and also perform, among other things, an educative role.

Public enterprises do not observe the principle of 'one enterprise, one union', which entails its own consequences. It is common to see more than one union operating in an enterprise and this multiplicity itself is not conducive to industrial peace. The emerging issues affecting the workers begin to be viewed, not on merit, but on political expediency. This points to the need for a rational policy for the recognition of trade unions. No less is the need for proper training of the union leaders so that they may be made aware of their true role, tasks, responsibilities and obligations.

Impact on Public Enterprises

The ecology is apt to penetrate into the anatomy and physiology of organisations bound by it, and public enterprises in India bear ample evidence of the ecological effects. Indeed, there has been such an intense intermingling of the two over the years that it is not often possible to say which bears the impact of ecology and which of the enterprise itself. The cumulative effect, however. is that many a public enterprise is not managed in accordance with accepted professional norms and standards. Political overtones are overriding and dominate the technical and functional aspects of public enterprise autonomy. The personnel practices are largely ascriptive and continue to be so despite the existence of the Bureau of Public Enterprises and of the Public Enterprises Selection Board. Many of these undertakings have remained 'topless' for fairly long periods, which perhaps is indicative of how much the government is concerned about their effective functioning.

Appointments are not always made on professional grounds: proper 'contacts' and 'pulls' are often more important than qualifications. This entails several consequences. The managers of these undertakings are prevented from concentrating on their jobs single-mindedly as they have necessarily to spend their time and energy in strengthening their contacts with the top level functionaries in Delhi and mobilising support for their survival and promotion. No less serious is the problem of frequent changes at the top and middle levels of the undertaking. Nor does there exist a meaningful process of evaluation of the performance of the managers. The personnel practices are not performance oriented and are always kept vague - primarily to serve narrow partisan ends.

Besides, the attitude shown by the controlling ministry often betrays ignorance about the nature of the task being undertaken by the enterprise, and curbs the drive and initiative of the managers who are positively motivated. There is a singular absence of reward system for the higher performer. Nor does there exist any punishment scheme for the derelict. The worst that may happen to a poor performer is a mere transfer. A transfer in such cases becomes but a mechanism under which a functionary escapes the consequences of his wrong decisions and faulty actions: the man does not stay long enough to reap the fruits of his actions.

Many employees are deeply politicised, maintaining links with ministers and MPs. They do not hesitate in bypassing the regular hierarchy and establishing contacts with the politicians. All this cannot but have a demoralising effect on managers who, as a result, feel it prudent to pursue a policy of masterly inactivity. It is common knowledge that the nationalised coal fields in Bihar are a haven for anti-social elements. The railways, too, have to cope with similar problems. The total time loss due to strikes and lockouts in public enterprises during 1979 was 6.66 million man-days or 18 per cent of the total time loss of 37.10 million man-days for the year in the country.

8

Evolution of Civic Engagement

The micro-analysis has an ancient origin in the Athenian democracy, yet the relationship between rulers and ruled resulted in regarding the population as subjects to the ruler who had specific rights over them, frequently attributed to a divine source. Participation of the ruled in the political process slowly gathered weight in the Western world, for instance in the Magna Carta. Later, the writings of Locke and Montesquieu, the social contractide as, the American Declaration of Independence and the French Revolution began to emphasise a different relationship-making approach by citizens and elections of the rulers more and more wide spread. The extension of voting rights to previously excluded groups, the introduction of proportional representation, growing participation in elections, and increasing numbers of candidates for offices all were evidence of a developing more active role of citizens and of closing the gap between rulers and ruled. Still a gap remained, although in the cases of the New England town meetings or the Swiss cantons, for instance, the resurrection of the Athenian democracy began to find expression. The concept of grassroots became more and more prevalent in discussions of political affairs.

Attempts to close the gap found special expression in the introduction of forms of direct democracy, such as initiative, referendum and recall. They met, however, with mixed acceptance. A special way of attempting to close the gap was the idea of civic or citizenship education gaining familiarity and becoming a common feature of secondary education. In addition, widening involvement of governments extending beyond the traditional spheres into environment, health and resources resulted in the emergence of many interest groups, frequently emphasising single issues, which brought their concerns to government attention. This increasing concern for the public for affairs of the country was not limited to government only. It found also expression in the areas of business and even other social organisations. In all of the areas, the demand to listen to the participants as consumers became widely heard resulting in wider participation in their governance, in labour unions, and in involvement in governmental affairs. Corresponding to this we find also in public administration increasing acceptance of the involvement of public management employees.

To complete this picture, the appearance of a variety of non profit organisations has to be mentioned, which by their activities contributed to the closing of the gap mentioned above. Expanding Role of the Academy, the typical role of the higher learning institutions in the United States of the 18th and 19th centuries was to be isolated from the communities, concentrating only on the personal developments of the students. The academy was located on a hill looking down on its environment from a superior position.

As a result a town-gown conflict developed with the academy satisfied to remain in its ivy-covered building and preaching morality to the town. In such a situation, there was not much room for an academic consideration of politics and government. Courses related to these areas, if at all present, considered classical writings and constitutional arrangements. In time this began to change and more courses developed resulting ultimately in the creation of departments of government and political science. Coverage in those departments began to expand by adding different courses and stressing the actual conduct of public affairs.

The development of progressivism and good government ideas obviously could not have these departments immune of them. They became frequently sources of ideas and moral concerns closely related to the real political scene, obviously maintaining some form of neutrality. This appearing closeness brought also students into contact with the world of politics. Political and governmental speakers began to appear for guest lectures in classes and students visited political events and offices. Following that, internships in offices and political campaigns became a standard feature. Encouragement of such closer relationships became in the 1950s a concern of the Citizenship Clearing House financed by the Pew Foundation.

They were quite successful and, after several years, ceased operations. The introduction of different model programmes, such as Model Legislatures, Model United Nations, or Model Organisation of American States attracted wide attention in the 1960s, 1970s and 1980s. Programmes like the Washington, United Nations or London Semester allowing students to spend a semester away from the home campus in real political situations were very popular.

The idea of political participation of students and faculty gained wider acceptance beginning in the 1960s. This brought some closeness to the teaching, but at the same time created the danger of limiting neutrality and objectivity while allowing personal views to enter into teaching. In time, similar developments penetrated departments of economics, sociology and psychology. Areas of study and departments very closely related to actual life began to be established as "public administration, business administration or social work." Fields like journalism or education always had a close relationship to actual life. Even some of the natural sciences developed specific interests and involvement in such areas as environment, health or hazards.

The institutions of higher learning began to recognise also the need for a close relationship to secondary schools. And so, for instance, colleges and universities began to conduct workshops for teachers of specific fields such as social studies and offer programmes for high school students such as model legislatures or Model United Nations. These programmes brought hundreds of high school students to the campuses making them aware of problems faced by American states and by the world's countries.

The discussion of public affairs and the academy above showed a clear preponderance of macro approaches. Surely enough it was announced that a proper macro performance ultimately will bring about favourable micro changes. This did not necessarily happen and so the gulf between the two levels continued. Emphasis on the macro level involved a setting of high sounding goals-a free society, higher standards of living, involvement of citizens and better prepared students. These goals and others similar to them obviously were quite desirable, but they were never clearly identified and their achievement because of the impossible measurability was difficult to ascertain. This kind of approach was best described by Max Weber's ethics of ultimate ends. He analysed the effects of working toward high sounding, generally moral goals which gave motivation to efforts, pointed out directions and presented an idealised ultimate end. Such an approach could certainly bring with it great efforts and in many cases approximations of the desired goals. Yet it was never quite sure whether the ultimate ends were achieved, since all too often they were relegated to a future continuously moving away.

This obviously meant that the ultimate ends acquired a form of doubtful reality. One was working toward the high goals which were steadily moving away. With such movement also the initial motivation was weakening. Certainly there were some highly desirable results of the goal directed activities, such as in missionary work or in improvements of municipal government, yet by and large the ethics of ultimate ends did not bring about the expected and desired results. However, there was an important side effect of these efforts. They resulted in an increased participation of the affected people and groups. One could with pride point out, for instance, increased participation in elections, greater membership of organisations and so on. Establishment of correlation between higher participation and goal achievement was never clearly evident.

It is, however, again difficult to prove that such an increase resulted in the achievement of the set goals. To state it generally, the ethics of ultimate ends with its emphasis on high sounding goals despite of the increases in participation and information does not bring about the desired effects. Some of the very desirable changes on the macro level do not transmit to the micro level in any expected manner.

Our critical analysis of the macro approach to high sounding goals showed that they have substantial short comings. This does not imply, however, any disregard for goal setting and planning to achieve them. It rather becomes necessary to consider how proper goal setting and planning may playa role in solving the problems we are facing. These problems are evident in any kind of observation. They were very well described by Madeleine Albright, former US Secretary of State, during celebrations of the 25th anniversary of the Solidarity movement in Poland. She stated them as coercion, corruption and complacency, the three Cs.

During a September 2005 speech at the University of Kansas, Lech Walesa, the former President of Poland, discussing the current situation in the world pointed out two issues we are facing. One is globalisation which according to him must be based on a value system ... that gives all people an equal chance to achieve success. The second is that today you can still find a lot of people who are not satisfied with things".

These current problems cannot be solved by the macro approach alone, since they have existed for a long time and their solution has been frequently attempted by this kind of an approach. Their situation today becomes increasingly difficult as a result of spreading violence, such as used by Islamic fundamentalism and of a very high incidence of natural disasters such as hurricanes, floods and earthquakes. It becomes, therefore, necessary to try a different approach which could be based substantially on Max Weber's ethics of responsibility. How would this be different from the macro approach? Weber points out that the achievement of any goals at any institution depends on individual actions of the people involved in the institutions concerned. They have to be motivated to act and more than that they have to be responsible for the results and consequences of their activities.

Demands of Civic Engagement

Civic engagement to be effective requires first and foremost an understanding of and information about current problems. Depending on the area of expected involvement this means exact, and, as much possible, complete data on the respective community or institution. What is needed next is the recognition that the elites have not been able to solve the manifold problems facing communities and organisations. Surely enough, they have been constantly approaching solutions, but their efforts did not always produce the desired results. High sounding goals have been attractive, but all to frequently they remained in the verbal realm involving only some of the affected groups and individuals. Involvement of as many groups and individuals as possible is a demand of civic engagement.

This kind of involvement is based on the recognition that not only the elites, but everybody is responsible for the failing accomplishment of the goals. This failure is to a large extent due to the previously discussed setting of high sounding goals and looking for perfection, leaving out more pragmatic solutions related to the ways of goal achievement. What is also missing is the specific description and assignment of responsibilities of the affected individuals and groups. What has been said is related not only to areas of politics and government as consistently was stated above.

This is important to mention again since we are facing interconnections of all areas of life. Any activity in one area will have an impact on others. Reference to chaos theory makes this evident. In addition to that we again have to refer to global interconnections which make any activity on the local or organisational level important because of its worldwide implications. Responsibility for the results and their consequences plays a central role in civic engagement.

It is essential to keep in mind that it is not only institutional responsibility within the existing frameworks, but first and foremost individual responsibility related to one's goals and values.

Civic Engagement in Action

Civic engagement is more than membership in an organisation and participation in it, even if it were involving some activity. It goes beyond such focus of involvement looking for more effective activities. What makes civic engagement different is, as indicated, the emphasis on responsibility for individual actions and this means responsibility for results and for their consequences. Such an understanding obviously places individual actions within an organisation in a focal position. Connected with it is also .the awareness that one's activities and their results have an impact on the activities of others. We have here, therefore, a system of interrelationships. To make the activities of an individual and his responsibilities more meaningful, the concept of vocation is central.

One called to do a certain work. This understanding of vocation may have a religious foundation, but makes sense also with a secular base, such as "professional," "issue related," and so on. It becomes now necessary to show how civic engagement can actually operate indifferent settings. Let us start with a community. Here the individual before becoming engaged has to learn about the community, then indicate one or a few areas of community concern affecting his or her, learn more about them and finally become involved in them by joining committees, forming groups of people with similar interests and so on.

Here it is essential that the expected results should be definite, their consequences recognised, and also there results being periodically evaluated. What has been said about communities refers similarly to political activities and non-governmental organisations. The steps of involvement are essentially the same. Of special concern is the work in administrative positions. Here there are no problems if there is no conflict between organisational and personal goals. If, however, a discrepancy arises then civic engagement demands that this conflict be clearly expressed.

An administrator, therefore, committed to civic engagement cannot in a covert way act against organisational goals, but has to state his or her position clearly. If this is impossible then civic engagement requires a separation from the organisation and pursuit of one's goals within the indicated community procedures.

Even in the area of business and economics such engagement is possible by paying attention to the activities of owners or managers. We know of such engagements in the field of labour relations or consumer relations. What is missing in many cases and falling short of civic engagement is the recognition of responsibilities and results. An interesting example on a large scale is developing in Germany with nationwide protest activities against high natural gas prices.

The results of these activities are clearly expected in lower prices and the leading people accept their responsibilities in case of failure. In a representative governmental system, civic engagement becomes more difficult. Yet even here an individual and any group may find problem areas affecting them and proceed in ways similar to community activities. Ultimately also candidacy for elected office is possible, with both individual candidates and electoral campaign groups following the patterns of civic engagement.

Any discussion of civic engagement has to take into account the necessity of assessing and evaluating their activities. Only if the results and consequences of the engagement are evaluated and a positive correlation with the intentions is evident may we regard civic engagement as effective. Obviously in a case of lacking correlation the entire involvement has to be reconsidered. A word of caution is also necessary. All civic engagement activities due to their nature have to be nonviolent. This establishes a clear limitation for any kind of civic engagement. Finally civic engagement has nothing to do with mass activities which always are definitely emotional and do not view possible results and their consequences all. Mass activities emphasise the protest activities, such as the French Revolution or the inti fada, with the protestation having priority ever the envisaged results. Civic engagement is not only peaceful, but essentially also individualistic and goal rational.

Role of Academy

The academy has to decide what role civic education will play in it making education its focal point, since the academy's purpose is education. This means first and foremost creating a climate for teaching which would place civic engagement in a central position. Civic education has to find a place in any academic area, on both the under graduate and graduate levels, with political science as a core. Due to globalisation realities, courses in international relations and foreign governments are essential. The form civic education will take in any discipline goes beyond such standard forms as guest lectures, visits, internships, and model programmes depending substantially on the imagination of the involved faculty. For any such effort to be effective, knowledge of American government is indispensable. Of special concern here are international students.

They have to be made aware of the American system and led to a recognition that civic engagement can playa great role in the development of their native countries. The global implications of any civic engagement activities need also specific consideration. The involvement of faculty in civic engagement has to be clearly stressed and recognised by assigning to it a place in any assessment of evaluation activities. The academic institution as such has also to be involved in civic engagement which requires involvement of the administrative personnel in community affairs.

Academic personnel should be expected to playa central, but by no means authoritative role, in their communities. Similar involvement is expected from the faculty in their communities and also in their professional associations. The academy is expected to playa model role in civic engagement. As stated, this involves a role for students, faculty, and administrative personnel. Their involvement should provide a model for the role of similar institutions. This also means that the institution itself should practice civic education. Ways have to be found to make it an open institution and that the civic engagement climate created finds also expression in the administrative conduct of the academy.

A discrepancy between the teaching of civic education and the internal lack of it being practiced would make the entire prospect of civic education questionable. Civic education, especially in its global elements, provides means to address the many problems we are facing. It is the academy's role to take a leading position. Lech Walesa, who was quoted above, at the same September 2005 lecture stated: If you fail to get involved ... others will do it for you." We know very well what the involvement of others has brought about in communities, in social life, in economic concerns, in public affairs, in the world and in the academy.

●●

9

Administrative Relations

Under the constitution if a state government fails to carry out the administration of the State in accordance with the provisions of constitution or if the State fails to run State administration according to constitutional directions of the central government, the President is empowered to declare failure of constitutional machinery in the State. If such a declaration is made and emergency declared, the central government takes over the administration of the State. It will appoint an adviser or team of advisers which will help the central government to run State administration in the desired manner. Administratively the federal structure, for that particular State becomes unitary.

It will thus be observed that in the administrative field the centre can tune state administration in the manner it likes. But normally the centre will allow maximum autonomy to the states within our constitutional framework. In fact, some of the States have been making a demand for more autonomy to the States but that is not being accepted. It is felt that need of the hour not only in India but all over the world is strong and powerful centre which can deal effectively with ever increasing complex problems of present day society.

LEGISLATIVE RELATIONS

In Indian federation there are states as well as Union Territories, each state has a legislature. Some of the states have unicameral, while others have a bicameral legislature.

But legislature in every state has a control over the administration. The legislature is very useful forum for the opposition for exposing the weaknesses and drawbacks of the administration.

Legislative Assembly. Lower House of the state legislature is called Legislative Assembly. As compared with the Legislative Council it is far more powerful.

Qualifications. A person for membership to state legislature should be a citizen of India of not less than twenty five years of age; should be hold any office of profit and should posses such other qualifications as may be prescribed in that behalf by Parliament by a law.

Tenure of Office. Every Legislative Assembly is constituted for a period of five years from the date of its first meeting, after which it is dissolved. The assembly can be dissolved earlier also.

Salary and Allowances. All the members of the legislature are paid a monthly salary which varies from state to state. In addition, they get the allowances during the sessional days. They are provided with residential quarters, free travel and medical facilities.

Composition. The Legislative Assembly of each state consists of not more than five hundred and not less that sixty members. These members are chosen by direct election from territorial constituencies in the state. Each person who has attained twenty-one years of age is qualified to vote. If the Governor feels that the Anglo-Indian community has not been properly represented he may nominate two representatives of that community to the Assembly. It may be mentioned that some seats are reserved for the scheduled castes, tribes and other backward classes, but this a temporary phase and will disappear in the course of time.

Presiding Officer. The President Officer of the Legislative Assembly is the Speaker. He presides over the meetings of the assembly. He decides about the resolutions, adjournment motions and points of order. He fixes time limit for the speeches. He certifies whether a bill is money bill or not. The Speaker maintains order and decorum in the assembly. For his assistance he gets the help of Sergeant-at-arm. If any body shows any disrespect to the Speaker or violates the privileges of a member, he may be punished by the Speaker.

The Speaker is elected for a term of five years at the first meeting of the assembly. He can resign his office or can be removed by a notice of fourteen day by a simple majority of votes in the assembly. While the proceedings to remove the Speaker are continuing, he will not preside over the meetings of the assembly. His salary and allowances etc. are determined from time to time. In a word, the Speaker of the State Assembly has exactly the same position in the Legislative Assembly as the Speaker of the Lok Sabha. As and when the office of Speaker is vacated by resignation or removal the Deputy Speaker discharges the duties of the Speaker.

Power and Functions. The powers of Legislative Assembly can be classified under three main heads :

1. Executive Powers. The executive powers of the state legislature are exercised by the Legislative Assembly. The Council of Ministers is controlled by the assembly. It is said that the Legislative Assembly dictates the government. This control of the assembly is exercised in three ways namely :

(a) The members of the assembly can ask questions and put supplementary questions to the ministers relating the department and the minister is supposed to satisfy the members.

(b) They can table ajournment motions.

(c) The constitution provides that the Council of Ministers is responsible to the Legislative Assembly collectively.

(d) They can put short-notice questions.

(e) In the end the assembly can pass a vote of no confidence against the Council of Ministers and in case such a vote is carried, the Council of Ministers will have to resign.

2. Financial Powers. The Legislative Assembly has complete control over the state purse. Removal of old taxes and the levy of new ones is down with the consent of the assembly. Even the money spent by the Governor from the Consolidated Fund of the State is to be approved by the Assembly later. No money can be spent without the consent of the assembly. A money bill can originate only in the Legislative Assembly.

3. Legislative Powers. The state legislature makes laws on the subjects enumerated in the State List and also in the Concurrent List. If there is any conflict on the scope of a law passed by the State on a concurrent subject (on which the Union Parliament also has the right to legislate) and such a law goes against the law of the Union on the same subject, it is the law of the Parliament that prevails over the state law.

LEGISLATIVE COUNCIL

In some states there is bi-cameral system of legislature. In such a system the Upper House is called Legislative Council. The Upper House is a not as powerful as the Legislative Assembly which is the Lower House of the legislature. It is a permanent body and is not dissolved with the dissolution of Legislative Assembly after the expiry of 5 years.

Tenure of Office. The Legislative Council is a permanent body. Its every member elected for six years. One-third of its members retire at the end of two years. The Constitution provides that the Legislative Council of a state is not subject to dissolution.

Composition. The total membership in the Legislative Council of a State shall not exceed one-third of the total membership in the Legislative Assembly of that State. Strength of a Legislative Council will however, in no case be less than forty. The members of the Legislative Council are elected indirectly. The distribution of seats in a Legislative Council is as follows :

(i) One-third of members of Council are elected by electorates consisting of members of municipalities, district boards and such other local authorities in the state as the Parliament may specify by law.

(ii) One-twelfth of the members are elected by the electorates consisting of persons who have been engaged in teaching for a least three years in educational institutions not below the standard of secondary schools.

(iii) One-third of the members are elected by members of the Legislative Assembly of the State from amongst who are not members of the Assembly.

(iv) One-twelfth of the members elected by the electorates consisting of persons residing in the state who have been graduates with a three-year standing.

(v) The remaining one-sixth members are nominated by the state Governor. These nominated members are persons of standing in such fields as literature, science, art, co-operative movement and social service.

Presiding Officer. The Presiding Officer of the Legislative Council is the Chairman. He conducts the proceedings in the

Council.He also maintains order in the House and safeguards privileges of the members. He gets salary, allowances and other benefits and privileges as are determined by law.

The Chairman and Deputy Chairman are elected by the members of the Legislative Council. The Chairman of Legislative Council shall vacate his office if he ceases to be a member of the Council. He may also resign his office and can also be removed from his office. In the absence of the Chairman, the Deputy Chairman discharges his functions.

Powers and Functions. Legislative Council is a very weak body. It has more formal functions than real ones. These may be summed up as under :

1. Executive Powers. The Council has practically no executive powers. It is so because the Council of Ministers is not responsible to this House and a vote of no confidence against the Council of Ministers in the Council, does not make it obligatory for the former to resign. Still, the Council can influence the working of the government. If the Council is not satisfied with the performance of the government it can, through questions and adjournment motions, bring the government to disrepute and make it unpopular by exposing its defects. By these methods it can very much lower the prestige of Council of Ministers in the eyes of the people.

2. Legislative Powers. Theoretically the Legislative Council has co-equal powers with the assembly in so far as ordinary bills are concerned. A non-money bill is enacted only when both the Houses approve of it. But in practice there are limitations on the powers of the Council here also. The Legislative Assembly has an upper hand.

3. Financial Powers. In the financial sphere the Council has no control whatsoever. No money bill can originate in the Council. Its opinion or recommendations on money bills do not mean much either. It can only delay a money bills for a period of fourteen days, within which period, if it does not return to bill, it will be deemed to have been passed. it can suggest amendments to money bills but it is for the assembly either to accept or reject these.

Legislature and Administration. An effective and powerful instrument of control in the State over administration is the state legislature. It is a forum where the administration and administrator can be exposed without least danger. Each department of administration is headed by a minister, who is responsible to the legislature for the execution of policies and programmes of his department. A member of legislature can put any questions on the minister about the working of his department and he is obliged to answer that unless such a reply can lead to revealing state secrets. Similarly a member in the legislature can control the administration by moving 'call attention' or 'short notice' question. On such occasions the administration is on its toes to provide information available without any grudge and grumble. Similarly the legislature controls administration at the time of budget.

These are only indirect methods though which a state legislature controls the administration. There are also direct methods when legislature as a whole directly control administration. A legislator can bring to the notice of government, corrupt, under-hand and illegal methods adopted by a public servant. He can allege that a public servant has misused his authority and position. We know that in Punjab, the legislators submitted a memorandum against Late Partap Singh Kairon, the then Chief Minister of Punjab, to the President of India pointing out certain irregularities. The outcome was Das Commission. Similarly in Punjab memorandum was sent to President of India, incorporating irregularities committed by Prakash Singh Badal Ministry. In fact, in India, there is perhaps no states in which charges have not been levied against the government, regarding corrupt and illegal means for amassing wealth, with the help of administration. The legislatures can control administration by means of 'Committee on Assurances' and Estimates Committee' 'Public Accounts Committee' and so on. In these committees the administrator is face to face with the legislator to explain the position of his department. We also find that in the States the constituencies are not as big as parliamentary constituencies. Therefore, a legislator comes into close contact with the constituents.

Thus in the state the legislatures mould the administration. These give guidelines and policies for implementation to the state governments. Thus in a state, legislature is guide and philosopher of administration. Of course the scope of state activity has considerably increased which has resulted in the less time for the legislature to supervise, yet the very fact that the legislatures can take administration to task at any time, is in itself a sufficient guarantee that the administration will not go much wrong.

Legislative Assembly. It is lower house of State legislature and every Indian citizen can become its member. Members of Assembly get monthly salary and other allowances. The tenure of the assembly is 5 years. The members are elected on the basis of universal adult franchise. Seats are however, reserved for the persons belonging to scheduled castes, scheduled tribes and other backward classes. The presiding officer of the Assembly is Speaker who is responsible for maintaining decorum in the house. He conducts the proceedings of the House. The assembly has executive, financial and legislative powers.

Legislative Council. It is upper house of state legislature. Each member is elected for a period of 5 year and 1/3 of its member retire after every two years. It is an indirectly elected House. The House is presided over by a Chairman who performs the same functions as the speaker in the assembly. The Council also exercises executive, legislative and financial powers.

Legislature and Administration. Legislature exercises indirect control over administration by putting questions on the ministers, moving call attention and short notice questions and ultimately by passing a vote of no confidence against the Council of Ministers. Directly an administrator is controlled by the legislature at the time of meetings of committees of the legislature where he is face to face with the legislators.

In a state broad policy guidelines are given by the legislature whereas the administrator is required to implement them. Thus the control is real and effective.

ADMINISTRATIVE RELATIONS

The administrative relations between the Union and the State as envisaged under the Constitution, largely follows the pattern laid down by the Government of India Act, 1935. The arrangement is designed to serve a two-fold purpose : first, to ensure effective federal executive control of matters falling within the legislative jurisdiction of the Union Parliament and second, to minimise the possibilities of conflict between the Union and State administrative machineries.

The General rule is that the executive power in respect of all these matters on which the Union Parliament can legislate, belongs to the Union Government, while the executive power in respect of the matters specified in the State List belongs to the State Government. Now, the existing arrangement is that some of the matters like customs, income-tax, railways, post offices, defence are directly administered by the officers of the Central Government, while the administration of the rest, and the execution of the union laws generally is entrusted to the State authorities. This is particularly evident in the judicial sphere. All the courts, with the exception of the Supreme Court, are State Courts. In this respect there is a striking contrast between the American and Indian federal system. In the United States there is a complete set of federal executive and judicial officers for the executive and interpretation of federal laws. In India it is unlikely that a complete system of Union officers and courts to take exclusive charge of the Union laws will ever be established. Therefore, the Union Government depends largely on State authorities for execution of its laws. However, this administrative coordination between Union and the State is a two-way traffic. If certain federal matters are administered by State authorities, officers of Union Government occupy higher positions in State administration. Thus the administrative systems of the Union and the States though distinct, yet are not altogether separated from each other.

Union Direction of any Control of State Administration. The Union and State administrative relations are so organized in India as to enable the Union Government to exercise considerable control over the administrative machinery of the State. Thus it is clearly provided that the executive power of every State shall be so exercised as to ensure compliance with the laws made by Parliament, and that the executive power of the Union shall extend to the giving of such directions to a State as may appear to the Government of India to be necessary for that purpose—(Articles 256, 257). If the State Government fails to carry out the directions of the Union Government, the President acting under Article 365 may proclaim a breakdown of the constitutional machinery of the State and place all the powers of State Government in the hands of the Union Government. Apart from this drastic action that can be taken against a State Govenrment the Union Government exercises general powers of direction and control in several other matters which concern the Union as well as the States. Thus, the superintendence, direction and control of all elections whether to Union Parliament or to the State Legislatures are vested in the Election Commission appointed by the President. The judges of the High Courts are appointed and can be transferred by the President. The financial accounts of all States are under the supervision and control of the Comptroller and Auditor-General of India. The President has been given special powers in respect of the welfare of schedueld tribes and backward classes. Thus the Constitution has conferred wide authority on the Union Government to exercise control and direction over the State Executive.

Besides, the Union Government may give directions to a State as to the construction and maintenance of the means of communications declared to be of national and military importance and measures to be taken for the protection of the railways in the States. Under Article 253 the President may, with the consent of the State Government, entrust to is functions in relation to any matter to which the executive power of the Union extends.

Mention may also be made of Article, 355 which imposes a duty on the Union to protect every State against external aggression and internal distrubance and to ensure that the Government of every state is carried on in accordance with the provisions of the Constitution. The fulfilment of the obligations may sometimes require Union intervention in purely State matters.

Inter-State Council. Though the federating units are autonomous within their own territorial limits, yet the Constitution of India empowers the Parliament to provide for the adjudication of any dispute or complaint with respect to the use, distribution, or control of the water, or in, any inter-State river or river valley. Parliament may by law also provide that neither the Supreme Court nor any other court shall exercise any jurisdiction in respect of any such dispute or complaint. Provision has also been made for the creation of Inter-State Councils charged with the duty of : *(i)* inquiring into and advising upon disputes between States; *(ii)* investigating and discussing subjects of common interest to some or all States ; and *(iii)* making recommendations on any subject and, in particular, recommendations for the better co-ordination of policy and action with respect to that subject. Parliament also possesses the power to impose restrictions upon inter-State trade and establish such authority as it considers appropriate for enforcing the povisions of the Constitution with regard to such trade and commerce.

In addition to these powers which the Parliament may exercise in regard to the States in normal times, the Constitution vests general powers of direction and control over the States in times of national emergencies. When a Proclamation of Emergency has been issued by the President and is in operation, the Union Government can give directions to any State as to the manner in which the State's executive power should be exercised; during such periods Parliament is also empowered to make laws conferring powers and imposing duties upon the Union or its officers regarding matters which are not enumerated in the Union List. As stated earlier the consequences of the various emergency provisions will be to suspend the legislative and the executive authority of the State even in respect of matters which have been specifically allotted to them by the Constitution. For all practical purposes all the governmental powers will be concentrated in the hands of the Union and the federal government will be transformed into a unitary government for the time being. This clearly establishes that Centre enjoy precedence over States as regards control over State and concurrent subjects are concerned particularly during abnormal times.

FINANCIAL RELATIONS BETWEEN CENTRE AND STATE

An appraisal of the financial relations it may be firstly noted that the Constitution does not enumerate separately the heads of taxation. The power to tax is included in the power to legislate. Thus the subjects which are enumerated in the Union List are within the purview of Central Government for purposes of taxation and similarly the State Governments have the power of taxation in respect of subjects enumerated in the State List. The three lists of powers given in the Seventh Schedule divide the sources of revenue between the Union and the States as follows:

(A) The Union Sources

(a) Taxes on income other than agricultural income.

(b) Custom duties including expert duties.

(c) Taxes on capital value of assets, exclusive of agricultural land of individuals and companies ; taxes on capital of companies.

(d) Estate duty in respect of property except agricultural land.

(e) Terminal taxes on goods or passengers carried by sea, air or railway.

(f) Corporation tax.

(g) Taxes other than stamp duties on transaction in stock exchanges and future markets.

(h) Rates of stamp duty in respect of bills of exchange, cheques, promissory notes, bills of lading, letters of credit, insurance policies, transfer of shares, debentures, proxies and receipts.

(i) Duties of Excise on tabacco and other goods manufactured or produced in India except alcoholic liquors for human consumption and opium, Indian hemp and other narcotic drugs and narcotics.

(j) Fees in respect of any of the matters in the Union List except fees taken in any court.

(k) Taxes on sale or purchase of newspapers and on advertise-ments published therein.

(B) The State Sources

(a) Land revenue.

(b) Taxes on agricultural income.

(c) Taxes on mineral lights subject to limitations imposed by law.

(d) Taxes on land and buildings.

(e) Duties on succession to agricultural land.

(f) Estate duty in respect of agricultural land.

(g) Taxes on the entry of goods into a local area for consumption, use or sale therein.

(h) Excise duties on alcoholic liquors for human consumption, and opium, hemp and other narcotic durgs.

(i) Tolls.

(j) Taxes on professions, trades, callings and employments.

(k) Taxes on consumption or sale of electricity.

(l) Taxes on sale or purchase of goods other than newspapers.

(m) Capitation taxes.

(n) Rates on stamp duty on documents other than those subject to Union stamp duty.

(o) Taxes on luxuries, entertainments, betting and gambling.

(p) Taxes on advertisements other than those published in the newspapers.

(q) Taxes on animals, and boats.

(r) Taxes on goods and passengers carried by road or inland waterways.

(s) Fees in respect of any of the matters in the State List.

The Concurrent List does not contain any subject in respect of which taxation may be levied.

The division of the resources as given above does not mean that the party to which a tax is assigned is the sole authority to determine it and is entitled to all the proceeds of that tax. So far as the taxes in the State List are concerned, they go entirely to the State but it is different with the Union taxes, the proceeds of many of which are assigned to or shared with the States. The Constitutional distinguish four categories of Union taxes which are available, whole or in part, to the States:

(a) Duties levied by the Union but collected and wholly appropriated by the State : Stamp duties in respect of bills of exchange, cheques, promissory notes, bills of lading, letters of credit, policies of insurance, transfer of shares, debentures, proxies and receipts and excise on medicines and toilet preparations containing alcohol.

(b) Taxes levied and collected by the Union but whose proceeds are shared between the Union and the States. The tax which comes under this category is income tax.

(c) Taxes levied and collected by the Union but wholly assigned to the States : duties in respect of succession to property other than agricultural land; terminal taxes on goods and passengers carried by rail, sea or air; taxes on railway fares and freights.

(d) Taxes which are levied and collected by the Union but whose proceeds may be distributed between the

Union and the States if Parliament by law so provide. Union duties of excise other than such duties of excise on medical and toilet preparations fall under this category.

Grants-in-aid. The Constitution also provides for Grants-in-aid to the States. Thus, Assam, Bihar, Orissa and West Bengal receive grants-in-aid in lieu of export duty on jute and jute products. Apart from the Union Government's constitutional obligation to provide grants-in-aid to the States for financing approved schemes for the welfare of the Scheduled Tribes and for improving the standard of administration in Tribal areas. Article 275 of the Constitution makes a general provision for Union grants-in-aid to the States. It is for the Union Government to fix the extent of these grants and lay down the conditions under which they are to be administered. It need not be stated that Grants-in-aid are potent instruments for the extension of Central control and direction of the States

Borrowing Powers. The Constitution also makes certain provisions in respect of the borrowing powers of the States. A State can borrow only within India and it cannot raise a new loan without the consent of the Union Government if there is outstanding any part of a previous loan and guaranteed by the Union or owned to it. The Government of India may, subject to such conditions as may be laid down by or under any law made by Parliament, make loans to any State provided that the limits set by Parliament to Union loans are not exceeded.

During the Proclamation of Financial Emergency the President may empower the Union to give directions controlling State's financial activities and require State Money bills to be reserved for his consideration.

It will be clear from the above description of Union-State relations that every effort has been made to make the

Union Government much stronger than what Central Governments are usually found to be in other federations. The emphasis is more on the authority of the Centre than on the autonomy of the State. As a matter of fact interference and dictation by the Centre is not only so prohibited but authorized as a normal procedure of the functioning of the Constitution. The absense of equal representation to the States in the council of States ; the power given to the latter chamber to declare by a two thirds majority any subject to be of national importance, and then to enable the Union to give directions to make a law thereupon; the power of the Union to give direction to the State Government; and the power given to the President practically to suspend the State Constitution in times of emergency—are some of the exceptional features of the Indian Federation which have lead the critics to remark that the Indian Federation is only a quasi-federation or better still as a unitary federation.

DISTRIBUTION OF POWERS

The Constitution of India, as stated already, has established a federal form of Government characterised by a high degree of centralisation. The essence of a federal system in the system is the division of powers between the Central and State Governments by the Constitution. However, the scheme of distribution differs from other federal countries and embodies its peculiar needs. Keeping in view its hoary past which kept India subjugated due to disintegrative and divisive forces. Hitherto the framers of a federal constitution have divided the governmental powers in either of the ways; the specific powers of the Centre are enumerated and the residuary powers are left to the units; or the powers of the unit are specified and the balance is left for the Centre. The former scheme has been adopted in the United States of America and Australia, while the latter in Canada. The word, 'Federation' is not found any where in the Constitution.

Three lists. The Indian Constitution, following the precedent set under the Government of India Act of 1935, divides the governmental powers into three lists—The Union List, the State List and the Concurrent List. The distribution is remarkably elaborated and detailed and attempt has been made to cover the whole field of all possible governmental activity as far as the human mind can visualise at present. If still some powers are left unspecified, they are vested in the Centre. The Union List contains these matters on which the Union Parliament has exclusive right to frame the laws. The State Legislatures have the exclusive powers of making laws with respect the matters enumerated in the State List. As regards the Concurrent List, both the Union Parliament and State Legislature have concurrent powers with the provision that, in case of a conflict, the Central law must, to the extent of repugnancy, prevail over the State law. If, however, the State law has been reserved for and received the assent of the President, it will prevail unless and until Parliament passes a new law overruling the provisions of the State law.

The Union List contains 97 subjects including such subjects as defence; atomic energy; citizenship; railway; posts and telegraphs; foreign affairs; shipping; airways; banking and insurance; currency and coinage; mines and minerals; opium, war, peace and treaties; etc. The State List contains 66 subjects and includes public order; police; jails; local government; education; agriculture and forests; public health and sanitation; roads, bridges, ferries, municipal tramways and traffic therein; ponds and the prevention of cattle tress pass; irrigation and canals of wards; industries; weights and measures except establishment of standards; inns and inn-keepers ; betting and gambling; state public services; etc. The concurrent list contains 47 matters and includes such sub-welfare; price control; factories; electricity; newspapers; legal, medical and other processions; charities and charitable institutions; stamp duties other than judicial stamps etc.

From a perusal of the three lists it is quite clear that the Central Government has been given very many powers. The total number of subjects specified in the Union List is as much as 97 as compared to 66 that are enumerated in the State List. Besides, the Union Parliament has powers to make laws in respect of 47 items included in the Concurrent List. It is true that the State Legislature also is empowered to make laws on matters specified in the Concurrent List, but as told already in case of an inconsistency between the State Law and Union, the latter supersedes the former. It would not be an exaggeration to say that whenever the Union so desires the Concurrent matter can for all practical purposes be converted into Union matters.

Functions

The Ministry is responsible for the administration of the finances of the Central Government and for dealing with financial matters affecting the country as a whole. It arranges for raising the resources for developmental and other requirements and regulates the taxation and borrowing policies of Government, It deals with all problems connected with banking and currency and, in consultation with the Ministries concerned, arranges for the proper utilisation of the country's foreign exchange resources. In co-operation with the administrative Ministries, it controls the entire expenditure of the Government of India.

Organization. The Ministry is now organised in four Departments:

(a) The Department of Revenue and Insurance.

(b) The Department of Economic Affairs.

(c) The Department of Co-ordination.

(d) The Department of Expenditure.

Each Department is headed by a Secretary and there are a number of organisations under the control of each of the secretaries. The functions of each of the Department mentioned above are as under :

Functions of the Department of Revenue and Insurance. This Department is responsible for the administration of all direct and indirect Union taxes and for all matters relating to insurance. It advises the Government on fiscal matters, reviews tax structure, examines fresh proposals of taxation, promotes legislation for the modification of tax law and administers Gold Control regulations.

In respect of revenue matter, the Department is assisted by two statutory Boards under it. These Boards are :

(a) The Central Board of Direct Taxes which consists of a Chairman and three other Members.

(b) The Central Board of Excise and Custom which consists of a Chairman and two other members.

The Chairmen of the two Boards hold *ex-officio* status of Additional Secretary to the Government of India while the Members of the Boards are *ex-offico* Joint Secretaries.

The Administration of the Gold Control regulations is entrusted to the Gold Control Administrator who also holds *ex-officio* status of Joint Secretary to the Government of India.

The tax Credit Certificates (Export) Scheme is being administered by a Director appointed in the Department and six zonal and sub-zonal offices have also been set-up for this purpose.

Functions of the Department of Expenditure. The Department consists of following Divisions:

1. Establishment Division. Estabilishment Discussion is responsible mainly for the adminstration of the various financial rules and regulations including those relating to the conditions of service of the Central Government employees. The Head of this Division is also in-charge of the Staff inspection Unit.

2. Civil Expenditure Divisions. There are ten Divisions each headed by an Additional Secretary or a Joint Secretary. In addition to rendering financial advice to the Ministries/ Departments of the Government of India, nominated officers of these Divisions also function as financial representatives of Government on Board of Directors of various public sector undertakings and on the governing bodies of autonomous organisations which receive substantial financial assistance from Government.

3. Defence Division. This division is constituted with the Financial Adviser at the head assisted by four Additional Financial Advisers and a number of Deputy Financial Advisers attached to the various Principal Staff Officers of the Army, the Chief of Naval Staff, the Chief of the Air Staff and the Director-General of Ordinance Factories. This Division renders financial advice to the Defence Headquarters, the Defence Ministry and to the Officers directly subordinate to that Ministry. The Financial Adviser (Defence) is also a Member of the Board of the Border Roads Development.

4. Staff Inspection Unit. The function of the Staff Inspection Unit is to keep the staffing position in Ministries/ Offices functioning under the jurisdiction of Government of India under constant review in accordance with pre-determined programme of work-measurement studies. The Unit also undertakes *ad hoc* reviews, by special request, of Ministries/Offices not included in the programme as well as of the public sector undertakings. The other aspects of work study, such as procedures and methods etc., are the responsibility of the Department of Administrative Reforms under the Ministry of Home Affairs.

Functions of the Department of Economic Affairs. The Department of Economic Affairs prepares the Government's budget, makes periodic assessments of foreign exchange needs and resources and takes necessary steps to mobilise and allocate resources, both internal and external, in keeping with the country's Plans and develop-ment needs. The department works through the following Divisions :

1. Budget Division. It prepares the Central Govenment's Annual Budget (other than that for Railways) and Supplementary and Excess Grants for presentation to Parliament.

2. External Finance and Foreign Aid Division. It deals with all matters relating to foreign exchange and trade agreements with foreign countries.

3. Internal Finance Division. It deals with all matters relating to currency, coinage, banking, industrial finance and control of capital issues.

4. Economic Division. It advises the Department of Economic Affairs on questions of economic policy.

5. Administrative Division. It looks after the administrative matters of the Department as also the work relating to grants to various institutions and councils.

Functions of the Department of Co-ordination. The Depart-ment of Co-ordination deals with State Plans and State finances with particular reference to Central financial assistance to the State Government, scrutinises Central and State legislations having financial and economic implications, advises in regard to State Governments proposals for investment in industrial enterprises, irrigation, power and flood control projects, etc., with reference to the availabie resources, carries out studies in the financial fields of State Governments and is associated with the scrutiny of the proposals of the Central Ministries for large projects involving heavy capital outlays. It also studies specific, economic, industrial and operational problems and bottlenecks in consultation with the Ministries and departments concerned.

The Department was closely associated with the Planning Commission in all phases of the preparation for the Fourth Five Year Plan and the determination of the size of the Central and the State Plans for 1966-67, and the Central assistance for the State Plans, in the light of the resources in sight. The scrutiny and analysis of periodic progress reports from industrial and mineral projects in the public sector also continued to be one of the responsibilities of the Department.

RELATIONSHIP BETWEEN PLANNING COMMISSION AND FINANCE COMMISSION

Article, 280 of the Constitution of India provides for 'an independent, quasi-judicial expert body', termed as the Finance Commission, to recommend the principles and proportions of financial transfers from the Union to the State through the 'built' in balancing techniques. The role of the Finance Commission is regulated by the basic principles of federal finance, which attempts to meet the residuary budgetary requirements of the States, after taking into account the devolution of the proceeds of the Union taxes to the States. The philosophy behind it is that the states, being at different stages of development, are required to be brought upto minimum level thereby aiming at 'equal sacrifice and equal opportunity. In the light of this basic principle, the various Finance Commission evolved their own schemes for determining the quantum of statutory assistance to the States, with common line of emphasis on the need to meet the budgetary gaps of the States.

The process of planned economic development introduced radical changes in the entire fiscal context in the economy since 1951-52. The criterion of 'budgetary needs', inherent in the Finance Commission's recommendations was put into, "insignificance by the impact of Plan expenditure, growing as it did in all these years of economic planning. The formulation of plans at the State level, their incorporation in the National Plans and their implementation at the State level, formed a big charge on the Union exchequer, in fact if not in theory. The tax sources of the States having been relatively narrow and inelastic, their financial resources for putting through the Plan schemes had to be supplemented by increasing assistance from the Union." As a consequence of these changes the criterion of the 'budgetary needs' a concept dealing with the gap in 'current revenues and expenditures for allocation of Union assistance' was replaced by the concept of 'fiscal needs' which is of much wider economic significance, and points out towards the gap in resources in an overall context of gross expenditure of the State.

The approach and thinking of the successive Finance Commissions was influenced deeply by such a gradual change in the Union-States financial relationship in the wake of the planned economic development. The first Finance Commission admitted the need to 'take into account' not only the 'budgetary needs' but also the 'fiscal needs' emerging out the execution of development programmes of the country. The same view was endorsed by the second Finance Commission which recommended Central assistance to the States so as to enable them to put through the Plans but was left to the Third Finance Commission, to embody this view, in quantitative terms, in its recommendations. The Fourth Finance Commission, "guided by its terms of reference to take only non-Plan expenditure into account, calculated the non-Plan revenue gap on the basis of its scrutiny of the estimates submitted by State governments and recommended its complete elimination through Union assistance." Similar changes in the scope of Finance Commission were made just by altering the terms of reference and by any Constitutional amendment. As it has been rightly stated that "otherwise excepting the limitations arising out of the terms of reference, there is nothing to preclude the Finance Commission to take into consideration requirements arising out of Plan expenditures too." Nowhere in these Articles is there an expressed or implied indication that the total revenues of a State should be utilized only revenue expenditure... It is abundantly clear to my mind that the reference in the main part of clause (1) of Article, 275 to grants-in-aid to the revenues of States is not confined to revenue expenditure only... There is no legal warrant for excluding from the scope of the Finance Commission all capital grants; even the capital requirements of a State may be properly met by grants-in-aid under Article, 275 (1), made on the recommendations of the Finance Commission... The legal position, therefore, is that there is nothing in the Constitution to prevent the Finance Commission to take into consideration both capital and revenue requirements of the States in formulating a scheme of devolution and in recommending grants under Article 275 of the Constitution."

The role being played by the Planning Commission regarding the allocation of Union assitance to the States is much wider as well as much more effective and decisive. Precisely speaking, "its role is confined to the needs arising out of additional current outlays and the total expenditure on capital account which is projected while formulating the Five Year Plan. The Planning Commission helps in the formulation of the State Plan, ship-shapes them in overall perspective of the nationwide strategy of economic growth. For the purpose, it considers the budgets of the State governments in their entire including the non-Plan revenue and capital expenditure, and then the quantum and Union assistance of the States is determined.'

The overlapping between the Planning Commission and the Finance Commission is witnessed in the flow of Union assistance since the advent of area of planned economic development. Very often the functions, as discharged these two bodies, 'have resulted in contradictions, disturbing thereby the harmony in the Union-States' financial relations.

Developments Caused by Overlapping

1. The estimates that are placed by the State governments before the two bodies are not consistent because of the fact that 'as the Finance Commission is engaged in filling the 'revenue gap', there is a temptation for the States present figures which underestimate their resources. On the other hand, under pressure to increase their Plan size and show the necessary resources for them in their submissions to the Planning Commission, they consistently overestimate their resource-raising potentialities and capitalities at current rates of taxation and prices and underestimate their non-Plan expenditure liabilities, as the more the undertake to raise, the more they are likely to get.

2. The isolated way of functioning of these two Commissions head led more developed States 'to fudge the figures'. Since according to the provisions, the statutory assistance under the Finance Commission's awards is given to those States which have 'a gap in their non-Plan revenue account', these States seem indifferent to the Finance Commission or 'manouver a gap in the revenue account' but the approach is 'reversed' when they deal with the Planning Commission.

3. State manouver the distinction between Plan expenditure and non Plan expenditure, worked out by the two Commissions for the purpose of allocation of central assistance. These is a widespread confusion.

4. In the circumstance wherein the Plan expenditure its progressively increasing, "the non-Plan expenditure in so far as it is functionally related to the Plan expenditure, also increases likewise.' It is opined in this regard that 'fast which

one body considers as relevant is totally overlooked by the other.' It is further pointed out that 'since it is the total expenditure which is pertinant. It should be the total assistance that must be the concern of the any body charged with the allocation of Central assistance.'

5. The idea behind the grant of staturtory assitance is to bring-up the backward States to a minimum level in comparison to the relatively more developed States. This is also one of the prime objectives of the Union assistance formulated by the Planning Commission. The overlapping occurs when 'in order to aim at balanced regional development, the Planning Commission allows for the relative backwardness of a State or region while formulating the strategy, structure and substance of a development Plan. The Finance Commission ignores, however, the Plan expenditure of the State which is designed to aim at, among levelling the regional economic disparities.' This dichotomy in the functions of the Planning Commission and the Finance Commission in determining the quantum of Union assistance to states have developed many inconsistencies.

It has been pointed out that, "One of the main objectives of Central assistance to State has been to ensure that the States implement effectively those schemes and projects which have a certain rationale in the overall context of national economy. In other words, the pattern of assistance devised was designed to facilitate the use of Central funds in channels predetermined in the Plan. When it was found that these objectives were not achieved on account of lacunae in the procedures underlying the release of central assistance, many reforms were introduced to simplify the procedures. Even then the main objective of ensuring that the funds were used so as to achieve certain results has remained largely unfulfilled. Instead what has achieved is an artificial uniformity in the schemes and projects of different States." This situation necessitates the formulation of a clear policy of plan assistance.

Suggestions for Improvement

1. The Planning Commission has been made responsible for making an assessment of the matrial, capital and human resources; framing development Plans for the most effective and balanced growth of the economy; determinating of priorities; and determining the nature of machinery to secure due implementation of the Plans with a view to raise the rate of overall economic development of the country. Planning Commission has been increasing the quantum of assistance in every Five Year Plan. It is suggested that "in a planned economy, its needs and resources will have to be viewed *in toto*. The allocation of resources will have to be consistent with the objectives and utilisation of resources is a point responsibility of the Centre and States. The old federal principle, which regards all the constituent units as independent of each other in their own spheres, has to give place to what may be called the idea of cooperative federalism. All the arrangements for Centre-State transfers of resources will have to be based on the consideration of rapid economic growth without prejudice to the idea of "federal justice."

It is a commonly supported view that in the context of overall economic development, the dominant role played by the Planning Commission should be retained. However, the functions and respective spheres of operation of the Planning Commission and the Finance Commission, relating to the 'Union assistance' should be statutorily defined.

2. The Planning Commission should be made a statutory body to give it 'a position of something more than an advisory body'. "A mere advisory committee of experts can wield but feeble weapons against Central ministries and State governments which are chafing at the restrictions imposed upon them by a Plan, and all trying to go their own ways, often in the genuine conviction that their sectional interests coincide with the national interests. Unless there is a strong

countervailing force, these centrifugal pulls can distintegrate a plan very quickly... What the Indian system, with all its faults, avoids is the situation, so dismal to the serious planner, in which the experts sit isolated and neglected it small black rooms, drawning up projections of economic development and making policy recommendations which few of the politicians read and none feel committed to it."

3. The area of jurisdiction of the Finance Commission and the Planning Commission should be demarcated in clear and definite terms 'by either suitable amendments in the Constitution by conventions'.

4. The Plan-assistance from the Union to the States must not be specific schemes/projects oriented in the State Plans.

5. There is a need for a well established, sound but flexible institutional framework for Union-State financial relationship under the Constitutional framework.

6. It is further suggested that the Finance Commission is appointed every five year to go into the problems of 'inter-State inequalities of income and other disparties and recommend adequate equalising financial transfers.'

6. It is also suggested that the suggestions of the Planning Commission 'in respect of Union Plan-Grants and the Union loans to the States should be accorded a statutory sanction.'

●●

10

Planning for Administration

A governmental system created to maintain order, administer justice, regulate international relations, defend the nation, and impose and collect taxes for the expense of these activities is not equipped for positive task of guiding, and controlling the conservation, development and utilization of the national resources of integrating its economic and social life... It has become increasingly clear... that decisions taken in a moment of crisis, or from a purely departments point of view, or under organized pressure from some particular interest, or on traditional lines, or with a wholy inadequate knowledge of the material facts and probable consequences, and not good enough.

Thus planning is an integrated effort of the following interlinked steps:

1. Object Determination. The object of planning is decided at the first hand. For this purpose data is collected from various sources : primary and secondary, both, to deal with all the aspects of the problem. It involves extensive examination of the various alternatives before taking the final decision.

Object Determination is a political function because it is a matter of policy.

2. Selection of the Best Course of Action. After testing the various alternative methods, it becomes imperative to choose the best of all the alternatives. The best course of action is implmented and follow up programme starts from here.

3. Determination of Various Ways and Means. After determining the obectives to be achieved the next step in the planning process is to find out the various ways in which the objects may be realised here various suggested methods are tested to find out the most suitable method to achieve the target. Sometimes all alternatives may be tasted through actual operation.

CHARACTERISTICS OF PLANNING

1. Planning is Regional and Dynamic Process. Planning devised in the past has its inseparable link with the present. The chain of planning never stops unless it fulfills its aim and object. It is the outcome of rational intellect, and thus it never proceeds to achieve futile aims. To quote Pfiffner and Presthus in this context.

"Planning is rational because it demands a systematic analysis of several possible means and ends, followed by a selection of those means though best suited to the designated end."

2. Planning is Flexible according to the Necessities. Though planning is not matter of daily change, yet, it is not changeable always. It is desirable that flexibility must be inherent in the planning process. It must have the capacity to absorb all the changing contingencies of the time.

3. Planning is Comprehensively Integrated Progress. Planning is not restricted to any particular place or subject. It includes many subjects concerned with the development of the nation and society.

4. Planning is Basically a Staff Function. Planning is undertaken though in very small amount at all the levels of the organization. It is also necessary for the personnels working at different levels of plan implemenation to be aware of the planning. Thus, primarily, it is a staff function.

5. Planning is the Synthesis of Various Programmes. Planning covers varied programmes which touch the interest of the human beings. It covers agriculture trade, indusry, road and transport, fisheries, educaion, health, welfare etc. Planning process is the synthesized whole of thsese varied programmes.

NEED FOR PLANNING

Planning, which has become the creed of the administration is a modern concept but an old phrase. Plan refers to the systematic achievement of the 'social goals'. It is a positive step to create facilities not an aggressive attack on the supporters of 'laissez-faire' theory. Prof. Arthur Lewis presents a lively picture of this situation in following words:

"The control exercised by the market is none the less real and powerful because it is invisible. In a free economy production is controlled by demand. Capitalists cannot produce what they like; self-interest drives them to produce what they can sell, and that is determined by what people demand, and by how much they demand of it. Production for profit is thus, by 'the invisible hand', transmuted into production for use. By the same agency the distribution of income is controlled. Producers cannot charge what they like for the forces of competition are ever driving prices down to the level of costs, and for ever driving capitalists to improve their efficiency.

The case against the invisible control, in favour of state control cannot proceed by way of black denial. It is obvious that the invisible hand exists, and that its influence is beneficial. Neither can the case be founded, as some suppose, on attacking the self-interest which is the driving force of the market economy. For every economic system devised for ordinary human beings must have self-interest as its driving force. This does not make an economic system anti-social. The purpose of such a system, indeed the every nature of an economic system, is the mechanism through which, by making what society needs most become what is the most profitable to the individual, it transmutes individual self-interest into the public good. Even if the economic system were completely planned from the centre it would need a mechanism by which those who planned well, or executed their orders well, were rewarded above those who planned badly or were poor executants.. No, the case against the market economy is not that it does not tend to promote the social good. The dispute is whether state control could not do better, either as an alternative, or as a supplement.

Following lines written by Prof. L.D. White reflects the importance of Planning in the modern times :

A primitive society, bound by its customs and taboos and relatively static from generation to generation, can dispense with planning. Government in contemporary society necessarily implies planning in some measure, even the kind that would attend the ideal state of Herbert Spencer. The management of a more police state demands some foresight and arrangements, the management of a garrison state or a beleaguered state much more. In a state that propose action to improve the lot of its citizens, planning becomes a function increasingly important complex, and hazardous. For better or for worse, most states now accept such a responsibility.

The world-wide movement for the better ordering of social life by conscious community action has sprung from two distinct sources. One group of planning activities is founded on the basic idea of town planning. This source unfoled rapidly into metropolitan and regional planning, emerged into the field of national planning for the best development and utilization of all types of resources, and became concerned with political, social and economic problems.

The other main current of thought began with the national economic life as a whole, with special reference to the "strategic controls" through which the national economy could be guided into desired channels with a minimum of direct intereference with the individual. It was essentially an attempt from the centre to create a better ordering of the national economy or to acehieve some definite purpose (such as national defence) which without guidance from the center it would be difficult to secure.

Any organisation if it wants to achieve success and energetically wants to avert collapse it must go for planning. Without planning the objectives can be realised in the present days of competition. Thus, "all organisations must plan if they are to achieve their ends."

To achieve following Objectives; Planning has become significant in life of the people :

(a) Speedy realisation of goal; through a systematic and integrated approach to the problems.

(b) Creation of better social services, especially for those who are 'have not's'.

(c) Achievement of maximum in less time due to collective effort.

(d) To raise the standard of living, education, and routine life of the individuals.

(e) Removal of poverty, unemployment and other economic backwardness.

(f) To avoid a lop-sided development of the country.

(g) To fight effectively the contingencies before the nation or any part of it.

(h) To gain fast development.

(i) To remove various social evils like, wide inequality in the income levels beggary : Illiteracy, etc. Thus, planning remains the only 'lamp of Alauddin to remove backwardness and poverty of the underdeveloped nations. It is equally essential for the far-developed countries to maintain their standard in all the fields.

(j) To have proper economic use of the nation's precious resources.

KINDS OF PLANNING

Planning differs in its scope and also in nature from place to place. It may be undertaken to achieve social and economic goals and also to beautify road and building. The concept of planning is also used in varied sense which also causes differentials in the opinion of the individuals. L.D. while writers in the context :

"In civil government the function of planning is less well-understood and accepted. The reason lies partly in confusion as to the meaning of the terms. Some planning is acceptable to most persons, some is violently opposed by a great many. Officials, high and law, may be concerned with all kinds."

Following are the different kinds of Planning:

1. National Planning. National planning is undertaken to solve some problems at national level in the country. Basically it proceeds to solve national problems in the economic field, the scope of this kinds of planning extends to all the sectors *i.e.*, primary (Agriculture etc.) secondary sector (industries etc.) and service sector. National Planning has been termed by L.D. White as the most inclusive of all planning. He opines. "The most inclusive and in the United

States the most challenged, is planning designed to control in some measure the economic system, at the expense of free-enterprise such as the Russian-five-year plan and the British Labour Government nationalisation programme."

The five year planning in India is also a natinoal plan. The nationalisation of banks in 1969, was also a part of the national planning in India.

2. Error Removing Planning. This kind of planning seeks to point out various errors in the national planning as a whole. But it does not direct the economic planning in the country. Prof White comments:

"A second type of planning is concerned with the correction of violent swings of the economic cycle without impairing the essential features of free capitalistic enterprise."

3. Regional Planning. Regional planning is done with the view to implement programme to a particular region and locality. The state planning in India is one of the striking examples of the regional planning. **Prof. White** remarks :

"A third type of planning is more modest designed to direct and facilitate the future growth of communities or regions."

Various corporations and industrial plants in India have been set-up for regional development. Damodar Valley Corporation is one of the striking examples of plants set-up for regional developments.

4. Town Planning. Town-Planning is as old- as the human history. Town planning is undertaken to organize the housing and roads etc. To quote Prof. White :

A fourth types, less far ranging is planning of which the immediate objective is often no more than the most effective construction of city plant and facilities : streets, sewers, public buildings. The secondary consequence of planning in these matters of course, are extremely important; the free flow of traffic, the convenience of citizens, the facilitation of private building, and the like-zoning.

5. Socio-Economic Planning. This type of planning is wider in its scope than all the types referred above except the national planning. It is a comprehensive kind of planning which seeks the development in social and economic field. This kinds of planning is a direct attack on the 'laissez-faire' in economic and political fields. It seeks to secure economic equality and remove poverty, socio-economic planning aims at securing social welfare of the individuals.

Socio-economic planning may be complete or partial. Complete planning refers to the complete control of the government over their resources. In the case of partial planning, government's control is not complete; but limited to some kinds of productions and undertakings.

6. Governmental and Non-governmental Planning. Planning does not refer to the government control and regulation only. But it is a part of the national or regional planning. To quote Prof. White :

Planning then, "is a term that covers a lot of territory. It means different things to different persons. The considerations that lead some persons to condemn one type are hardly relevant to others. Public officials have become involved in all, to a greater or lesser degree, and the onward flow of public affairs they will not be able to extricate themselves."

Nearly all the enterprises whether on their own land or on a foreign territory implement their programmes according to the pre-planned programmes. This kind of planning is known as non-governmental planning.

Administrative planning or governmental planning refers to all the activitives of the government... Which the national government performs to secure the national objectives. The administrative planning "can be divided roughly into policy, programme and operational planning. This division is based on the levels the main objectives and the subject matter which each type deals."

India's five year planning envisaged by the Planning Commission is the example of Administrative or Governmental Planning.

Long-Range Planning. Long-Range Planning sets big objective to be achieved in a long period of time and it also provides some agency to look into the graphical progress of such plans. In India in 1957, the Planning Commission was provided with a separate Division of experts to look into the growth of the long-set objectives: We find a concrete description of long range planning in the following paragraph of Prof. White :

"Planning as a term used in the context of public administration is not equivalent to making decisions on basic policy. The meaning of the two terms can be differentiated although the progress designated by them approach each other and a sharp line of distinction is difficult to identify. The consideration of basic policy is a duty of both legislative and administrative bodies a fact which further confused the differentiation. Determination of policy however, is primarily the responsibility of legislatures; the preparation of plans for its achievement is primarily the duty of administrative agencies. Such policy matters involve a choice between competing goals or objectives-ends that are bound-up often with values purposes that affect the broad interests of the people or a part of them. Planning in the context of administration, begins where general policy stops; it is concerned with means by which ends can be brought to fruition. From one point of view it can be argued that the Constitutional Convention of 1787, was a planning body; but for the purposes of this analysis it would be classifed as body concerned with policy not planning; with ends and with basic organisation, not with means."

Programme Planning. Programme Planning to the setting up of objectives to complete varied programmes. The provisons under this planning is made to secure the completion of those various steps falling under any programme of the planning policy. This system of planning grew in 1890, in U.S.A. When the federal administration worked to improve the cities.

White calls programme planning as the "horse of another colours". To quote his lines :

"Programme planning is a horse of another colour. It, too, is a normal inevitable phase of large-scale management, public or private federal, state, or local. It raises, however, no basic issues of the role of government in the economy. Programme planning is the determination of the specific steps to be taken to put in operation and bring to fruition a policy already agreed upon. To the extent that the policy decisons are ambiguous or vague, or administratively unfeasible, programme planning may actually affect policy; in principle its purpose is merely to implement policy through the most economical use of resources.

The nature of the programme planning is similar to the task planning. It starts with the study of the various jobs to be done. Leading to the identifications of in principal parts and their divisions and sub-divisions, the relations between them the boundaries of each *vis-a-vis* the others, and the types of procedures that will be required. This is visualisation of the whole operation often occurring before any part of it has taken physical four.

The second phase of the programme planning is the estimation of volume of the programmes. The third phase of programme planning is concerned with the staff being entrusted to implement the plans at various levels with due foresight and intellect. The last aspect of the programme planning in the forecasting of the shifting rate of flow of work.

Their function is not one that normally forms a part of their school experience at any level; and the art is one acquired by practice rather than by reading.

PLANNING MACHINERY AT STATE LEVEL

Planning Machinery at the State Level. At the State level there is no Planning Commission but there is a State Planning Department which is directly under the Chief Ministers. The department keeps close touch with Central Planning Commission and the various departments of the State, co-ordinating their programmes for development and formulating the development plan for the State as a whole. The plan prepared by it is put first to the Council of Ministers of the State, then to a State Development Board or Planning Advisory Committee which usually consists of State Ministers and important non-official representatives and finally to the State Legislatures. The suggestions made by the Planning Commission are generally kept in view, otherwise the procedure of planning at the State level is practically similar to that at the Centre.

Planning Boards for State Envisaged. The Planning Com-mission has suggsted to State Government that every one of them should establish a State Planning Board.

These Boards, it has been suggested, could be set-up, more or less, on the lines of the Planning Commission and they could assist the State Governments in the formulation of the main policies and solution of the basic problems of implementation.

These boards, in the view of the Planning Commission, could have the Chief Ministers of the States as their Chairman and could also include the State Finance Minister as members. Like the Central Planning Commission, the State Boards could each have two or three full-time members who possess special experience and knowledge of planning and economic problems.

The states have been also given the hint that the Statistical Bureaus in the states could function in close association with the State Planning Boards which could gradually develop their own expertise on planning.

Case for Boards. The Planning Commission seems to be of the view that State Planning Boards would be able to tackle planning problems more comprehensively than individual departments of State Governments who are mainly concerned with the implementation of specific projects, and solution of particular problems. The State Planning Boards it is felt, could also assess the proposals of individual departments and help them to plan in a more systematic way and with better perspective. The State Planning Boards could also coordinate the developmental scheme of the State better.

The information of the State Boards, in the opinion of the Planning Commission, will also facilitate improvement in the quality of planning and help in the evolution of more flexible procdures on matters like central assistance and annual planning.

If is also felt that the State Planning Boards could contribute much in bringing about closer collaboration between the Planning Commission and the States in drawing up the plan for long term development.

Planning at District and Block Levels. Below the State level an attempt is made to undertake the work of planning at the District and Block levels. This is done jointly by the offiers of the various development departments and the members of the District Councils or Block Councils and/or the non-official representatives. The Distirct Collectors and the Block Development Officers are responsible for co-ordination at the district and block levels respectively.

Planning at Village Levels. An experiment is being made to carry the process of planning the village level. The village plan is to be prepared by the Village Panchayat or Council and Co-operatives with the help of the development and the extension staff at the block and the village levels.

Planning Committees on Primary, Secondary and University Education in Punjab. The Government of Punjab constituted Planning Committee on Primary, Secondary and University Education which started functioning straightway in early sixties so that the blue prints of the schemes could be prepared well before the draft plan is to be prepared. This procedure obviated the possibility of hurriedly divised schemes finding place in the Plan and enabled the department to devote all necessary thought and attention for careful consideration the various aspects of all the schemes likely to be included in the plan. The same process and emphasis continued in subsequent plans.

The Committees met once every three months for considering ideas and proposals put forward to each of them by their respective sub-committees. The sub-Committee in each case was presided over by the Deputy Director concerned, helped by one or two members of the Planning Committee who were chosen by the Deputy Director. The Sub-Committees met once in a month or once in six weeks to collect and formulate ideas for the Fourth Plan.

COMPOSITION OF PLANNING COMMISSION

Even since Dada Bhai Naoroji published his paper on poverty of India in 1876, the Indian leaders had urged the necessity of co-ordinated action in the economic field as a means to the economic development of the country. As the struggle for national independence progressed, its social and economic aim became more definite. Much useful programme in the field of national planning as adopted by the National Planning Committee which was set-up in 1938, by the Indian National Congress, with Shri Jawaharlal Nehru as its Chairman. The work of this Committee was, however, unfortunately, interrupted due to the outbreak of the Second World War during which period, many of its members were sent to jails. In 1944, the Government of India set up a separate Department of Planning and Development schemes to be undertaken after the war. Towards the end of 1946, the Advisory Planning Board which was set-up by the Interim Government of India, recommended the appointment of a Planning Commission to devote, continuous attention to the whole field of economic development and to suggest methods and means to rebuild the shattered economy of the country.

As on July, 1992, the Planning Commission consisted of Prime Minister as the Chairman, a Deputy Chairman, Finance Minister, Defence Minister, Agriculture Minister, Minister of State for Planning and other members. One person of administration can be a members secretary. It may be stated that Finance Minister is the *ex-officio* whereas other Ministers are associated in their individual capacity at the sweet will of the Prime Minister.

As already said for administrative purposes the Commission has a secretary who is assisted by a Joint Secretary and Deputy Secretary. They are further assisted by senior administrative staff, senior and junior research staff, junior administrative clerical staff.

Functions

1. To make an assessment of the material, capital and human resources of the country, including technical personnel, and to investigate the possibilities of augmenting such of

those resources as are round to be deficient in relation to the nation's requirements.

2. To formulate a plan for the most effective and balanced utilization of the country's resources.

3. To define the stages in which the Plan should be carried out and to propose the allocation of resources for the due completion of each stage on a determination of priorities.

4. To determine the nature of the machinery which would be necessary for securing the successful implmentation of each stage of the Plan in all its aspects.

5. To appraise from time to time the progress achieved in the execution of each stage of the Plan and to recommened the adjustments of policy and measures that such appraisal might show to be necessary.

6. To indiciate the factors which are tending to retard economic development, and determine the conditions, which in view of the current social and political situation, should be established for the successful execution of the Plan.

7. To make such interim or ancillary recommendations as might to appropriate on a consideration of the prevailing economic conditions, current policies, measures and development programmes, or an examination of such specific problems as may be referred to it for advice by Central or State Government or for facilitating the duties assigned to it.

Organizations of the Planning Commission. To begin with the Commission consisted of fifteen members—The Prime Minister (Chairman), twelve full time members (including the Deputy Chairman). Full time Deputy Chairman of the Planning Commission, Ministry of Finance and Defence. The Planning Minister used to be assisted by a Deputy Minister and Parliamentary Secretary. But now its composition has undergone a change as explained above. The Statistical Adviser to the Cabinet is an additional *de-facto* member of the Commission.

The office of the Planning Commission is headed by a Secretary who is also Secretary to the Cabinet. The office consists of three main organs : *(1)* Programme advisers, *(2)* General Secretariat, and *(3)* Technical Divisions. The Programme Advisers (Programme Administration) have the status of *ex-officio* Additional Secretaries to the Government of India. Assistance to the members of the Commission in matters requiring field study and observation is provided by a team of three senior officers known as advisers. These officers have considerable experience of administration in the States and they help the Commission in keeping close touch with the Progress of planning and its implementation.

The General Secretariat consists mainly of three branches—Plan co-ordination, General co-ordination and Administration, and an Organization and Methods Section. It is staffed by members of the Administrative and Central, Clerical and Secretarial Services. The General Secretariat performs both co-ordinating and house-keeping functions. It concerns itself primarily with matters of common interest to the commission and keep in touch with questions of general policy, bringing to notice and seeking according to the needs of a case, the advise of Secretary, Deputy Chairman, or individual members or the Commission as a whole.

The Technical Divisions perform the most important work and constitute the back bone of the office of the Planning Commission. They vary in size, but ordinarily, ahead of a research unit is described as Chiefs and where a less senior officer is incharge he is known as Director. Chiefs and Directors are assisted by Assistant Chiefs. Each research unit consits of some research staff like Senior Research Officers, Research Officers and Investigators and some Secretariat staff. There are in all about 20 such, Technical Units in the

Planning Commission. The senior positions in the Technical Divisions are occupied by subject specialists. It is in these Divisions that various types of data are collected and put in shape to help in the formulation of plan programmes and policies. The Technical Divisions are responsible for scruitny and analysis of schemes and programmes to be included in the plan, preparation of material for the reports for the plan, conduct of technical studies and research, follow-up on plan recommendation examination of reference from Central Ministries, State Government and voluntary agencies in regard to plan programmes and projects.

The Planning Commission has been criticised to be a super cabinet or a parallel government having as many departments as the number of members. It was emphasised that it should be concerned more with techniques of planning than the implementation and execution of plans. It was further asserted that it is a white elephant. To avoid it from politicization the Deputy Chairmanship has passed from Planning Ministership to the Economists.

White Elephant. The disclosures made by the Indian Institute of Public Administration about the Planning Commission's internal organization will inevitably provide further ammunition to critics of this body which has lately been under heavy fire. A study by the Institute, revealed that the Commission's sanctioned staff has increased about five times in 11 years—from 224 in 1951-52 to 1,131 in 1963-64. Evidently, the staff has doubled with each five year plan, conforming to Parkinson's law with vengeance. Established soon after Indpendence to expedite national development, the Commission has itself developed much faster than the country.

Its early composition was vehemently criticised on the plea that none of the 15 members of the Commission, according to the Institute's report drawn up by a professor of Economic

Policy and Administration, had any background of business and industry. Only one member (excluding the five Ministers) had experience of general administration and only three had handled technical and scientific responsibilities.

It is also stated that as much as 45 per cent of the Commission's total expenditure is incurred on the emoluments of the higher level staff and barely 28 per cent on these of the other functions. It is indicative of its lop-sided structure. Another hurdle in planning and occassional delay in execution is attributed to faulty the distribution and redistribution of subjects among the members during their tenure.

Little wonder that, despite colossal expenditure, the commission has failed to build-up an Institutional framework adequate to the semi-starved, ill-clad and ill-housed mases. The basic problems of proverty and unemployment remain unsolved. How can the country's administrative machniery be streamlined when the Planning Commission itself has a cumbersome and top-heavy establishment which lives in a ivory tower and has ceased to be effective? Planning in a developing country is indispensable, but it ought not to bring more burdens in place of blessings. The trend towards interminable sacrifices, all in the name of Planning and in pursuit of the elusive hope for a prosperous tomorrow was checked by Mr. Lal Bahadur Shastri whose down-to-earth policy in favour of immediate returns had come as a great relief. For a practical approach free from ideological shackles, a thorough overhaul of the Commission and a drastic cut in its "supersecretariat" was the crying need of the hour. A drastic change in its composition and clear definition of its task *vis-a-vis* the cabinet resulted in marked improvement in its affairs. There is still a scope for improvement.

A.R.Cs' Recommendations

(a) The commission secretariat should be recognised in order to focus its activities around two principal functions *viz.*, *(i)* Plan formulation and revision. *(ii)* Plan appraisal and evaluation to reduce waste of money and top heavy personnel.

(b) The Commission recommended that the members should be chosen for their expertise, wisdom and knowledge of handling men and affairs.

(c) The planning Commission should be diverted of its executive functions so that it may concentrate on the planning and evaluation functions.

(d) Long research activities should be taken away from Planning Commission.

The Government accepted all the recommendations of the A.R.C. and reorganized the commission and its secretariat in 1969. The reorganized commission organized itself into secretariat branches for dealing with the work concerning *(i)* Administrative work in the Planning Commission and *(ii)* Co-ordination.

NATIONAL DEVELOPMENT COUNCIL

India having a Federal Constitution, it is vary important that there should be close co-operation between the Planning Commission and the States. For this purpose National Development Council has been constituted which consists of the Prime Minister of India, Chief Ministers of all the States and the members of the Planning Commission. The Ministers of the Central Government also participate in its meeting and the council makes recommendations to the control as well as to the State Governments. The meetings of the Council are hold at least twice a year. The main functions of the National Development Council are as follows :

1. To review the working of the National Plan from time to time;

2. To consider important questions of social and economic policy affecting national development;
3. To recommend measures for the achievement of the aims and targets set-out in the National Plan including measures to secure the active participation and co-operation of the people, improve the efficiency of the administrative services, ensure the fullest development of the less advanced regions and sections of the community, and through sacrifice borne equally by all citizens, build up resources for national development.

The National Development Council has been evolved as an administrative agency to achieve the fullest co-operation and co-ordination in planning between the Central Government and State Governments and to bring about uniformity of approach and unanimity in the working of the National Plan.

COMPOSITION OF THE NDC

The National Development Council includes the Prime Minister as Chairman, the Chief Ministers (or their nominees) of all States and the members of the Planning Commission.

Role of NDC. The former Vice-Chairman (V.T. Krishnamachari) emphasised the role of NDC in these lines : "It provides a forum in which the Union Minister and Chief Ministers of States discuss the plans at important states in their formulation. Plans are also approved at its meetings after competition and before they are presented to the Parliament and the State legislatures. In this way, the national characters of the Plans is emphasised. The council also considers social and economic policies affecting the country from a national point of view so that their necessary, uniformity may be secrured. In this way, it gives a lead to the country on broad issues of policy and promotes collective thinking and joint section on mattters of national importance."

Working of the Planning Commission. The Planning Commission prepares the Plan and after that it is placed before the NDC for its approval. At this Stage the Union and State Governments are involved in the process of decision making. When passed by NDC the plan is presented to the Parliament for its final approval. There are two opinions of the positions of the position Commission *vis-a-vis* the National Development Council. First, the NDC is superior since it is decision taking authority. Michael Brecher feels that the NDC "has relegated the Planning Commission to the status of a research arm." Second, the real centre of authority is the Planning Commission since the fundamental decisions are taken by it and these are just formalised when placed before the NDC. The real controller is the Prime Minister as he shapes the proposed plan initially in the Cabinet meeting and then in the Planning Commission. In this view quite a large body like the NDC is mere formality as the decision of the Prime Minister cannot be pre ruled by a few Chief Ministers of political party other than that of the ruling party.

Planning Commission and the Centralisation of Power Factors. The Critics of the Indian federal system argue that the Planning Commission is held to be the instrument through which a steady shift of power to New Delhi has been manipulated. It was, therefore realised at a very early stage that, if the Plan was to be a National Plan, some machinery "had to be devised by which the State Governments could be nabled to participate in formulation of the plan and over-all policies underlying it." It is also argued that in reality, "the Sates had no role to play in the formulation of the Plan." The creation of NDC was to sort out such problems and it "was clerly conceived as a federal body, though notion in formulation of National Plans and in bringing about a national consensus regarding Plan policies."

It is a matter of debate whether NDC has served the desired purpose when it was reconstituted in 1967, to include all Union Ministers according to the recommendations of the Administrative Reforms Commission. It gave set back to the Chief Minister. The single dominant party system under the leadership of Mr. Rajiv Gandhi, the NDC is merely a bigger platform where the state Chief Ministers put their formal seal of approval on the policies already laid down by the Prime Minister of India.

Criticism of the Working of the Planning Commission. On the following grounds the working of the Planning Commission has been criticised :

(i) It appears as an agency of the Prime Minister because he appoints the members according to his individual judgement and there is no criterion in regard to the qualifications.

(ii) According to the convenience of the Chairman (i.e., P.M.) the strength of the Planning Commission may vary from time to time.

(iii) The term of the members depends upon the Prime Minister.

(iv) The Planning Commission should act as an advisory body without Prime Minister because, it is due to the presence of the P.M.

(v) The Planning Commission is not only an advisory body rather it works as an effective decision-making body surpassing the jurisdiction of statutory bodies like the Council of Ministers and the Finance Commission.

(vi) The Planning Commission is not answerable to the Parliaments and dissident member is required to submit his resignation.

Evaluation. The National Development Council has been fairly successful in bridging and linking the Union

Government, the Planning Commission and the various State Governments. It has served as an effective forum for discussions and free exchange of ideas and has created a sense of high responsibility on the part of the State Governments for making plans a success.

However, there are persons who view the growing powers of the Council as a danger to the privileges of the Central and State Cabinets. They charge the N.D.C. for usurping authority and functioning as a 'virtual super cabinet'. Thus, Brecher writes in the biography of Pt. Nehru, "The N.D.C. was etablished as a supreme administrative and advisory body on planning...It lays down policy directives invariably approved by the Cabinet. Since their inception the N.D.C. and its Standing Committee have virtually relegated the Planning Commission to the status of a research arm". H.M. Patel, retired I.C.S. expresseed a similar view; "Among the Advisory Bodies to the Planning Commission is included the N.D.C. This is surely unaccurate, as is clear from its composition. The N.D.C. is a body obviously superior to the Planning Commission. It is indeeed a policy makig body and its recommendations cannot but be regarded as policy decisions and not merely as advisory suggestions." Santhanam is a little more unsympathetic to the Council when he says : "The position of the NDC has come to approximate to that of super cabinet of the entire Indian Federation, a Cabinet functioning for the Government of India as well as for the Government of all States". Mr. A.P. Jain, ex-Food Minister, charged the N.D.C. for acting arbitrarily. He felt that N.D.C. encroaches upon the functions which constitutionally belong to the other bodies Council of Ministers at the Cenral and State levels. Sometimes, it acts without thorough knowledge of the subject and without proper consultation of the various Ministries. Thus, in 1956, it fixed targets of food produtcion in the Second Five Year Plan without prior consultation of the Food Ministry. Similarly, in 1958, the Council decided in favour of State Trading without making sure as to the capacity of the State Governments to enforce controls under State Trading. In Mr. Jain's opinion, the Council is incompetent, both by law and by the nature of its composition, to take high-level national decisions.

The only defence that can be given to the N.D.C. from the above criticism is that it is neither a constitutional body nor a statutory body and hence, its recommendations have no binding force. Rather, it is a creature of the Union Cabinet and as such its role is only advisory in nature. It is only a high ranking policy-making body and it's for the Cabinet to decide as to the degree of weight its recommendations should carry. By the very nature of its composition, the Council is likely to gain more and more influence and prestige but this should not be taken as a potential danger to the powers of the Union and State Cabinets.

There can however, be two dangers which may adversely affect the working of the Council. Firstly, if the members from the State Governments make this Council as a forum for the ventilation of their grievances; and secondly, if the present one party character of all the States and Centre gives rise to multiple party charcters. There have been two such occassions when Janata and Janata Dal Government came in power at the centre for living period *i.e.*, in 1977 and 1988-89.

THE STRUCTURAL BASIS OF PLANNING IN INDIA

By the nature of its composition and the manner of its functioning, the Planning Commission has helped define many of the basic aims of development and the institutional changes required for their realisation. In the light of economic and other developments major structural changes have been taking place with time and quite often at the turn of unexpected situations or on the basis of study and research by specially constituted commissions, committees and expert groups. The national planning agency is gradually diminishing its role concerning the formulation of fundamental, social and economic policies. These are now taking shape in a greater degree from public debates in Parliament and State Legisature and from the play of new social and political forces within the community. The press and the public opinion are helping build a kind of national consensus for further rapid changes in the economic and social fabric.

The work of the Planning Commission at the Centre and of the planning bodies in the States is, therefore, now related more to the secondary levels of policy to analysis of experience, evaluation and apppraisal, considering comments and forecasts based on current developments, and the formulation of long and medium-term investment and consumption goals and of annual plans. The process of planning and development is inevitably marked by greater flexibility and adaptation to changing conditions.

Planning Agencies. The work of plannig agencies now calls for greater use of advanced statistical and other computational techniques and for profounder understanding of the economy and of changes occurring in the social structure, including motivations and tensions. Not that the tasks are less important than before, but the changes in them are an indication of the transformation which has taken place over the past few years. In turn, this transformation calls for a certain re-orientation of planning, for closer links between planning for development and the current management of economy and for greater contact between the work of the planning agencies and the universities and other centres of socio-economic resarch.

CENTRE-STATE RELATIONS IN PLANNING

When the Planning Commission was constitued it was assumed that it would assist and advise both the central and the State Governments. At that time it was far from clear how the Planning Commission would in fact function in relation to the States. Over the years, in the context of planning, a pattern of Centre-State relationships has taken shape. The main elements in this pattern can be briefly described.

The Five Year Plans embrace the entire range of developmental activities. Responsibility for legislation and execution derive from the Constitution, but consideration of policies bearing on development and the setting of developoment goals and the preparation of plans to fullfil them have been regarded as tasks to be undertaken by the country as a whole, jointly by the Centre and the States in co-operation with one another. At the first meeting of the National Development Council, in November, 1952, and at many subsequent meetings of the Council, Jawaharlal Nehru stressed that the Chief Ministers of the States bore intimate responsibility for the Plan in all its phases. As Chief Ministers, they shouldered heavy responsibility for the whole of India and had to look upon every question from a national point of view. Both in their preparation and their implementation, therefore, the Five Year Plans have developed as a continuing partnership between the Centre and the States.

For many years, the more important policies and directions on priorities have either emerged from or have been considered and approved in meetings of the National Development Council or in conferences of Chief Ministers or in inter-State conferences and other similar fortuns. In future, the National Development Council could play even larger role both as a body and through its committees.

ROLE OF THE STATES IN PLANNING PROCESS

Since assessment of resources and their mobilisation are necessary basis for the formulation of five year and annual plans, review of the financial position of States and of measures to mobilise resources for the future has been undertaken systematically by the Planning Commission in co-operation with each State. Since the Third Five Year Plan, the major directions on resources mobilisation come from a committee of the National Development Council, including Chief Ministers and others pressed and resolved at the official level. By convention, the Planning Commission's representatives have participated for many years in inter-departmental committees of Secretaries and other senior officials. If issues involving policy in which the Planning Commission had a special interest remained unresolved at official level, steps were taken to discuss them in meeting of the Planning Commission to which the representatives of the Ministers concerned were invited. In this way, to the maximum extent possible, agreed views could be submitted to the government. Where there might have been difficulties in reaching a common view betwween the Minister and any Member concerned, in the Planning Commission, further discussions were arranged at the level of the Commission and, more often than not, agreed views emerged.

PROPOSALS FOR REFORM IN THE PLANNING COMMISSION

Over the past few years, the strength of the Planning Commission has diminished seriously. If thought is given to the range of subjects which planning embraces and the responsibilities which, as a body, the Planning Commission is required to fulfil in relation to the Centre and the States and the national economy, it has been suggested that six full-time Members instead of five at present would do better justice to the technical work of the Commission. Planning calls for much intensive study and thought on the part of the Members and for collective consideration of different aspects of development. For the Planning Commission to be able to function as a body of competent individuals who have a distinct contribution to make and endeavour to reach conclusions and recommendations of real value of the Centre and the States implies an enormous amount of application, teamwork and cohesion. These latter elements have to be provided largely by the Deputy Chairman who would need to give all his time to the work of the Commission. It is physically impossible for even a gifted individual to fulfil his policial responsibilities as a Minister, including responsi-bilities in Parliament and, at the same time, to devote the attention needed to the study of problems in depth, both individually and jointly with his collegues. The Deputy Chairman of the Planning Commission has to gave the greater part of his time for coordination of work on the Plan as a whole, co-ordination with States, review of the current economic trends, and the preparation of perspective plans for the eocnomy.

The question is sometimes raised whether the full time Members of the Planning Commission should be responsible for any specific subjects or should function only as a collective body, considering matters placed before them and generally keeping in touch with developments. This concept is more appropriate to the judicial than to the executive branch of government. Every aspect of development involves extensive study and, therefore, calls for a degree of specialisation.

ANNUAL PLAN DISCUSSIONS

Apart from annual plan dicussions, each year the Planning Commission and the Planning Board of a State could jointly review progress and consider problems requiring special attention. If States have adequate planning machinery, a great deal of consideration of detail which now enters into discussions on planning could be undertaken by them. The work of the Planning Commission would be facilitate and all necessary references to the Centre avoided. Technical and analytical work required in planning has to be undertaken on scientific lines equally for individual State as for the Country as a whole. Systematic training programmes should be developed both for planning in general and for planning in scientific fields and at area level. Implementation by local authorities has to be observed more closely and reported upon authoritively. All these steps will become easier if the planning apparatus in the States is strengthened.

Parliament has a vital and continuing interest in the success of planning and in keeping itself informed about policies proposed and problems encountered in giving effect to the plans. Therefore, it is necessary to designate and senior member of the Council of Ministers as the Minister of Planning. The Planning Commission now has a full-time Deputy Chairman, the national interest may be best served if the Minister of Finance, who is in a position to take a view of the national economy as a whole, also functions as the Minister of Planning and provides the essential link with Parliament.

The State governments may create a common pool of managerial, Technical and accounts service officers taken from various departments and exising State enterprises to induct professionalisation, sense of security and of involvement among the senior state personnel of State government undertakings. The general trend is away from departmental undertakings and towards the increased use of semi-autonomous or independent agencies, public corporations and government companies.

For the developing countries, in which managerial skill is scarce, it is normally better to have functional members of a board who come from within the enterprise and serve concurrently as management heads of functional units. Whether a board is a policy board, a functional board or a mixed one, it should include some members who have a broad outlook and some who are specialists in management and/or in the substantive area in which the enterprise operates. Such a combination enables a board to both serve the public interest and make correct policy decisions from a technical point of view.

●●

11

Policy of Legislative Control

The Legislative or Parliament plays an important role in making administration accountable. There are several means through which Parliament exercises control over public administration. Some of the important means are : questions, discussions and debates, motions and resolutions on specific administrative actions and matters of great concern. Members through financial control, through budget and Parliamentary committees, Call attention motion can draw the attention of the Minister concerned to a matter of urgent public importance; such matters comprise national security and unity of the nation; drought or flood problem, maintenance of essential services; law and order problem; improper functioning of the administrative machinery; scarcity of essential commodities; foreign actions adversely affecting country's interest, border incidents; and serious incidents involving Indians abroad, for example, during Gulf War due to pressure of public opinion administration made arrangements through Air India Special flights to safely evacuate Indians from Iraq. Parliamentarians also get opportunity to hold administration accountable through budgetary process at the time of general discussion on the budget, discussion and voting of demands for grants and consideration and passing of both the Appropriation Bill and the Finance Bill. In this way, legislature through its power over the public purse seeks to insure administrative accountability. Besides the standing committees such as public accounts committee on subordinate legislation, committee on government assurances and so on, of the Parliament which facilitate and exercise of the power of administrative accountability. There are consultative committees attached to the ministries and Parliamentary committees of investigation. The committees are empowered to ask for files, information and other documents from government officials. Not only this, the officials may be called for evidence. It is interesting to note that in the proceedings of the committees, public servants are put hard to defend their policies and actions on grounds of laws, rules and their perception of public interest and in such situations administrative accountability becomes more meaningful. It has been noted that scant attention is paid to the results and findings of the committees by the legislatures and their reports are hardly considered on the floor of the house, thus, the results of their labour are shelved. Although the reports of all the Parliamentary Committees are not normally debated in Parliament yet they have great informative values because they enable the members of Parliament who sit on the committees to study in detail the working of the administrative machinery and suggest improvements, whenever necessary. Thus, Parliamentary committees contribute to a considerable extent to the efficient working of Parliamentary democracy. After having consideration, action on such reports must take place. Further, the power of administrative accountability would be actively operationalised only with the active participation in its exercise by them. Ultimately the success of the legislative devices for ensuring administrative accountability largely depends upon intelligence and enlightenment of legislators.

The system of post-audit of the Governmental accounts is also among the important means of control and insuring accountability as it seeks to ensure that the funds sanctioned by the legislature are spent by the approved authorities for the same purpose for which they are appropriated. It means that actual spending is compared with authorised expenditure in order to detect the extent of administrative accountability for public spending. It is thought that this system of control loses some of its effectiveness when government finance becomes more complex in terms of variety of items purchased and complexity of financial arrangements, it is because of multiplicity of economic activities and almost every nation has found it advisable to allow sufficient atitude to the government in planning public spending, shifting the head of accounts and even aggregates of government expenditure.

In Indian federation there are states as well as Union Territories. Each state has a legislature. Some of the states have unicameral, while others have a bicameral legislature. But legislature in every state has a control over the administration. The legislature is very useful forum for the opposition for exposing the weaknesses and drawbacks of the administration.

Legislative Assembly. Lower House of the state legislature is called Legislative Assembly. As compared with the Legislative Council it is far more powerful.

Qualifications. A person for membership to state legislature should be a citizen of India of not less than twenty five years of age; should not hold any office of profit and should posses such other qualifications as may be prescribed in that behalf by Parliament by a law.

Tenure of Office. Every Legislative Assembly is constituted for a period of five years from the date of its first meeting, after which it is dissolved. The assembly can be dissolved earlier also.

Salary and Allowances. All the members of the legislature are paid a monthly salary which varies from state to state. In addition, they get the allowances during the sessional days. They are provided with residential quarters, free travel and medical facilities.

Composition. The Legislative Assembly of each state consists of not more than five hundred and not less that sixty members. These members are chosen by direct election from territorial constituencies in the state. Each person who has attained twenty-one years of age is qualified to vote. If the Governor feels that the Anglo-Indian community has not been properly represented he may nominate two representatives of that community to the Assembly. It may be mentioned that some seats are reserved for the scheduled eastes, tribes and other backward classes, but this a temporary phase and will disappear in the course of time.

Presiding Officer. The Presiding Officer of the Legislative Assembly is the Speaker. He presides over the meetings of the assembly. He decides about the resolutions, adjournment motions and points of order. He fixes time limit for the speeches. He certifies whether a bill is money bill or not. The Speaker maintains order and decorum in the assembly. If any body shows any disrespect to the Speaker or violates the privileges of a member, he may be punished by the Speaker.

The Speaker is elected for a term of five years at the first meeting of the assembly. He can resign his office or can be removed by a notice of fourteen day by a simple majority of votes in the assembly. While the proceedings to remove the Speaker are continuing, he will not preside over the meetings of the assembly. His salarly and allowances etc., are determined from time to time. In a word, the Speaker of the State Assembly has exactly the same position in the Legislative Assembly as the Speaker of the Lok Sabha. As and when the office of Speaker is vacated by resignation or removal the Deputy Speaker discharges the duties of the Speaker.

Power and Functions. The powers of Legislative Assembly can be classified under three main heads :

1. Executive Powers. The executive powers of the state legislature are exercised by the Legislative Assembly. The

Council of Ministers is controlled by the assembly. It is said that the Legislative Assembly dictates the government. This control of the assembly is exercised in three ways namely :

(a) The members of the assembly can ask questions and put supplementary questions to the ministers relating of the department and the minister is supposed to satisfy the members.

(b) They can table adjournment motions.

(c) The constitution provides that the Council of Ministers is responsible to the Legislative Assembly collectively.

(d) They can put short-notice questions.

(e) In the end the assembly can pass a vote of no confidence against the Council of Ministers and in case such a vote is carried, the Council of Ministers will have to resign.

2. Financial Powers. The Legislative Assembly has complete control over the state purse. Removal of old taxes and the levy of new ones is done with the consent of the assembly. Even the money spent by the Governor from the Consolidated Fund of the State is to be approved by the Assembly later. No money can be spent without the consent of the assembly. A money bill can originate only in the Legislative Assembly.

3. Legislative Powers. The state legislative makes laws on the subjects enumerated in the State List and also in the Concurrent List. If there is any conflict on the scope of a law passed by the State on a concurrent subject (on which the Union Parliament also has the right to legislate) and such a law goes against the law of the Union on the same subject, it is the law of the Parliament that prevails over the state law.

LEGISLATIVE COUNCIL

In some states there is bi-cameral system of legislative. In such a system the Upper House is called Legislative Council. The Upper House is not as powerful as the Legislative Assembly which is the Lower House of the legislative. It is a permanent body and is not dissolved with the dissolution of Legislative Assembly after the expiry of 5 years.

Tenure of Office. The Legislative Council is a permanent body. Its every member elected for six years. One-third of its members retire at the end of two years. The Constitution provides that the Legislative Council of a state is not subject to dissolution.

Composition. The total membership in the Legislative Council of a State shall not exceed one-third of the total membership in the Legislative Assembly of that State. Strength of a Legislative Council will however in no case be less than forty. The members of the Legislative Council are elected indirectly. The distribution of seats in a Legislative Council is as follows :

(a) One-third of members of Council are elected by electorates consisting of members of municipalities, district boards and such other local authorities in the state as the parliament may specify by law.

(b) One-twelfth of the members are elected by the electorates consisting of persons who have been engaged in teaching for a least three years in educational institutions not below the standard of secondary schools.

(c) One-third of the members are elected by members of the Legislative Assembly of the State from amongst who are not members of the Assembly.

(d) The remaining one-sixth members are nominated by the state Governor. These nominated members are persons of standing in such fields as literature, science, art, co-operative movement and social service.

(e) One-twelfth of the members elected by the electorates consisting of persons residing in the state who have been graduates with a three-year standing.

Presiding Officer. The Presiding Officer of the Legislative Council is the Chairman. he conducts the proceedings in the Council. He also maintains order in the House and safeguards privileges of the members. He gets salary, allowances and other benefits and privileges as are determined by law.

The Chairman and Deputy Chairman are elected by the members of the Legislative Council. The Chairman of Legislative Council shall vacate his office if he ceases to be a member of the Council. He may also resign his office and can also be removed from his office. In the absence of the Chairman, the Deputy Chairman discharges his functions.

Powers and Functions. Legislative Council is a very weak body. It has more formal functions than real ones. These may be summed up as under :

1. Executive Powers. The Council has practically no executive powers. It is so because the Council of Ministers is not responsible to this House and a vote of no confidence against the Council of Ministers in the Council, does not make it obligatory for the former to resign. Still, the Council can influence the working of the government. If the Council is not satisfied with the performance of the government it can, through questions and adjournment motions, bring the government to disrepute and make it unpopular by exposing its defects. By these methods it can very much lower the prestige of Council of Ministers in the eyes of the people.

2. Legislative Powers. Theoretically the Legislative Council has co-equal powers with the assembly in so for as ordinary bills are concerned. A non-money bill is enacted only when both the Houses approve of it. But in practice there are limitations on the powers of the Council here also. The Legislative Assembly has an upper hand.

3. Financial Powers. In the financial sphere the Council has no control whatsoever. No money bill can originate in the Council. Its opinion or recommendations on money bills do not mean much either. It can only delay a money bill for a period of fourteen days, within which period, if it does not return to bill, it will be deemed to have been passed. It can suggest amendments to money bills but it is for the assembly either to accept or reject these.

Legislature and Administration. An effective and powerful instrument of control in the State over administration is the state legislature. It is a forum where the administration and administrator can be exposed without least danger. Each department of administration is headed by a minister, who is responsible to the legislature for the execution of policies and programmes of his department. A member of legislature can put any question on the minister about the working of his department and he is obliged to answer that unless such a reply can lead to revealing state secrets. Similarly a memb in the legislature can control the administration by moving 'call attention' or 'short notice' question. On such occasions the administration is on its toes to provide information available without any grudge and grumble. Similarly the legislature controls administration at the time of budget.

These are only indirect methods though which a state legislature controls the administration. There are also direct methods when legislature as a whole directly control administration. A legislator can bring to the notice of government, corrupt, under-hand and illegal methods adopted by a public servant. He can allege that a public servant has misused his authority and position. We know that in Punjab, the legislators submitted a memorandum against Late Partap Singh Kairon, the then Chief Minister of Punjab, to the President of India pointing out certain irregularities. The outcome was Das Commission. Similarly in Punjab memorandum was sent to President of India, incorporating irregularities committed by Prakash Singh Badal Ministry. In fact, in India, there is perhaps no states in which charges have not been levied against the government, regarding corrupt and illegal means for amassing wealth, with the help of administration. The legislatures can control administration by means of 'Committee or Assurances' and Estimates Committee' 'Public Accounts Committee' and so on. In these committees the administrator is face to face with the legislator to explain the position of his department. We also find that in the States the constituencies are not as big as parliamentary constituencies. Therefore, a legislator comes into close contact with the constituents.

Thus in the states the legislatures mould the administration. These give guidelines and policies for implementation to the state governments. Thus in a state, legislature is guide and philosopher of administration. Of course the scope of state activity has considerably increased which has resulted in the less time for the legislature to supervise, yet the very fact that the legislatures can take administration to task at any time, is in itself a sufficient guarantee that the administration will not go much wrong.

Legislative Assembly. It is lower house of State legislature and every Indian citizen can become its member. Members of Assembly get monthly salary and other allowances. The tenure of the assembly is 5 years. The members are elected on the basis of universal adult franchise. Seats are however, reserved for the persons belonging to scheduled castes, scheduled tribes and other backward classes. The presiding officer of the Assembly is Speaker who is responsible for maintaining decorum in the house. He conducts the proceedings of the House. The assembly has executive, financial and legislative powers.

Legislative Council. It is upper house of state legislature. Each member is elected for a period of 5 year and 1/3 of its member retire after every two years. It is an indirectly elected House. The House is presided over by a Chairman who performs the same functions as the speaker in the assembly.

Legislature and Administration. Legislature exercises indirect control over administration by putting questions on the ministers, moving call attention and short notice questions and ultimately by passing a vote of no confidence against the Council of Ministers. Directly an administrator is controlled by the legislature at the time of meetings of committees of the legislature where he is face to face with the legislators.

In a state broad policy guide lines are given by the legislature whereas the administrator is required to implement them. Thus the control is real and effective.

In India, the principal methods of Legislative control are of three types, that is, control over *(i)* policy, *(ii)* departmental acts, *(iii)* finance.

The various methods of exercising such control are :

Debates and Discussions. The parliament may exercise control through various debates and discussions which provides an opportunity for the review of governmental policies and their implementation. The more notable occasions for discussion among these are during the president's inaugural speech to both houses of parliament, the budget speech of the finance minister or during the introduction of new legislative proposals.

There are also some other occasions, when various aspects of administration are put up for legislative comment or criticism.

Resolutions or Motions. The legislature has the power to pass resolutions on any matter or move motions to censure a particular minister of the government as a whole. The most important motions are calling attention motion, adjournment motion, privilege motion and the no- confidence motion. A resolution is only meant to be recommendatory whereas censure motions, if passed, make it compulsory for the government to resign.

Questions. In a parliamentary form of the government, legislative questions become the most continuous and vocal method of the people's representatives to exercise their scrutiny over the acts of omission and commission of the government. During the question hour in parliament any member can ask any question seeking information on any matter. The minister concerned replies to these questions with the aid of the bureaucrats and secretaries in his department. If the answer given to a question does not satisfy the questioner, supplementary questions can also be asked to which ministers are expected to give satisfactory replies. The main purpose of the question hour is to ventilate public grievances and to draw the attention of the people towards various facilities of the government. Since the question may cover any field or branch of administration, the public officials are constantly alert, conscientious and responsible for their official acts.

Budgetary Control. In every democratic country, the legislative controls the nation's purse-strings. No money can be spent by the executive without legislative sanction. The budget proposals are extensively debated in parliament before being voted upon. With the ruling party enjoying a majority in parliament, in parliamentary democracies the demand for grants can neither be rejected nor reduced, but provides an opportunity for a general review of public policy. It is also the duty of the parliament to see that the money sanctioned has been spent economically and in accordance with the guideliness laid down by it. This requires proper audit of governmen expenditure which is the duty of the Comptroller and Audito General of India. The auditor general while auditing th governmental expenditure examines whether the money spen had legislative sanction and whether it was spent for th purpose for which sanction was made. It also examine governmental expenditure from the principles of econom and financial propriety.

Parliamentary Committees. Modern parliaments are so overburdened with work that they neither have the time nor technical expertise or knowledge to go into the details of the working of various administrative agencies and governmental departments. Thus the parliamentary committee system was evolved to act as a watchdog on public administration and governmental functioning. Some of the important committees of Parliament in India are : Public Accounts Committees, Estimates Committee, Committee on Public Undertakings, Committee on Subordinate Legislation and so on.

The Public Accounts Committee examines the reports of the auditor general regarding the propriety of expenditure incurred by government departments. The Estimates Committee examines the budgetary estimates sent by different ministers to suggest economies in expenditure.

The Public Undertakings Committee is responsible for scrutinising the reports and accounts of the public sector undertakings in India to see whether they are being managed in accordance with sound business principles.

The main purpose of the Committee on Subordinate Legislation is to exercise a necessary check over delegated legislation which is a typical legislature outgrowth of modern parliamentary states. The legislature usually lays down the broad principles and outlines of laws delegating authority to the administration to bill in the details. The above committee in India is charged with the responsibility of seeing whether the powers delegated by the parliament have been properly exercised within the framework of the parliamentary statute delegating such authority.

Limitations of Legislative Control

The relative ineffectiveness of legislative control in the modern age is a universal phenomenon in all democratic countries. Legislatures neither have the time nor expertise to effectively control all spheres of administration. Their control is sporadic in nature and that too meant to highlight certain acts of omission and commission, which might have been brought to their notice by the public or the press. In the presidental form, congressional control over administration is very limited in nature and scope. In parliamentary countries like India, legislative control is considerably reduced and restricted in effectiveness due to the following reasons :

(a) The executive plays a key role in formulating policies. The legislative leadership therefore rests more with the government.

(b) The expansion in the volume and variety of administrative work has led to the increasing incapacity of the legislatures to effectively control the ever-growing bureaucracy.

(c) Budgetary control is also limited by the fact that since voting is always on party lines any government with the required legislative majority can get any demand for grant passed in Parliament. Hence, legislative control over administration is more illusory than real or substantive in nature.

EXECUTIVE CONTROL OVER ADMINISTRATION

Executive control is an internal control over administration exercised either by the superior over the subordinate within the chain of administrative hierarchy or by other parallel agencies in the executive branch of the government. Administrative structure is hierarchical in nature. One level controls the other and none is outside the chain of command.

Types of Executive Control. The executive control is exercised in many ways. Most of the means of control are formal provided by the laws of the country but some of them are informal depending upon the good sense of the public servants. The system of internal control may be studied under the following heads :

1. Political or Ministerial Control. Ministerial responsibility is the cardinal principle of Parliamentary democracy. The executive branch of the government consists of Ministers as members of the Cabinet. Each Minister is individually incharge of a portfolio consisting of one or more departments and thus, he is the chief executive so far that portfolio is concerned and is responsible for the official working of the subjects under his charge. In running the administration of concerned department (s) he has to control the actions of civil servants under him so that they may help in implementation of the policies. This leads to the sensitive complex issue of relationship between the minister and the civil servant.

2. Administrative Control within the Hierarchy. In the above point we have discussed the political command structure but there is a hierarchical command structure in the permanent executive. Administrative head of the department is secretary. The department is divided into wings, under the charge of Joint or Additional Secretary; a wing is sub-divided into divisions headed by deputy Secretaries;' each division is further divided into branches, under the charge of Under Secretaries; and then comes the Section, presided over by Section Officer. The principle of Secretarial procedure is that each paper must pass through the proper authorised channel both in its outwards and inward journey. The Secretariat is the 'headquarter' which has hundreds and thousands of field offices located throughout the country. These field offices work under the direction and control of the Secretariat. There are a number of techniques and devices through which the headquarter's administration controls the field agencies. The devices include prior approval of individual project, promulgation of service standards; budgetary limitations upon the operations; and approval of the appointment of key subordinate personnel; audit, inspection, reporting and investigation, etc. Luther Gulick discussed and distinguished between three types of headquarter field-relationship. For example, All Fingers; Short Arms, Long Fingers, and Long Arms, Short fingers, Under the first, the headquarters office deals directly with the field units without any regional units, under the second type regional units are there but these are located in the central office and not in the field; and under the third type, territorial units are located in the entire area away from the Central office.

3. Personnel Management Control. An important means of control is the Centralisation of establishment of personnel functions. The Chief Executive has a centralised personnel office. This office controls the methods of recruitment, salaries, promotions, conditions of service etc. An uniformity in personnel matters throughout the administrative organisation of the Government is maintained. This is advantageous in preparation of projects, and estimates etc. The system of giving rewards like increments, rise in salary, promotion, etc., are very powerful instrument of control in the hands of the executive. Likewise public servants can be reprimanded, censured, removed and dismissed from the service if they do not behave in a desired way. These examples persuade the public servants to avoid undesirable behaviour and improving their performance on desirable lines.

4. Budgetary Control. To carry out the functions of the government the budget provides necessary finances. The activities of the public servants can be controlled by controlling the finances made available to them through budget. If budgetary system is effective, no official can escape its control. The budgetary control is exercised by the Ministry of Finance, through a system of hierarchy of financial powers. The other parts of this control are the expenditure reports sent by the central audit conducted by the C & AG. Appleby said that India has a faulty system of budgetary control. Expenditure control is exercised to an oppressive degree and converts the budgetary system into a fault finding system.

5. Control by Staff Agencies. There are two important staff agencies which also exercise control over various ministries, departments and other administrative agencies. The important agencies are : the Plannning Commission and the Department of Administrative Reforms, which is now part of a full fledged Ministry named Ministry of Personnel, Public Grievances and Pensions. The administrative wing of the new Ministry functions as the top agency for improving administrative capability on a continuing basis. The Planning Commission suggests new policies or programmes and coordinates policies and programmes started by other agencies of the government and maintains effective liaison with the central ministries and State Governments.

6. Professional or Administrative Ethics. In due course of time, every profession develops a code of conduct and behaviour for its members, Medical and Legal professions have organised so well that they have shaped formal means of enforcing their ethics on members. However, the legal and medical professions have formal and legal methods of enforcement of their code of conduct for the sake of pride in their profession. Public services have also become a professional career and in many countries it has evolved its own code of ethics. In India there is a very voluminous code of conduct for civil servants. It lays down in great details what a civil servant should do and should not do. It even goes to the extent of specifying the need for reporting to the government even bonafide transactions with the members of the family and close friends. However, these tight controls have not inculcated the necessary sense of duty and discipline in the civil servants. At present, it is a very serious matter that our civil servants have also involved in numerous scams along with the politicians. Thus, they are not observing the conduct rules which often suffer from numerous loopholes.

There are many methods of executive control of administration, but according to E.N. Gladden, there are three important controls of the executive on the civil service, namely, political directions through ministerial administrator, the operation of the national budgetary system and recruitment by an independent authority.

Policy Making. It is the task of the Chief Executive to frame administrative policies. In the USA, the president determines the broad outlines of administrative policy. He has the power to delegate the policy making powers to various heads of departments within the overall framework of his guidelines without in any way delegating his main responsibility of direction, supervision and control. In a parliamentary government, it is the cabinet which is in charge of policy making, overall direction and coordination of the different branches of administration, besides individual ministers exercising control over public officials in their respective departments.

Budgetary System. It is the executive which is responsible for the framing of the budget, getting the demand for grants passed in parliament, and then allocating necessary funds to each department for expenditure. Every department submits its annual financial demand to the executive before the budget is framed, which has to be first approved by the cabinet before it finds its place in the final budget estimates.

Recruitment. The broad principles of recruitment are laid down by the Chief Executive. The ministers themselves select the secretaries and deputies of their departments. Other recruitments to the civil service are, however, done on the recommendation of an independent recruiting board—the Public Service Commissions—in most democratic countries. In the USA the Chief Executive seeks senatorial approval of the official appointments he makes but he has the exclusive power of dismissal of his cabinet and top aids.

Executive Law Making. Delegated legislation becomes an important tool of exercising executive control over public officials. Most of the laws passed by the parliament provide a broad framework and the minor details are filled in by the administrators in their daily application of laws. This is an important method of executive control over administration and can be used in controlling administration by laying down rules and regulations to be observed in the implementation of a particular law concerned.

Executive controls are very important because they are self-corrective and continuous in nature. However, the effectiveness of these controls depends much on the civil service-minister relationship specially in the higher echelons of the bureaucracy. The minister who is an amateur in administration has to depend on the administrative abilities of his secretaries in the departments who are considered experts in the field. Since government comprises both the wings (political and permanent) of the executive, and effective coordination between the two leads to harmonious functioning of the administrative departments. The minister and his administrator colleagues should work together as a team based on mutual trust and undertanding. The minister should lay down policies and supervise wherever necessary without interfering in the details of administration. Before taking important decisions the minister should take all respresentative opinions into consideration though he is not bound by any advice. The civil servants on their part can influence, persuade or advise the minister in whatever way they choose, but it is their official duty to implement a policy as faithfully as possible once a decision is taken by the minister.

JUDICIAL CONTROL OVER ADMINISTRATION

Judicial control over administration means the powers of the courts to examine the legality of the officials' acts and thereby to safeguard the rights of the citizens. It also implies the right of an aggrieved citizen to bring a civil or criminal suit in a court of law against a public servant for the wrong done to him, in the course of discharging of his public duty. L.D. White explaining the importance of Judicial control writes, "The system of formal external control over officials and their acts falls primarily into two main divisions—that exercised by the legislative bodies and that imposed by courts. The purpose of legislative supervision is principally to control the policy and the expenditure of the executive branch, the end sought by judicial control of administrative acts is to ensure their legality and thus protect citizens against unlawful trespass on their constitutional or other rights."

CASES OF JUDICIAL INTERVENTION

Judicial intervention is restrictive in nature and sometimes limited in its scope. Firstly, the courts cannot interfere in the administrative activities of their own accord. They can intervene only when they are invited to do so by any person, who feels that his rights have been infringed or are likely to be infringed as a result of some action of the public official. Secondly, the courts cannot interfere in each and every administrative act, as too much of judicial action may make the offices too much conscious and very little of it may make them negligent of the rights of citizens. In the words of L.D. White, "At one extreme, the vigour of judicial control may paralyse effective administration, at the other the result may be an offensive bureaucratic tyranny, exactly where the balance may be best struck is a major problem of judicial administration relationship."

1. Lack of Jurisdiction. Every officer has to act within the limit of the authority given to him and also within a specified geographical area. If he acts beyond his authority or outside the geographical limits of his powers, his acts will be declared by the courts as *ultra vires* and hence ineffective. As, for example, in India it is expressly laid down in the Constitution that no government employee shall be dismissed by an authority below in rank the authority which appointed him otherwise the action of dismissal shall be declared *ultra vires* due to lack of jurisdiction. In the case of R.P. Kapur, I.C.S., Commissioner, Patiala Division, the Court held that the Governor of Punjab could not suspend Mr. Kapur because he was appointed by the King in Great Britain and after Independence, it was the President of India and not the Governor who could exercise this power—Governor being lower in rank than the appointing authority.

2. Error of Fact-Finding. There may be cases in which the official has erred in discovering facts. He may wrongly interpret facts or ignore them and thus may act on wrong presumptions. This may affect a citizen adversely and so there may be ground for bringing a case in a court of law.

3. Error of Law. A public servant may misinterpret the law and may impose upon the citizens duties and obligations which are not required by law. A citizen who has suffered on account of this has the right to approach the court for damages.

4. Abuse of Authority. If a public official uses his authority vindictively to harm some person, the courts can intervene and punish him if he is found guilty of using his authority to take a personal revenge.

5. Error of Authority. Above all, public officials have to act according to a certain procedure as laid down by laws and if they do not follow the prescribed procedure, the courts have a right to question the legality of their action, on appeal from the party affected. For example, law requires that an employee should be served with the notice of the charges before any action of suspending or dismissing him can be taken against him. Suppose the officer takes the action against him without serving a proper notice, then his act shall be declared null and void by the court.

JUDICIAL REMEDIES FOR SUING THE GOVERNMENT

Judicial remedies are available against the Government officials in the cases mentioned above. Judicial control can be in the form of suing the State or the Government itself or the public official concerned for his wrongful acts. The position regarding the suitability of the Government and public officials differs in the countries following the system of Rule of Law or the Administrative Law (Droit Administration). The Rule of Law system prevails in England and her Dominions and other Commonwealth countries including India and the U.S.A. and Belgium. The Administrative System is practised in France and other countries of continental Europe. The systme of Rule of Law implies that everybody, high or low, official or private citizen is subject to the same ordinary law of the land and that the official cannot take shelter behind the State sovereignty in defending himself. To repeat what Dicey said : "with us (English) every official, from the Prime Minister down to a constable or a collector of taxes is under the same responsibility for every act done without legal justification as any other citizen." That means that the State cannot be held liable for the wrong acts of its officials even if they had done an injury to a citizen while working in their official capacity and that the officials themselves are personally liable for their wrongful acts.

This remedy is hardly of any use because the damages decreed by the courts cannot usually be recovered due to the impecunious condition of officials. An agitation was carried in England to improve the system. After long agitation the position was improved by the passage of the Crown Proceeding Act of 1947, which makes the Crown *i.e.,* the State liable for torts committed by its servants. But there are two exceptions, namely *(i)* the prerogatives of the crown to defend the realm, the administration of armed forces, labours and aliens, and suppression of disorder are outside the field of liability and a certificate from the Government to this effect relieves it of such liability, and *(ii)* the state is not bound to produce before the court secret documents by way of evidence.

In U.S.A. subject to a few exceptions, the State ins still immune from fortuous liability of its officials. The exceptions are the admiralty and maritime jurisdictions, and the power given to Post Master General to settle claims involving personal injury or property; the damage claimed not expecting $ 500. In regard to states also, the general position is the same, *i.e.,* no state can be sued in tort except with its own consent expressly given, usually by statutory enactment. The federal government cannot be sued in State Courts nor State Governments in federal courts.

In India the suability of the State is governed by Article, 300 of the Constitution. The Article provides that the Union of India and the Government of a State may sue or be sued, but the circumstances in which a suit against them would lie are to be laid down by the Parliament and the State Legislatures, and subject to such legislation, the position would continue to be what it would be "If this Constitution had not been enacted". The position is that State is suable for contracts but the position about the torts is not clear. In the Case of Rao *vs.* Khusal Chand, the Bombay High Court has held that the Government cannot claim any immunity from illegal acts under S. 176 of the Government of India Act, 1935, when it illegally requisitions land under the Bombay Land Requisition Ordinance. Except in case of strictly 'sovereign' acts, the Government of India is liable for all unlawful acts of its servants. Recently, the question of liability of the State Government arose when the Supreme Court upheld the Rajasthan High Court's Order, allowing compensation of Rs. 15,000 against the State for the tortuous act of one of its employes—driver of a Government jeep who knocked down a person on the footpath, causing him multiple injuries, which resulted in his death. The State's main contention was that it was not liable for the tortuous act of its employee. Dismissing the appeal of the State of Rajasthan, the Chief Justice, Mr. B.P. Sinha, of the Supreme Court, in his judgment delivered on February 2, 1962 held that a state would be as much liable for the tortuous acts of its employees, committed during the course of their employment, as any other employer.

However, two years later the Court all but departed from the previous decision. It was an interesting case. Ralia Ram was arrested by three constables on a wrong suspicion of carrying stolen property and taken to a police station in Meerut. Gold weighing 103 tolas and silver weighing more than two maunds were seized from him and kept in police custody.

When Ralia Ram was later released, the silver was returned to him but, oddly, not the gold. He field a suit for the recovery of the gold valued at Rs. 11,000. The State alleged that the gold was in the custody of Mohammed Amir, head constable, who had misappropriated it and gone away to Pakistan, and contended that it was therefore not liable for the loss.

The trial court held that the police were negligent and that the State was liable to compensate Ralia Ram for the loss. On appeal, the Allahabad High Court set aside the decree and dismissed the suit, Ralia Ram went in appeal to Supreme Court and the Chief Justice held that negligence was no doubt committed by the police officers but even so the State was not liable for this act.

A distinction was thus made between the sovereign functions and non-sovereign functions of the State. The liability of the state for the tortuous acts of its servants extends only to the non-sovereign functions and not to sovereign functions. Since the distinction between the two kinds of functions is not always logical or clear, therefore, the court observed: "Before we part with this appeal, however, we ought to add that it is time that the Legislatures in India seriously consider whether they should not pass legislative enactments to regulate and control their claim for immunity in case like this on the same lines as has been done in England by the Crown Proceedings Act, 1947. It will be recalled that this doctrine of immunity is based on the common law principle that the King commits no wrong and that he cannot be guilty of personal negligence or misconduct, and as such cannot be responsible for the negligence or misconduct of his servants. Another aspect of this doctrine was that it was an attribute of sovereignty that a State cannot be sued in its own Courts without its consent. This legal position has been substantially altered by the Crown Proceedings Act, 1947."

The Law Commission examined the whole issue of liability of the State for the wrongs of its servants and laid down three fundamental principles on which legislation should proceed in our country. These principles were :

(a) The State should be liable, without proof of negligence, for breach of a statutory duty imposed on it or its employees which causes demage.

(b) The State should be liable if in the discharge of statutory duties imposed upon it or its employees, the employees act negligently or maliciously, whether or not discretion is involved in the exercise of such duty.

(c) The State should be liable if in the exercise of the powers conferred upon it or its employees the power is so exercised as to cause nuisence or trespass of the power is exercised negligently or maliciously causing damage.

In 1965, the then Union Law Minister, Mr. A.K. Sen, introduced a Bill in the Lok Sabha, the Government (Liability in Tort) Bill. It provides, fairly enough, that "Government shall be liable in respect of any tort :

1. Committed by an employee of the Government or an agent employed by the Government:

(i) while acting in the course of his employment; or

(ii) while acting beyond the course of his employment if the act constituting the tort was done by the employee or agent on behalf of the Government and is ratified by the Government;

2. Committed by an independent contractor employed by the Government or any of his servants or workmen in dosing the act contracted to be done for the Government.

The Bill not only excludes the armed forces from the application of these clauses, but also the police forces from the purview of those proposed legislation on the ground that "the case of a police constable is not distinguishable from that of a soldier". This is, in fact, the main weakness of the proposed law. The Bill for reasons best known to the Government was not brought on the Statute Book.

ADMINISTRATIVE LAW SYSTEM

Administrative Law, in the countries where the system of Administrative Law prevails, the liability of the State for the wrongful acts of its officials is fully established. There the officials are tried not in the ordinary courts of law but in the administrative courts which award damages from the public funds to the aggrieved individuals. The State may later deal with its officials at fault as it thinks fit but so far as the citizen is concerned he sues and obtain damages from the State.

The protagonists of this system contend that, firstly, it frees the administrative authorities from the jurisdiction of the law courts and hence secures promptness, fearlessness and efficiency in administrative action. Secondly, it is contended that the Judges, who are only experts in the law and know nothing about the technicalities of administration or executive exigencies should not be entrusted with the task of settling administrative disputes. Administrative disputes should be decided from the point of view of public and not from the legal point of view. Hence, the necessity of administrative law which ensures decisions of administrative actions by administrative experts. Thirdly, the system provides remedies to the citizens against the wrongful acts of the officials, whether high or low, at a very low cost and rather with greater ease than is possible under the Rule of Law System. The French Council of State has been working with perfect smoothness, independence and impartiality and people look upon it with respect, pride and confidence. According to Mr. C.K. Allen. "The remedies of the subject against the State in the France are easier, speedier, and infinitely cheaper than they are in England today. It has become a maxim of constitutionalists and a bulwark of French democracy that the Council of State is the greater buffer between the public and the Bureaucracy."

CERTAIN EXCEPTIONS OF THE RULE OF LAW

It may be mentioned here that even in countries following the Rule of Law system, there are certain people like the Head of the State who enjoy legal immunity and are not amenable to the ordinary courts of the land. For example, the British Monarch is completely immune from legal liability in respect of any of his or her acts done in public or private capacity. "The King can do no wrong" is a legally accepted phrase in England. The American President is also immune from any legal proceedings during the term of his office. He can only be impeached by the Congress and it is only after his removal from office that he can be tried in ordinary courts for crimes committed by him as President. In India, personal immunity from legal liability is granted to the President of the Union and Governors of the States for any act done in exercise of their powers and duties as laid down in the constitution. During their term of office they are immune from any criminal proceedings even in respect of their personal acts. Civil proceedings in respect of their personal acts are permissible even during their term of office but only after two months written notice stating the nature of the proceedings, the cause of action, name, address, etc. of the party concerned, and the relief claimed. The Ministers have however, no such immunity and they are, therefore, liable for crimes and torts and are amenable to the ordinary courts.

The other officials can be sued both in civil and criminal cases. Civil proceedings can be instituted against an offical for anything done in his official capacity after the expiry of two months' notice. No such notice, however, is necessary when the official is to be proceeded against for an act done outside the scope of his official duties. When criminal proceedings are to be instituted against an official for the acts done in his official capacity, previous sanction of the President or the Governor as the case may be is to be obtained.

EXTRAORDINARY JUDICIAL REMEDIES

In addition to the judicial remedies of suing the Government or its officials, citizens have the following extra-ordinary remedies also against the excesses of public officials:

1. Habeas Corpus. Habeas Corpus literally means "to produce the body of". The writ of Habeas Corpus is accordingly issued by the courts in the nature of an order calling upon the person who has detained another to produce the latter before it in order to let it know on what grounds he has been confined and to set him free if there is no legal justification for the confinement. The purpose of this writ is, thus, to determine whether the person is legally detained or restrained in his liberties.

The writ of Habeas Corpus is granted as a matter of the right and not at the discretion of the court, *i.e.*, the court is obliged to issue it if there is *prima facie* case for supposing that the person is unlawfully deprived of his liberty. It is something very particular that our constitution declaring India to be a Sovereign Democratic Republic and providing a lengthy Chapter on Fundamental Rights of the citizens should authorise the Parliament and State Legislatures to pass laws providing for the Preventive Detention of a person in times of peace. It is indeed a great limitation on the citizens' right to liberty. But it cannot be helped as there are still some anti-social and subversive elements in our country and to prevent them from becoming a serious threat to the welfare of society or a danger to the security of the state, it is necessary to exercise detention power under the Preventive Dentention Act. It is worth mentioning here that this power cannot be used arbitrarily used by the executive. A person cannot be detained for more than 3 months unless the cause of his detention is investigated by an Advisory Board consisting of persons of the status of the judge of a High Court within that period and the Board has reported that there is in its opinion sufficient cause for such dentention. In a democratic country, Preventive Dentention Act providing restrictions on the liberties of the people, seems most obnoxious. The earlier it is scrapped, the better it would.

2. Writ of Mandamus. Mandamus literally means "a mandate" or "a command". The writ of mandamus is a command issuing from a common law court of competent jurisdiction directing any person, corporation or inferior court requiring him or them to do some particular thing specified therein which appertains to this or that office and is in the nature of public duty. In short, it is writ issued to a public official to do a thing which is part of his official duty but which he has so far failed to do. This writ cannot be claimed as a matter of right.

This writ can, therefore, be issued on the fulfilment of certain conditions. Firstly, the petitioner must prove that he has a legal right to the performance of a legal duty by the respondent.

Secondly, the right must be a public right and duty sought to be enforced as a public duty.

Thirdly, the petitioner should ordinarily be the same person whose right is being infringed.

Lastly, the petition must be preceded by the demand for performance of the duty by the respondent and a refusal by the latter, *i.e.,* the petitioner must prove that he has made a demand for the performance of duty relating to his right upon the public official and that the official had refused to perform it.

3. Prohibition. The writ of Prohibition is a judicial writ issued by a superior court to an inferior court for the purpose of preventing it from usurping jurisdiction with which it is not vested. This writ then commands the Lower Court not to do a thing which it is not legally competent to do. This writ can be claimed as a matter of right. Prohibition should be differentiated from Mandamus.

Firstly, a Prohibition writ can be claimed as a matter of right while the Mandamus cannot.

Secondly, Mandamus can be available against any public authority or official, but 'Prohibition' can be issued only against judicial and quasi-judicial tribunals. It is not available against purely administrative or legislative authorities or acts.

Thirdly, 'Prohibition' does not require any personal right of interest on the part of the applicant but in the case of 'Mandamus', he must prove his personal legal right.

Though the writ of Prohibition plays some part in connection with the control of administrative tribunals with quasi-judicial functions it is of little significance as a measure of control over administration by the courts.

4. Injunction. Injunction is a writ issued by the court requiring person to do or restrain from doing a thing. It is called "mandatory" when it requires the defendant to do a thing and "preventive" when it requires the defendant to refrain from doing it. Mandatory injunction thus would appear to be resembling Manadamus because they both command the respondent to do a thing but actually there is a difference between the two. Mandamus cannot be issued against private persons while the injunction is usually directed to the parties in the dispute whosever they may be.

5. Certiorari. Certiorari literally mean to be certified or to be made certain. The writ of Certiorari means the direction of a superior court to an inferior for transforming the records of proceedings of a case pending with it for the purpose of determining the legality of proceedings and for giving more satisfactory effect to them than could be done in the inferior court concerned. The writ of Certiorari resembles the writ Prohibition as both of them are meant to supervise the work of the judicial authority, but Certiorari is something more than the writ of Prohibition. Prohibition is only preventive and curative. Prohibition prevents an inferior court from proceeding with a trial but Certiorari enables the superior court to send for record of the proceedings and other of the inferior court, to enquire into its legality and to quash the order if found beyond its jurisdiction.

6. Quo-Warranto. Quo-Warranto literally means, 'What warrant or authoirty'? The writ of Quo-Warranto is issued by the court to enquire into the legality of the claim which a party asserts to an office or franchise and to oust him from its enjoyment if the claim be not will-founded or to have the same declared forfeited. The conditions necessary for the issue of the writ are that the office under dispute must have been created by the Constitution or by a statute and should be public and not a private one. Secondly, the tenure of the office must be permanent, *i.e.,* it should not be terminable at pleasure. Thirdly, the persons proceeded against must have been in actual possession and user of the office. The purpose of this writ is thus to try a claim to a public office. The burden of proof to prove his title is on the respondent. The usual judgement in such proceedings is that of turning out of office.

The Supreme Court of India has been empowered under the new Constitution "to issue directions, orders or writs in the nature of Habeas Corpus, Mandamus, Quo-Warranto and Certiorari for the enforcement of fundamental rights of the Indian citizens," and the High Courts have been empowered within their jurisdiction "to issue to any person or authority directions, orders or writs for the enforcement of fundamental rights and for any other purpose." Thus, it would be observed that the powers of the Supreme Court are wider than mere issuing of the traditional writs as it can issue other directions, orders or writs also as may be necessary in a particular case. Secondly, these writs can be issued even against the Government in our country while in England, these writs are issued only against persons. Thirdly, powers of High Courts are in certain way wider than those of the Supreme Court.

Limitations of Judicial Control

The judicial remedies mentioned above under the "Rule of Law" system provide an effective control against official excesses of abuse of power and in protecting the liberties and rights of the citizens. But judicial control has certain limitations. In the first place, all administrative actions are not subject to judicial control. There are many kinds of administrative actions which according to the Constitution cannot be reviewed by the law courts. Then, there is a tendency on the part of the Legislature also to exclude by law certain administrative acts from the jurisdiction of the judiciary. For example, in India, the Administration of Evacuee Property Act, 1950 vests final judicial powers in the Custodians and Custodian General of Evacuee Property and the law courts have no jurisdiction to interfere in the decisions made under this Act.

Secondly, even in those administrative actions which are within its jurisdiction, the judiciary cannot by itself take cognizance of excesses on the part of official. It can intervene only on the request of somebody who has been affected or is likely to be affected by an official action. Human nature being what it is, legalism is the last sphere in which it would like to enter. We are always reluctant to enter the precincts of judiciary and prefer to continue to put-up with minor injustices of administration.

Thirdly, sometimes the remedies offered by the law courts are inadequate and ineffective. In many cases, especially relating to business activities, mere announcement of an administrative action or even a reminder concerning a proposed action may cause an injury to the individual against whom not even a suit can be filed in the law court.

Fourthly, the judicial process is very slow and cumbersome. The courts follow certain set technical pattern of procedure beyond the comprehension of a layman and then the procedure is so lengthy that it cannot be known as to when the final judgment shall be given. There have been instances when the cases have been pending with the courts for years together. Some time the decision of the court come when the damage has been done beyond repair : "Justice delayed is justice denied." An aggrived person cannot wait indefinitely to avail himself of the judicial remedy. The dilatory judicial procedure will not in any way console the sufferer or reconcile his affected mind. Tired of the delay he will loose hope and become a victim of bureauracy.

Fifthly, judicial action in incredibly expensive and cannot therefore be taken advantage of by many people. Filing a suit means paying the court free, fee of the lawyer engaged and cost of producing witnesses and undergoing all inconveniences which only those who can afford can bear. This keeps many people away from the court who prefer to suffer.

Lastly, the highly technical nature of the most of the administrative actions saps the force of judicial review. The judges are only legal experts and they may have little knowledge of the technicalities and complexities of administrative problems. Their legal bent of mind may higher them in arriving at a right decision. They have to follow the prescribed procedures and observe some formalities. W.A. Robson writes, "The liability of the individual official for wrong doing committed in the coures of his duty is essentially a relic from past centuries when government was in the hands of a few prominent, independent and substantial persons so called Public Officers, who were in no way responsible to ministers or elected legislatures or councils. Such a doctrine is utterly unsuited to the Twentieth Century State, in which the Pubic Officer has been superseded by armies of anonymous and obsecure civil servants acting directly under the orders of their superiors, who are ultimately responsible to an elected body. The exclusive liability of the individual officer is a doctrine typical of a highly individual Common law. It is of decreasing value today, and is small recompense for an irresponsible state."

●●

12

Civil Service

The Civil Service performas numerous functions in the modern state, most important of which are as follows:

1. Advice. One of the important functions of civil service is to offer advice to the political executive. Ministers are laymen, without much knowledge of the technicians of administration. They rely on the advice of senior officials who are reservoirs of information and knowledge concerning the subject-matters which they administer. Ramsay Muir has stated this function of rendering service to the ministers in an emphatic style. He wrote, "He (the minister) has obtained this position because of his achievements in the general field of politics. In a majority of cases he has no special knowledge of the immense and complex work of the department over which he presides. He has to deal with a body of officials who have been giving their whole time in quietness to the study of the problems of the office, during the years when he has been making his position in world, or talking fluently on platforms. They bring before him hundreds of knotty problems for his decision, about most of which he knows nothing at all. They put before him their suggestions supported by what may seem the most convincing arguments and facts. Is it not obvious that unless he is either a self-important as or a man of quite exceptional grasp, power and courage he will ninety-nine out of hundred cases simply accept their view, and sign his name on the dotted line?"

The business of the government, if it is to be well done, calls for the steady application of long and wide views to human problems. It is the peculiar function of the civil service to set wider and more enduring considerations against the exigencies of the moment, in order that the parliamentary convenience of today may not become the parliamentary embarrassment of tomorrow. Sir Josiah Stamp righly observed, "I am quite clear in my mind that the official must be the main spring of he new society, suggesting, promoting, and advising at every state."

2. Programme Planning. Although planning is the function of the political executive, but there is a sense in which it may be said that these are the civil servants who perform the function of planning. The ministers depend upon the civil servants who collect the material, arrange it and devise policy. The ministers discuss the policy drafted by the civil servants and make changes here and there. Although the preparation of budget and planning, the periodic adjustments of the revenue structure is a responsiblity of the Minister for Finance, yet in practice it is the Finance Secretary who does all this. It is in fact the civil servants who determine the industrial policy, the food policy etc. It is, of course, true that determination of policy is the task of the political executive, yet it nevertheless remains the fat that the actual work of policy formulation is done by the civil servants.

Moreover, in the field of delegated legislation the civil servants has ample scope of influencing the policy. The legislature passes the Acts in general terms to execute and implement which certian rule and regulations are required. The civil servants, who put the law into execution, determine the specific steps to be taken in order to bring to fruition a policy or a law agreed upon by the legislature. In order to execute that policy the civil servant has to take up the work of programme planning. Through the main purpose of programme planning is to execute the policy, yet it may actually affect the policy. It need not be emphasized that the success of any new policy will depend ultimately upon good programme planning.

3. Production. Civil service exists to perform services in the broadest sense of the term. Its primary purpose is production. Things produced may be tangible objects such as kilograms of fertilizers and rules of concrete roadway or less tangible such as cases of legal disputes decided or school children educated. Every official is to secure the most affective utilization of personnel. He supervises his subordinate employees. The supervisor must cultivate attitudes that is conducive to co-operation, energy and loyalty.

It is thus clear that the civil service is essential for the present day civilization. The civil servants serve the public with the spirit of service. They work for the welfare of the community. Referring about the civil service, S.E. Finer observes, "The civil service does not exist to make a profit. Hence its member's incentive is, in the last resort, to draw a salary, and not, by taking risks, to make a lot of money. Secondly, it is public. Hence it actions are subject to persistent scruitiny and liable to disavowal. This again limits its flexibility and enterrprise. Thirdly, civil servants and their Ministers must face constant informed criticism from Parliament. This fortifies their unreadiness to take changes. Finally, its services are vital. This forces it to pay special care to its staff relations, and, in order to prevent disaffection or dispute, to cultivate equality of a treatment at the possible expense of quality of service." With the expenditure activities of the state, their role is increasing day by day. It was not without reasons that Ramsay Muir said, "Parliament is a tool in the hands of permanent civil service." In India the civil service can play a still greater role as it gained freedom in the recent past and it making efforts to rebuild its economy by following the latest policy of liberalization of economy. It is a switch over from earlier stance of socialistic economy. The civil servant is now the humble servant of the people to work for them and help in their welfare. The common man should be made to feel that the civil servants exist for his welfare and that his co-operation with the civil servants is ncessary in the task of rebuilding India.

However, red tapism, bureaucrative attitudes of high borrowed I.A.S. officers and rempant corruption give a contrary impression regarding the current role of civil services in India. They have become suppliant tools in the hands of corrupt Ministers and gained the vicious circle exploiting the treaming millions at every step. I have an very few exceptions who can boost of impartiality and unimpeachable integrity.

CIVIL SERVICE IN A CHANGING SOCIETY

The aim of the British Rule in India was to maintain its hold over the country. The Government was interested in the collection of taxes, maintenance of peace and law and order. The few public utility services hat were started, were to fulfil the main object of the British Rule, viz., to keep its control over the country. Indian society was feudal with agriculture as the main profession of the people. The masses, groaning under the weight of poverty, under-nourishment and misery, started clamouring for equality. The main role of bureaucracy in India during the British Rule was nagative, i.e., it performed regulatory functions and made all efforts to crush people's moment for independence.

After independence, the National Government took up the task of modernising India through indusrialisation and undertook to provide all the amenities of modern life to the citizens. The negative concept of functions of State was replaced by democratic welfare State concept. Keeping in mind the democratic values of life of freedom and consent, a new equalitarian society was to be established. Standard of living of the teeming millions was to be improved. The administrative apparatus which was inherited from the old British regime was to be adapted, adjusted and renovated to fulfil the requirements of the new socialistic society. The role of the Civil Service was to change from mere law preservers to social welfare workers. Because of the democratic set-up of the Government. Civil Servants were called upon to work under the control of the representatives of the people. It was a marvelious phenomenon of human adjustment. The bureaucracy which was fighting and arresting political leader in British days, was called upon to work under the same leaders. Leaders who were despised by the bureaucracy were now to be obeyed and respected. Bureaucracy was to adjust itself to a democratic set-up with proper accountability and popular control. If an exmaple were needed of the power and capacity of adjustment and adaptability of the Indian Civil Service, the most important example is that of proper and harmonious relationship which existed beween the Ministers and the old bureaucracy in India from the very dawn of independence. No revolts no clashes were reported. The bureaucracy has adjusted itself smoothly to democracy and popular control.

Now bureaucracy has to adjust itself and undertake the gigantic task of reconstructing the Indian economy. India has embarked upon ambitious Five Year Plans, the main purpose of which is to improve the standard of living of the teeming masses and lay down the foundations of a socialist, democratic, equalitarian soceity.

The central objective of public and national endeavour in India since Independence has been the promotion of rapid and balanced economic development. The First Five Year Plan, while aiming at meeting certain urgent problems arising out of the war and partition, was calculated to strengthen the economy at the base and to initiate institutional changes which would foster more rapid progress in future. In both these directions the First Plan made a significant advance.

The Second Five Year Plan had to carry forward the processes initiated in the First Plan period. It was to provide for a large increase in production, investment and employment and was to accelerate the institutional changes needed to make the economy more dynamic and more progressive. The socialist pattern of society was to be established in India. The same objectives have been reiterated in the Third and Fourth Five Year Plans.

Essentially the socialist pattern of society means that the primary criterion for determining the lines of advance must not be private profit but social gain and that the pattern of development and the structure of socio-economic relations should be so planned that they result not only in appreciable increases in national income and employment but also in greater equality in incomes and wealth. The benefit of economic development must accrue more and more to the relatively less privileged classes of society, and a milieu should be created in which the small man has chances of rising in life.

For creating such an environment, the State has to take on heavy responsibilities. The Public Sector has to expand rapidly. It has to play a dominant role in shaping the entire pattern of investments—both private and public—in the economy and has to initiate developments which the Private Sector is unwilling or unable to undertake. The responsibility for new developments in certain major lines of activity which require the use of modern technology, large-scale prodution and a unfiied control and allocation of resources must be undertaken in the main by the State.

The essential objective is to secure rapid advance on democratic and egalitarian lines.

Within this broad approach, the Five Year Plans have been formulated with the following objectives in view:

(a) a sizable increase in national income so as to raise the level of living in the country;

(b) rapid industrialisation with particular emphasis on the development of basic and heavy industries;

(c) a large expansion of employment opportunities;

(d) reduction of inequalities in incomes and wealth and a more even distribution of economic power.

In new India the Civil Service has been called upon the manage State-owned industrial and commercial projects. Civil Servants have to advise the Government on the problems of planning. The Civil Servants have to execute planning. It is suited to the new tasks which it has been called upon to perform. The Civil-Servant, it is alleged, shows too much attention to precedent; he looks always to the past and eschaws and departure from tradition of the habitual way of doing things. He is essessively cautious. The one quality in which he excels is that of finding reasons, why a change should not be made or why a given course of action should not be pursued. His attitude is negative where it should be constructive. Moreover, he is so afraid of making a mistake or so lacking in self-confidence that he tries to avoid personal responsibility, and consequent passes on to some one else, if he can, any question involving decisions. This accusation was confirmed by the Committe on the Training of Civil Servants. It observed, "The faults most frequently enumerated are over-divotion to precedent, ... lack of initiative and imagination, ...procrastination, and unwillingness to take responsibility or to give decisions. We recognize that these faults exist in some measure....."

A Civil Service which is weak in the field of imaginative and creative suggestion is ill-suited for the new tasks, which require the spirit of initative, enterprise and even adventure. Cautious persons who 'play for safety' cannot undertake the modern expanding activities of the State. Keeping in mind these defects of bureaucracy and the requirements of new society proper selection, proper incentives to maintain effeciency and high morale of the Civil Service are requird. Right selection and adequate training shall determine whether Civil Servants shall be able to meet the challenge of society.

Economic Civil Service for India

State-control of the main means of production has been adopted as the corner-stone of Indian Economic Planning. The community has become the owner of a owner of a large field of national resources. Officials are responsible for organizing transport services, planning and development of new towns and running of State-owned industries. Public Corporations, which have been set-up to manage State-owned industries, are being run by officials in India. Civil Service has been called upon to perform many activities in the economic field. The question arises; Is the present Civil Service suited to the new tasks or a separate 'Economic Civil Service' should be set-up to manage the economic affairs of the State? Mr. A. D. Gorwala has discussed the problem of an 'Economic Civil Service' in his Report on Public Administration. It is said that the operation of controls, the running of State Enterprises of an industrial or commercial character, the manning of certain departments such as Industry and Commerce. Economic Affairs, etc., the implementation of certain development plans, should be left to the Economic Civil Service. Generally four different tyeps of personnel at one and the same time are covered by the phrase Economic Civil Service. They are :—

(a) The personnel competent to advice Government at the highest level of economic policy.

(b) The personnel competent at a lower level to collect and present the economic data on which advice regarding economic policy may be formulated.

(c) The personnel who have a grounding in economics and may be expected to discharge the duties of certain Secretariat and executive posts more efficiently than those who do not possess such knowledge.

(d) The personnel possessing the managerial experience and ability associated with efficient business.

It is said by the Advocates of the Economic Civil Service that the recruitment to this service shall be confined to persons with degrees in Economics. It may be said that graduates in Economics, do not necessarily possess administrative and managerial ability—a thing which is very essential for any kind of Civil Service. Mr. A.D. Gorwala rightly observes : "Officers of this class could not in any case come from raw degree holders. Economic grounding would certainly be of some use to those holding posts in departments where decisions have often to be made in the light of economic data and trends but there would be no particular advantage in confining recruitment to these posts to those with degree in Economics. An officer with general ability could be given the necessary economic training during the earlier years of service. On all grounds then, there would seem to be no case for a Special Economic Civil Service."

It can be suggested that there should be an industrial management service, consisting of persons who have industrial management training to run State owned industries. The Government of India felt the necessity of such Industrial Management Service, and announced a scheme known as "The Industrial Management Pool Scheme."

Indian Civil Services from East India Company to Indian Independence Act, 1947. Before the coming of Britishers on the political scene of India, the nation, both in the Hindu as well as Muslim era, did not know about civil service system in the present sense of the term. There were of course civil servants and each public servant had his allotted duties but all appointment, were made on patronage basis. The persons appointed could be removed from service as soon as they earned the displeasure of some superior officer. Moreover, there was combination of both the civil as well as military functions and the post, were transferable. It was during East India Company rule that the system of making recruitments through competitive examinations, and that of providing in service training was introduced.

Evaluation of the System. As the traders, in the form of East India Company began to get more and more political powers and the problem of administring the territories acquired by them became of serious magntitude, the Company thought of having a regular method of recruiting personnel for administering Indian territories. The servants of the Company enjoyed patronage of Court of Directors and were not only untrained an inexperienced but also corrupt and engaged themselves in private trade. Lord Clive set the ball rolling by forbidding Company's servants from engaging themslves in private trade and giving them some better service conditions. It was however, during the reign of Lord Cornwallis that a more serious thought was given to the problem and in 1793, covenanted services were created in India. Indians were virtually disallowed to join these services and only lower posts were kept open for them. It was however, soon realised that the officers of covenanted services, who were supposed to run Indian administration, did not know about country's social, economic and political life and thus were likely to be a failure. In order to overcome the difficulty Lord Wellesely established a College at Fort William to training such persons in India for period of 3 years before assigning them any administrative duties.

Beginning of Examinations. There was alround discontentment among the educated Indian who could get only inferior and lower jobs in the service of Company. These was growing demand in India that recruitment to these services should not be made on the basis of patronage but only through competitive examinations. The demand of th Indians was accepted and the principle of entry to civil services through competitive examinations was accepted. But the change in theory brought no actual change in the position of Indians. They were supposed to compete in England at comparatively young age, the cost of living was rather high, the atmosphere altogether different and the study of Latin a great hindrance. Age limit for entry to the service was very low. In 1860, it was further lowered to 19. The position was so tight that upto 1870, no Indian could find entry in the civil services.

The position was so grave and the demand for liberalising the rules so forceful that British Government was forced to set-up a commission to inquire into the method of recruitment to Civil Services. Credit goes to Sir Surendra Nath Banerjee who toured the whole country and aroused public opinion. The demand of Indians was that competitive examination should simultaneously be held in India and England and the age limit for entry should be raised. Aitchison Commission favoured the demand of Indians for entry to services upto the age of 23, but opposed the India of simultaneous examinations. In 1893, however, the House of Commons passed a Resolution accepting the second deamand as well.

Government of India Act, 1919. There was a pressing demand from the people of India that some remedial measures should be taken to meet the demand of Indians for providing opportunities for joining civil services. The formation of Indian National Congress provided an additional platform for raising our voice. The Montford Reforms accordingly recommended that simultaneous examinations should be held in India and England and that at least 33% of the total superior posts in the civil services should be filled through recruitment in India. Accordingly a five member Civil Service Commission was set-up in India. Indians were even now not satisfied, due to spread of English education and development of contacts of Indians with European nations, country had considerably awakened.

The Government of India Act, 1935. Between 1919 to 1935, it had become amply clear that the Indians shall not feel satisfied till they had been given some share in the superior services. Under the act of 1935 rules, regulations and appointments to certain categories of posts like I.C.S., I.P.S., I.P.S., were to by made by the Secretary of State, appointments to central services were to by made by the Governor General and those of the Provincial services be the Governor. Provision was also made for setting up a Federal Service Commission and Provincial Service Commissions. These Commissions were to make both recruitments as well as recruitment rules and also to conduct examinations when and where necessary. Appointment as well as service conditions of the Chairman and members of the Service Commissions were to be decided by the Governor General or the Governor respectively.

Assessment of the Civil Services before 1947. There was a lull in Indian for some time due to the outbreak of war and the situation did not materially change even after the close of the war. But on the whole very high tributes have been paid to the efficiency, ability and impartiality of Indian Bureaucracy before 1947. It was actually and in the true sense of the term the steel frame-work of Indian administration. But as it has rightly been said that at that time Indian Civil Service was neither Indian, nor civil, nor service.

Civil Services after 1947. After independence the position altogether changed. There was rapid expansion in our administrative set-up but a depleted service to cope with that. Many of the European civil servants either left India or requested for premature retirement, as they did not like serving under Indian masters. Similarly many civil servants belonging to Muslim community opted for Pakistan. Another serious problem was that the civil servants were required to change the psychology and way of thinking. From bossing they had now to think in terms of serving the nation.

In the conclusion, it can be said that the Indians had to fight very hard for entry into the civil services of their own country. This fact was clearly admitted by Sir Thomas Munro who said, "There is perhaps no example of any conquest in which the natives have been so completely excluded from all shares of government of their country as in the British India."

PLACEMENT SYSTEM OF CIVIL SERVICE IN INDIA

System of recruitment to Civil Services is becoming increasingly difficult and the whole method is becoming more and more scientific. This has put the systems of promotion from within as well as from without under serching criticism. It is also due to this that various methods, including those of finding suitable candidates, either by way of examination or oral tests, are being followed. But all these methods are only for finding out a suitable person for manning a post. The Commissions which are loaded with the responsibility of finding out such persons are only recommending and not appointing authorities. Thus few more steps are taken towards final recruitment after a person has qualified in the written examination or in any other prescribed test. Some such steps are :

1. Certification. After the candidates have ben examined and their merits assessed the Service Commissions in India draw a panel of qualified persons in order their merits and forward the same to the appointing authority for final appointment. This is called 'certification.' In U.S.A. however, 'rule of three' prevails under which for each post a list of three candidates is forwarded and it is for the department to select any one of the three condidates.

2. Orientation. For quite some time it was believed that orientation means inoducing a candidate to the job. But today whole concept has changed. Today each candidate is provided with elaborate information about the nature of work, rules and regulations of the organisation procedures to be followed and so on, so that a candidate is not lost before joining the department.

3. Appointment and Probation. Service Commissions are not the appointing but only recommending authrities. Appointments are made by the department concerned which requisitions candidates stipulating terms and conditions of service and also date of joining. Such a formal offer enables him to join his duties. But it is rather rightly said that competence of a person is not judged on the basis of his performance in the examination but only on the table on which he is required to work. Therefore, each fresh enterant in the service is kept on probation for some specific period. It is after satisfactory completion of this period that he is confirmed. During his probation period his performance is very carefully watched. In India usually the candidate is confirmed after completing his probation period, from the date of his appointment which is of considerable advantage to him in his subsequent service career.

4. Placement. After the person has been confirmed, it is essential that he should be properly placed. Without proper placement energies of the persons concerned, are likely to be wasted. If all persons are placed in accordance with their aptitude and inclination, the department concerned can derive maximum advantage out of him, otherwise not.

An Assessment of Recruitment System in India. Before independence, in India nepotism and corruption in recruitments was quite rampart. Virtually all higher jobs were open to well placed families and the poor or middle class people were denied all higher jobs. But with the independence a new chapter has been opened in our services where the merit and not the status or position of any person counts. All posts are filled up by the democratic means and methods. For all the higher posts there are competitive examinations, interviews and each candidate is supposed to qualify in such tests before getting a job. Of course some temporary or short term appointments are made by the deparments but these are exception to rule and not the rule itself.

Criticism on the System of Recruitment

(1) Or system of recruitment is not imaginative but rather aggressive.

(2) It has also been said that the system of viva voce is very undependable and should be replaced by psychological tests. In the words of Mr. A.D. Gorewala, "A fifteen minutes conversation with layman, although possessing the wide experience of public service commission, can be of no substitute for an expert psychological examination designed to give a scientific insight into the candidate's mental and emotional make-up."

(3) Then another criticism is that those on the board of interview are usually not well-equipped with latest methods and techniques of interviewing the candidates and thus fail to pick-up best available candidates. Through different techniques should have been followed for making recruitments to different categories of posts, yet that is not being done in actual practice.

(4) The interview system is usually given too much weight over the writen tests which every candidate qualifies after very hard labour.

(5) Interview of he candidate is conducted in most artificial environment and no efforts are made to keep the candidate at home. Still more problem is that several experts

sit on the Board to test the ability to new expectant to the post, who is supposed to be raw.

(6) The system of written examination is both defective and depends on chance—a risk which must be eliminated while making recruitment to civil service examinations.

(7) Our examination system, which is usually used for selecting candidates, is very defective and undependable. It is thus agreed that where the bases are not sound the superstructure is bound to be faulty and undependable. Not only this, but in most of the case syllabi prescribed for examinations are out-dated.

(8) There are many posts which have been kept outside the scope of Service Commissions. Autonomous bodies usually do not approach Service Commissions.

(9) The departments for whom the applications are invited and recommendations made by the Service Commissions, are at liberty to turn down their recommendations, which is certainly undersirable.

(10) Dr. Appleby has found fault with the system of certificating as well, when he says that, "The absurd limitation of a selection of a new appointee to a single individual, certified by the differences in individuals impotant to different kinds of position and reduces the probability that a needed person can be immediately engaged."

Suggestion for Improvement. The defeats in the system are not inherent. These can be removed by keeping as few posts outside the scope of Service Commissions as possible. Similarly, it is very much desirable that it should be made obligatory on all government departments to accept the recommendations of the Service Commissions and not to turn these down. One such suggestion can be that each Service Commission should have a research wing which constantly reviews the syllabii prescribed for different examinations and their relationship to the society and nature of jobs.

Too much weightage given to interview should be dispensed with even though new objective type test system has been introduced to remove subjectivity. Yet the problem still continues.

In spite of the fact that our system of recruitment has been criticised by few yet on the whole it has been appreciated by many. Of course there are charges that V.I. Ps. exert their influence. It is also said that departmental heads manage to get their own candidates in through the agencies of these Commissions but in spite of this our Service Commissions have maintained their impartiality. Let us hope that with the passage of time our Service Commissions will get rid of present allegations. In fact public opinion is even now exerting itself and a little variation from the recommendations of Service Commissions is not tolerated.

INDIAN ADMINISTRATIVE SYSTEM

India is an ex-colonial country and as such, has a mixture of the traditional strctures, behavioural pattern, modern political and economic structure borrowed mostly from Great Britain, the former rules of this country. Her administrative system is, according, a blend of the steal-frame of the colonial administrative system and the concepts and directions of the indigenous system established since independence. The Indian society is in a process of great transition and the political atmosphere is characterized by controversy and conflict about the importance, objectives and tecniques of developoment. There is a large middle-class sector which is well-exposed to western values and is deeply committed to change. This elite-class, comprising the top political leadership and the higher bureaucracy, has articulated new social, political and economic aspirations, to be communicated and implemented in past through old and new administrative caders functioning through new and modified structure.

Decentralization. The basic frame work of the administration is based on the theory of decentralization of structures and functions, under which autonomy and initiative are vested in the States and local units of Government. But it also accepts Central planning and direction, articulated both through the governmental machinery and the ruling political party which has enjoyed dominance continuously since independence—a dominance both at the Centre as well as in most of the States. Leadership, both political and administrative, is definitely committed to the welfare state concept. Alongwith the explicit goals of egalitariansim and social service, the administration is also enagged in the achievement of the vitual objective of integrating the people, both politically and emotionally, into a nation, This involves both communication of administrators with the most isolated sectors of the society and the development of a channel of identification, by both administrators and citizens, to the broad goals of the total society. The administrative system emphasises a public, not parasitic in its relation-ship to the administrative system but participant a public which is confident in the administrative hierarchy and is motivated to share in the responsibilities of development.

Penetration of Administration into the Lower and Peripheral Sectors of the Community. An empirical study of the elite-citizen interactions conducted, in Delhi State during 1964, indicates that the citizen base of the political system is being expanded, that the regime is consciously attempting to contact remote sectors of the society, communicate with them and involve them with the new system and its goals. However, lack of education and income status are a hindrance to bureaucratic penetration, with the result that the Indian Administration is out of direct contact with the bulk of the lower social classes, even in areas close to metropolitan cities.

One immediate consequence of this lack of contact between the administration and the citizen is that the public gets its image of the government on stereotypes laden with historical connotations, rumours and hearsay, indirect and informal secondary communication channels or through the local opinion or party-leaders in the village. Very often, this type of indirect contact is dysfunctional. Accordingly, the attitude of the Indian citizens towards their government is a complex and paradoxical mosaic of support and hostility—consensus and critique. "Almost all the citizens view administrative jobs and prestigious, most of them consider governmental programmes as worth-while, and less than half of them are critical of the job performance of the officials. But on the other hand, majority of them feel that officials are corrupt, that their dealings with the citizens are unsatisfactory, that the administrative machinery needs political pulls or illegal gratification for being moved to serve the ordinary citizen and that there is less possibility of getting redress against the high-handedness or incompetence of officials."

The relationships and interactions between the citizens and officials at the base of the administrative hierarchy are generally functional to the achievement of integrative and developmental purposes. They are more positive in the rural, as compared to the urban society and more supprotive among the illiterate and low class people than among the high caste and the educated classes. To broaden the base of adminitsration and to penetrate it further into the remote sectors of the community the administrator, particularly at the base of the hierarchy, where he comes in direct contant with the citizen, becomes the vital cog in the system. Officials, committed to innovation and democracy, can facilitate the involvement of the citizen with the social aspirations. This requires a major change in the recruitment system, and in the training and job orientation of the Civil Services from the colonial period to the present one.

Changes in the Civil Service. What ever scanty studies have so far been made in these directions, they indicate that there has been a slight boardening in the recruitment base of the services in India. No doubt majority of the higher and middle range positions in the services are still filled in by sons and daughters of the high-class families belonging to upper income groups, whereas lower ranks attract a majority of low income people from the middle and the low casts. In regard to training programmes there's is comparatively larger commitment now than before, particularly for the administrative classes and the Community Development bureaucracy. And in the training courses also there is an increasing emphasis on development programmes, democratic values, public relations and citizen cooperation. In spite of this, training programmes are on the whole unsystematic, sporadic and imbalanced. In most services, lower and middle level administrators get little or no training. Even among higher categories training courses have not yet been systematized, nor are their objectives properly spelled out. No doubt there is occasional mention of refresher courses and mid-service training programmes, yet these are carried on more as rituals and social get-together rather than as scientifically planned training programmes.

Change from Steel-frame to Aluminiu n-frame. Within the civil service, the old time emphasis on rank, status, seniority and rigid compartmentalization of the civil service into cadres and grades still continues. In personnel management there is more dependence on seniority than merit. Mobility within the ranks or services is impossible, with the result that each service—and their number is legion—is a closed corporation open only to its members who are recruited early in life and who stay there until the end of their official career. There is no competitiveness or opportunity of accelarated promotion for outstanding performance with the result that mediocrity gets an undue premium. Slow pacing, conservatism, formalism or proceduralism, a habit of passing the buck, lack of initiative and innovation are the inevitable consequence of such a personnel system.

Awareness of the New Role. However, it may be added parenthetically that, despite their social background, long and secure tenures and limited training, there great majority of Indian officials are incorporating, the welfare State and public service perceptions of their roles and although a large proportion of these officials reveal latent authoritarian dispositions, no strong relationship exists between these tendencies and the assumption of democratic job perspectives. In fact, there is a direct relationship between the democratic job perspectives and the training programmes, Officials who have had some kind of institutional training show greater propensity to the democratic and developmental role perceptions. Particularly in the development departments a subtle process of democratic socialism and communication is evident and sensitivity to public needs is higher where the official hierarchy communicates such an expectation and reinforces it with a training programme whose accent is clear.

Specialization. Another impact of the developmental progra-mmes on the bureaucracy is the increasingly higher degree of specialization within the services. During the last 30 years these has been more than 300 per cent increase in the technical staffs in Govt. services. Not only has the number of technical staff incrased but also there has also occured a proliferation of various specialists, professions and trades within the public services. However, in official hierarchy, and particularly in status and remuneration differentials, the generalist class enjoys a superiority over the technocrats. This has led to a dangerous conflict and bitterness between the generalists and the technocrats. The problem of generalist vs. specialist is not only a theoretical controversy borrowed from the British administrative milieu, but in the present day context of Indian administration, it is one of the most critical problems which is vititing the harmonious atmosphere in the administration of the country and is hampering the progress of many a developmental programme. The specialist feels that he is the main view of development administration and hence, must get a position of superiority in the administrative hierarchy, whereas the generalist has been clinging, and sometimes hopelessly, to his traditional and time-honoured status and role of superiority. A solution to this problem may be found in reforming the entire system of secretariat organisation. In this regard two factors are more important : firstly, that a clear line of demacration needs to be drawn between field services and the secretariat functions particularly between the Executive Department and the Secretariat, and secondly, there is a need for more specialisation within the administrative ranks. The old pattern of filling in Secretariat positions through a fixed 3-to-4 years tenure system has become more or less out-dated, because the administrative thinking, socio-economic planning, broad forms of management, like policy co-ordination and direction; whereas field administration requires different types to qualities, such as the capacity to execute programmes, the capacity to manage political and other pressures, and the capacity to achieve the planned targets with scarce resources. Therefore, administrative services need to be organised on functional basis, rather than on territorial basis, as is being done today. Broadly spaking administrative cadres may be of four different types, *viz., (i)* district of field administration, *(ii)* economic and financial administration, *(iii)* social welfare and community development administration, and *(iv)* general administration. These cadres should be organised nationally rather than State-wise.

Development and the Administrative System. An important question is : What has been the process of development in India since Independence and what shape it is likely to take in the future? The interpretations provided by the Western thinkers are not very helpful to us. For, their frame of reference is mainly the politico-administrative development of Western European Societies during the 19th and early 20th centuries which has been mainly unilinear and unicausal; that is, technological development led to economic development which led to political development which, in turn, led to administrative development. As against that, in India, as in the other present-day developing societies, the process of development is multillinear. Below is made an effort describe the mean ends of this process in India.

Firstly, every increment in the activization of the electoral process brings about a correspondingly large reconciliation of personal and sectional self-interest with the common good as interpreted by the legitimatized elite. This happens like this : every increase in the base of the electorate brings about a deeper penetration of the political process to larger and newer sections of the community; this accellerates the pace of political competition which, in turn, brings about a change in the structure and dispersal of power and influence; and this, in its turn, increases the capacity of the system for consultation, persuasion and accommodation of divergent interests and views.

This development is an enigma to both the Western democrats and the Communist and fascist authoritarians. For while in the West during the period their economic development, the arena of power was limited to an oligarchy; in the totalitarian countries, the process of politicization is completely controlled so long as economic development takes place. In fact, in the Western countries, not only was political power concentrated in the hands of the oligarchy during the period of economic development; but even economic power and wealth was vested in a small class, thus giving free play to economic exploitation and social injustice.

The second indicator for model-building is that with the increase in the process of political acculturation, the Indian

Politico-administrative System is becoming a fitter instrument for nation-building. Apparently, it does not appear so. For with the passage to time and with the broadening of the electoral base, a greater degree of fragmentation and diversification in the structure of political power here taken place. To the Western observers, this development appear to be an indicator of disintegration and chaos." To those thinker who believe that the only possible process of political acculturation to from ascriptive to 'associational' organisation, the secularization in traditional social cleavages and particularities and the politicians of traditional castes and communities appear to be inexplainable oddities. But although this process of development may not adhere to the Western model of political development, it nevertheless does bring about, in the Indian case, a transformation of a fundamentally plural society into a political community which is, for the first time on its history endeavouring to establish a legitimatized dominant political power centre getting its sustenance not from an outside military power or traditional sectarian or super-human authority but from the various regional and organisational political power centres which are taking shape under the spurt of political acculturation that is taking place from one general election to another general, or midterm, election. For the first time in her history, India's cultural unity is bring transformed into politcal unity.

The third indicator is in the field of economic development itself. In the Western model of development, economic development means the mobilisation of men and resources in the development process within a controlled political system. To accelerate the process of capital investment in modern industries, the political system permits accumulation of wealth in fewer and fewer hands.

Viewing the Indian development from the viewpoint of this model, the shift of our polity from one "dominant party system" to "fragmented political party" system and a similar shift in our economic plans from heavy industry to social welfare programmes are interpreted as the failure of India's planning and development.

But, India has deliberately chosen a participative strategy of mobilization. This strategy works against the creation of a unified certain power structure and tends towards central coalition of various power centres. This strategy is forced upon her not only due to her vast dimensions and pluralistic culture but is deliberatly selected in order to mobilize her immense manpower which is by far the most abundant resource available to her. So, if instead of looking upon economic development as a function of the accumulation and saving construct, we view it in the wider perspective of mobilization of the entire human and material resources involving people's participation, their motivation and morale, and the articulation of their demands and felt needs, then India, is certainly nearing the take-off stage of her development.

●●

Index